Religion in Primitive Society

RELIGION IN

PRIMITIVE SOCIETY

EDWARD NORBECK

RICE UNIVERSITY

HARPER & ROW, PUBLISHERS

NEW YORK AND EVANSTON

TO HANNAH, CROSBY, AND SETH

Contents

Preface

The intent of this book is to present from the point of view of anthropology—perhaps it is better to say from the viewpoint of an anthropologist—a discussion of religion dealing largely with peoples of simple ways of life, those whom we commonly call primitive peoples. The book is intended chiefly for an audience of students and other interested persons who are not professional anthropologists.

It has long been the contention of anthropologists that a knowledge of foreign cultures provides a better understanding of one's own way of life. According to popular thought, however, anthropologists study only primitive societies and the extinct cultures of long ago. The elaborate, living societies are the province of sociologists and other specialists. Anthropologists have in fact studied principally the simple societies of our world and they still pursue this traditional interest. But their fundamental concern goes beyond primitive societies. It centers upon the nature of culture, the culture of all mankind, and the efforts of anthropologists in recent years have tended increasingly to embrace the study of the great industrialized civilizations. These chapters in some measure reflect that tendency and it is my opinion that they are at all times relevant to an understanding of our own civilization and religions.

The objective study of religion which goes beyond the merely descriptive and historical has never been popular. Social scientists usually avoid emphasis on research in this field or else effectively bury their writings from all except professional colleagues by the nature of their professional interests and vocabularies and by publishing in journals and serials easily available only to fellow scholars. Debunkers of religion are extremely rare among contemporary scholars of the social sciences. I think that few wish to be debunkers. But the uneasy feeling seems to exist that any ''popular'' treatment of religion except outright rallying support will cause many persons to regard the writer as a biased subversive out to undermine the moral foundations which putatively hold society and nation together. The time and efforts of potential scholars of religion may be devoted with greater profit and comfort to any of the large number of questions and problems in fields which do not bear directly upon the subject of religion or which avoid treatment of it in any generic way. The modest beginnings of a comparative, scientific study of religion have, however, been made, and the problems, theories, and questions which these studies have presented will probably interest many persons who have lacked the opportunity to become acquainted with them. With this judgment in mind, a selective summary and critique of theories and interpretations of religion from the social sciences is included. The intent here, let me make it clear, is not to serve as a comprehensive abstracter of the work of others. I have included that which interests me and offer my own opinions.

To state the case briefly and more completely, I shall describe commonly recurrent elements of religion, whether primitive or civilized, centering the description upon the primitive. These data are offered for their own sake and also to serve as a necessary background for the interpretations which follow of the role of religion in human life. By ''role of religion'' I refer to what scholars more frequently label as the functions and functional relationships of religion, theories concerning the human needs which religion serves, its role with reference to society and the individual, its relationship to other parts of culture, and the nature and manner of change in religion. In the pages which follow, then, some well-worn paths will be traced again, if lightly, and some less-traveled routes will be explored.

Having stated what I intend to do, let me say what I intend not to do. I regard the question of truth versus lack of truth of religion as largely irrelevant to the objectives of this study, and I shall disregard it except insofar as discussion of conflict between naturalism and supernaturalism is useful in discussion of religious change. I shall pass no judgments on the relative superiority and inferiority of particular religious complexes.

I wish to thank Robert Anderson, George DeVos, George M. Foster, Robert F. Heizer, E. A. Hoebel, Frederica de Laguna, and Seth Leacock for suggestions helpful in the preparation of this book.

EDWARD NORBECK

ALL FAITH IS FALSE, ALL FAITH IS TRUE:

TRUTH IS THE SHATTERED MIRROR STROWN

IN MYRIAD BITS; WHILE EACH BELIEVES

HIS LITTLE BIT THE WHOLE TO OWN.

The Kasidah, Part Six

PART I. PRIMITIVE

RELIGIONS, AN OVERVIEW

Chapter 1. Introduction

Authors of books on religion which attempt to be comparative in scope or to deal with religion in a general sense are usually quick to state that religion is difficult to define. Their search for a definition has sometimes revealed the curious philosophy that "religion" has an inherent and unchanging meaning; it has suggested the pursuit of the Holy Grail, an unending quest for a desirable something lying perpetually in the distance. Sometimes the printed pages seem clearly to imply that the definition lies in wait, perfectly formed, for the truly diligent who has pursued it with enough skill and persistence to determine its innate nature.

Merely defining religion is obviously not difficult. We can repeat with ease and speed a great many scholarly and unscholarly definitions, all valid as definitions and many of them useful. The difficulty lies in devising a definition which suits the purposes of this book and which at the same time comprehends the large assortment of kinds of behavior and attitude which diverse opinion among readers might place under the heading of religion. Creating a definition which fully meets the latter requirement is, of course, an impossible task. Views as to what properly constitutes religion are not only numerous but also often exclude as superstitious or nonreligious many kinds of belief and behavior which other opinion might include and which the scholar would unfailingly include as being essential to the understanding of religion as a whole. A definition which might satisfy all readers and meet all vested interests is for these reasons both impossible and undesirable to realize. The intent here will not be to present *the* definition of religion but instead to offer *a* definition which it is hoped will be useful—and before our discussion ends we will find it necessary to amend that definition.

As a part of the process of outlining the boundaries of what we are calling religion, it is useful to discuss some of the views of anthropology, in particular the concepts of culture and ethnocentrism.

The concern of anthropology is man and all man-made things, both ideas and objects. Anthropologists look upon man as an animal, the product of many steps of biological evolution, rather than as the special creation of a divine being. But man is a highly distinctive animal which possesses a trait not found among other forms of life, the ability to symbolize.[1] By symbolizing we mean the arbitrary attachment of meaning to things. The principle form of symbolizing is speech. Man arbitrarily has assigned meaning to the kind of physical events called speech, events which in themselves have no inherent meaning. Other less important forms of symbolizing include writing, gestures and certain facial expressions, mathematical systems, and forms of art. Man is unique among living things because he provides for subsistence, protection, and the survival of his species principally by techniques resting upon this symbolic capability which no other living form possesses.

A large variety of lower animals such as monkeys, apes, dogs, cats, and some species of birds may learn to understand certain words uttered by human beings and also other of man's symbols, quite as Pavlov's dog learned to "understand" the significance of the sound of a bell before it was fed. Some lower animals may also be taught to produce reasonable vocal facsimiles of a few words of human speech, and many animals communicate with others of their species by sounds or other actions. These animals never themselves, however, arbitrarily attach meanings to objects, sounds, or other events. Even the ape, the animal most man-like in anatomy, physiology, and behavior, is completely unable to speak or otherwise to symbolize. We may teach an ape to react in a desired way to the

[1] Much of the discussion of symbolism and culture in this chapter is derived from the writings of Leslie A. White. See his *The Science of Culture*. (For complete publishing information for all references cited throughout the book, see the bibliography.

utterance of a modest number of words and to meaningful gestures which we make, but no ape himself arbitrarily attaches meaning to sounds to form words or symbols.

All forms of life are capable of learning of the kind we call conditioned reactions, and the conduct of their lives is based upon the increment of this kind of learning upon a body of unlearned behavior which they follow instinctively. No amount of perseverance on the part of human beings, however, will enable the ape or any other nonhuman form to engage in what we ordinarily call abstract thinking or in any way truly to participate in symbolic behavior. Nothing man can do will enable the ape to understand such abstractions as virtue and beauty, to distinguish virtue from lack of virtue, or to discriminate between a beautiful vase and an ugly one. As the example which is most relevant here, we may say that no ape can ever be made to understand and engage in religious behavior or to hold religious beliefs. Distinctions between holy and mundane, good and evil, supernatural and natural, and false and true religions may never be taught to an ape. The Christian significance of the cross is entirely lost to him, and, unlike man, he can never suffer from black magic or receive solace from prayer. If man were to lose his ability to symbolize, he would also lose much else. Gone would be his schools, machines, incest prohibitions, marriage ceremonies, calendars, wedding anniversaries, funerals, religion, and everything else except essentially that which apes have and which apes can do.

The foregoing is one way of saying that man and only man has culture. The ape and all forms of life including man maintain their existence by ways inherent in being the forms which they are. The manner of life of all animals but man is, however, strongly circumscribed, with only very limited variation existing as the result of individual experience or learning. All animals except man behave in ways that are almost wholly biologically predetermined or "instinctive" rather than learned. Whether produced under natural conditions or hatchery-raised (and thus subjected to some conditioning or "learning" through the agency of human beings), a trout free in a stream behaves essentially like any other trout of its species. The things which a lower animal learns from individual experience seldom or never spread to others of its kind. In any case, these learned things never become a part of trout, monkey, or beaver tradition. We cannot, in fact, properly speak of such things as trout, monkey, or beaver traditions. Only man has traditions, and only man has many, if often similar, ways of ordering life. By means of symbolizing he creates and transmits his creations to other human beings and to succeeding generations. Thus learning—for whether or not it constitutes learning in the conventional sense of knowledge, all symbolically based behavior must be learned—and the material products of learning accumulate to form what we may properly call traditions. These accumulations of learned things we call culture, the principal subject of study of anthropology.

As a working definition, we may now describe culture as a category of things and events of our universe which is distinguishable from all other classifications of things and events. It consists of ways of behaving, ideas, attitudes and material objects, all of which are interrelated and dependent for their existence, growth, change, and perpetuation upon man's ability to symbolize. Culture is man's technique of survival, the human equivalent of the teeth, claws, swift limbs, poison ducts, and other innate characteristics and capabilities which permit lower animals to survive. It is important to note well that our definition includes the idea that culture is learned rather than instinctive. Man, as an animal organism, also has non-learned behavior which we do not regard as cultural. But even the animal behavior of man, such as responses to the urges of hunger and sex, is strongly conditioned by learning (culture) and varies from society to society. Within the realm of religious behavior, as we will note, many kinds of behavior once thought to be innate and to rest wholly upon inferred biopsychological characteristics of man, now appear fairly surely to be culturally derived, i.e., learned, or at least strongly modified and channeled by cultural tradition.

One of the oldest premises of cultural anthropology is that culture —culture as a whole or abstract drawn from all cultures of the world and also each of the numerous species of culture such as Japanese, Greek, or Cheyenne Indian—comprises a system or an integrated unit. Culture, anthropologists believe, is not a fortuitous, haphazard growth unexplainable except insofar as its history of growth may be determined and stated. Instead, it is viewed as a whole composed of interrelated elements, functionally associated with one another so that if one important aspect of culture changes other aspects will undergo concomitant change. Culture is assumed to have characteristics of its own like any other class of phenomena in our universe. One of the principal concerns of cultural anthropologists has been to study culture and the interrelationships of its constituent parts and thereby to formulate generalizations concerning the nature of culture—the nature of its relationships to non-cultural factors such as the physical environment and man's physical organism, the internal relationships of its parts, and the manner of its growth and change.

A fundamental hypothesis, so far only implied, is that cultural phenomena are amenable to scientific observation and the formulation of scientific laws in quite the same manner as the phenomena of the physical sciences. Reiterated by many of his successors, the words of the pioneer anthropologist E. B. Tylor, published in 1871, state the view clearly: "The tendency of modern enquiry is more and more towards the conclusion that if law is anywhere, it is everywhere."[2] The manner of procedure and the problems of anthropologists in their attempts to shed light on the nature of culture are, in a general sense, precisely those of any other science, distinguished chiefly by the fact that objectivity has been more difficult to gain because the scholars of culture are in it and of it in their daily lives, so deeply immersed that a wholly detached view has never been attained.

Before going further, it is useful to consider the second of our preliminaries, the subject of ethnocentrism, a name given to a world-wide attitude of human beings. By ethnocentrism we mean the excessive centering of ideas and values around those of one's own culture so that the customs of people of different culture are depreciated and regarded as amusing, ridiculous, inferior, unworthy of serious consideration, immoral, or animal-like. We are all ethnocentric in some degree and the highly ethnocentrized person is, of

[2] E. B. Tylor, *Primitive Culture*, vol. 1, p. 24.

course, well adjusted to his own culture. Ethnocentrism may have real value for the individual in the conduct of his life within his native culture. The similar attitudes of nationalism, parochialism, and anthropocentrism—to list only a few of the named categories of attitude and behavior whereby one set of values is placed above others—have had important influence in the conduct of human affairs.

Examples of ethnocentrism are easy to find: the Christian view that having more than one spouse simultaneously is an inherently immoral act; the American attitude that it is cowardly and unethical to initiate war without formal declaration of intent (the ordinary procedure of many primitive peoples and, according to Japanese standards, a traditional and strategically desirable action unrelated to ethics); the idea of civilized man that eating grasshoppers, grubs, and other insects—common foods among many primitive peoples— is revolting, and the attitude of revulsion of many East Asiatics against cheese and other dairy products.

A common form of ethnocentrism is to regard persons of different race as being inherently inferior, a view which has no scientific basis. The question of physical or racial differences among human beings is the proper subject of a book different from that intended here. It is useful to us, however, to summarize in a few sentences some of the views of scientists who have concerned themselves with this topic. Attempts to explain differences in the cultures of peoples on the basis of racial differences are unwarranted and have yielded no sound results. Given the cultural opportunity, any variety of man living in the world today may have any culture known to the world. All living varieties of man are sufficiently alike so that con- sideration of physical differences may be omitted in the comparative study of cultures. Finally, race and culture have no inherent or necessary relationship and thus religion, as an element of culture, is unrelated except fortuitously to race.

The foregoing statements refer to the relationship between races, peoples, or societies and particular cultural conformations and not to individual, intrasocietal differences in biopsychological charac- teristics and cultural participation, which is quite a different matter and one which we will later give some attention. A considerable range of biological differences exists among the individuals of any race, population, or society, and these differences unquestionably have bearing on the kind and degree of participation in the culture, including the religion, of the society to which any given individual belongs.

Much ethnocentrism revolves about the term "primitive," which has come for many persons to connote inferiority and, when applied to human beings, to imply the mistaken notion of mental processes which are prelogical or qualitatively different from those of civilized man. Much of the writing on primitive religions until fairly recent years has reflected this view and it may still be found in current writings on religion despite the fact that it has no scientific support from anthropology. The word primitive is, however, firmly entrenched in our language. No adequate substitute has been offered, and there can be no serious objection to its use if the notion that primitive peoples are of another psychological order than civilized man is laid in its grave.

In the pages which follow there will be frequent references to "primitive" peoples, but no ethnocentrism or implication of physical or mental inferiority is intended. For convenience, we will also refer to primitive cultures, primitive societies, and primitive religions. By these expressions is meant the ways of life, the social organization, and the kinds of religious behavior of peoples of the world who have no substantial body of scientific knowledge and few or no elaborate mechanical devices; peoples who have little or no writing; and, as a rule of thumb, peoples whose manners of living are crude and simple as compared with our own.

The most luxuriant growth of ethnocentrism revolves about religion. In the history of the West, this attitude has been the rule rather than the exception. The missionizing nature of Christianity offers powerful support to this statement, and the reader may easily supply an abundance of additional evidence from personal experience.

The foregoing paragraphs are designed to serve two purposes with reference to our study of religion. One is to state that if we wish to go beyond invidious comparison we cannot define religion on the basis of the religious beliefs of our own or any other single culture and consider all else unworthy of attention as mere superstition. The second purpose is to state firmly that recourse to racial or biological differences among varieties of man in order to explain differences in religions has shown itself to be fruitless.

Returning now to the problem of defining religion, we have assumed by our title that religion represents something distinct from all other things, and we seem also to have assumed that religion is found among all peoples, at least all primitive peoples. Placing religion as a universal under the larger heading of culture, we need to make clear the characteristics which render it distinct from other elements of culture and thus finally formulate a definition which may be applied to all cultures.

Most attempts to distinguish the religious from the nonreligious have rested on the conceptions "holy" or "sacred" versus "profane." These terms and the ideas they imply are useful, but the words are tinged with troublesome emotional connotations and they reflect Christian religious ideas. To which of these two realms can one suitably assign the unholy, as distinguished from the profane, or mundane? In Christian thought the unholy has been labeled superstition or sacrilege rather than religion and thus seems to fall quite outside this bipartite scheme. The term holy also often implies attitudes of awe, veneration, and fear, emotions which do not always seem to be evoked by what we conventionally regard as the religious and it suggests that the profane entirely lacks association with these emotional states.

Anthropologists have commonly called religion a "cultural universal," one of the many things, including marriage, incest prohibitions, the family, and social organization, found everywhere in the world. No society ever observed has failed to display something readily identifiable to scholars as religion. No matter how bizarre and vastly different the foreign culture, it always contains these elements. Primitive peoples themselves sometimes label the religious and the nonreligious in a manner corresponding with our sacred and profane. The distinguishing traits of religion lie in an attitude extended toward certain ideas, objects, and acts; but the psychological state is not necessarily one of awe, veneration, or fear. Psychological states hardly if at all distinguishable from certain of the emotional reactions we commonly call religious are evoked by a variety of things never conventionally described as religious. The unfurling of a flag, the playing of stirring music such as a national anthem, and the words of a compelling orator appear to invoke subjective emotional states describable in terms indistinguishable from those which depict physiological and psychological states often associated with religion. What, then, can we safely and profitably use to distinguish the religious from the nonreligious?

The least constricting terms our vocabulary provides to enable us to set off the realm of religion from the rest of culture are the natural and the supernatural. Most if not all peoples make some sort of distinction between the objects, beliefs, and events of the everyday, workaday, ordinary world and those which transcend the ordinary world. Using this distinction, as others have done, we shall define religion as ideas, attitudes, creeds, and acts of supernaturalism. By ''supernaturalism'' we mean to include all that is not natural, that which is regarded as extraordinary, not of the ordinary world, mysterious, and unexplained or unexplainable in ordinary terms. Being extraordinary, mysterious, and unknown or unexplainable in terms of natural or ordinary things and events of the world, the supernatural may evoke various other attitudes. It may be associated with awe, veneration, wonder, or fear. A common denominator in subjective states which the supernatural evokes is an attitude of *apartness* from the mundane.

It is important to add that this definition of religion undoubtedly represents the extension to the primitive world of ideas of Western society. We have often been warned from within the ranks of anthropology that our classifications must represent native points of view. Unfortunately, we can never be certain that we know native viewpoints. Thoroughgoing attempts to present them are few and generally represent the ideas of a single interpreter. Strained through the culture of the observer, they are presented in terms of our own language, as they must in order to be comprehensible. Moreover, the use of native distinctions and classifications in religion or any other aspect of culture makes comparative study difficult if not impossible. For those who object to a definition of religion as supernaturalism, we offer the alternative of regarding this book as a discussion of supernaturalism. Few will find it easy to deny that, however religion is defined, supernaturalism has nearly always been its major distinguishing trait in both the scholarly and nonscholarly worlds. It would not be difficult to demonstrate that many who might object to this definition nevertheless make use of it to distinguish the religious from the nonreligious in primitive society.

Religion, as it is defined above, is a cultural universal. But a few more words—to be elaborated upon in the chapters which follow—are useful here. We may take special note that the definition contains no statements about ethics or morality, no reference to a single supreme being, and that it potentially embraces a wide variety of phenomena which fall quite outside the "proper" boundaries of modern Christianity. These are all deliberate and necessary omissions. Granting that our definition of religion makes it a universal human phenomenon, one might still ask if all systems of philosophy and patterns of behavior of the modern civilized world conventionally labeled religions fall within its scope. Certainly a few of the modern do not. Views of what constitutes religion are unquestionably changing, as seems inevitable since religion itself is undergoing great change. This is a subject to which we shall return.

A review of the preceding words can easily lead to a restatement of the distinction between the religious and the nonreligious. It is a very old idea: man interprets his universe in two principal and different ways and on the basis of these interpretations he is afforded patterns of behavior with relation to that universe so that he may know how to act. One of the kinds of interpretation we call naturalistic, the other supernaturalistic. Naturalism and supernaturalism are both ways of adjusting to the universe. Man's behavior has been based upon both of the principal lines of interpretation, separately, alternately, and in combination; and they have affected his life in ways of which he has not always been aware.

We may note in passing that when we speak of the primitive

world it is permissible in any civilized company to refer to supernaturalism. With reference to our own society, however, it is often regarded as a mark of militant atheism to refer to our religious faiths as supernaturalism. No attack of this sort is here intended, but for the time being, our definition of religion will rest upon supernaturalism and the structures, doctrines, attitudes, and practices which have grown upon supernaturalistic interpretations of the universe.

Chapter 2. Origins

It is often assumed that universal elements of human culture such as marriage, the family, and religion rest upon inherent physical or psychological traits common to all mankind. The universals exist, in other words, because of the nature of man's physical organism, and whatever cultural elaboration of form the universals might take, they serve to fill needs common to all mankind. Some understanding of universal culture traits, it is thus thought, may be gained from consideration of man's inherent attributes. When, as so frequently happens, culture traits of geographically isolated societies are similar and little or no possibility exists of the intersocietal diffusion of those traits, it seems reasonable to follow this line of thought and surmise that similar circumstances may have produced similar results.

We may see clearly the biological aspects of family organization, a culture trait found in varying form among all peoples. Without a social unit like the family, whether it is the small family of parents and offspring characteristic of the industrialized societies or one of the various forms of familial and kin groups of primitive society, human beings could not have survived. Human young mature slowly and must be nurtured for many years before they are able to fend for themselves. Family organization, it has been suggested, is a biological inheritance from the unknown evolutionary predecessors of man. Man's nearest living relatives, the gorilla and other modern apes, who are thought to share with him common ancestors in the geologically speaking fairly recent past, also must care for their young for long periods and they tend to live in family-like units. The human family also serves other functions of biological or

14

psychological nature, the satisfaction of sexual needs of the procreating pair and—it has been suggested—innate psychological needs of intimacy and affection, although these needs might be met in other ways.

The physical basis of religious behavior, if indeed any truly specific physical factor of the kind does exist, remains obscure. Although many theories of the origin of religion have been based upon biological (that is, inherent psychological) considerations, the theories reflect great disagreement with one another, as do all other attempts to explain the genesis of religion. Concern with ultimate origins has, as a matter of fact, become extremely unpopular in the social sciences. This unpopularity appears to be largely the result of frustration; the study of ''origins'' has seldom yielded results regarded as positive, and it has often emerged with strongly conflicting theories. The opinions of modern scholars are that the origins of religion remain unknown and that no theory presented or presentable can be more than reasonable speculation. Social science today most frequently devotes its efforts to other problems; and, on the question of origins, contents itself with stating that the data necessary for formulating sound and verifiable hypotheses of the genesis of such things as language and religion are lost in an ancient past from which we have no reliable techniques for recovering them. A French linguistic society has for many years prohibited as worthless the reading at its convention of papers on the origin of language. Recent works on religion written by sociologists and anthropologists usually omit entirely the subject of origins or allude to theories only in passing as curious, mistaken efforts of the past. The trend of inquiry into religion by social scientists of the past several decades has instead revolved chiefly about the sociocultural role of religion. The prevalent attitude toward origins is that even if the factors which gave rise or which give rise to religious behavior were clearly understood much else of greater importance about religion would remain unclear and that the only justifiable approach to the study of religion or any other subject is to deal with data which are observable and verifiable.

The stand of modern scholars toward theories of the origin of religion seems reasonable, but endorsement of it does not imply that the subject is uninteresting or entirely beneath notice. Scholars of religion of the late nineteenth and early twentieth centuries devoted much attention to speculation on this subject. As has often been stated in criticism, most of the theories of origin which they advanced were formulated introspectively by pondering how ideas of supernaturalism might have arisen if the scholars were themselves simple tribesmen. This criticism seems hardly telling, and the many writings on religious origins are by no means valueless. In connection with the question of the genesis of religion, they have presented other hypotheses which have served as the foundation for modern studies. We offer no apologies for presenting in brief form the more famous of these sometimes well-reasoned if unverifiable hypotheses.

Most theories of the origin of religion include or imply an evolutionary scheme of development beginning from various "origins" and following varying routes of growth to a common culmination in monotheism. Few attempts have been made to classify the theories. They are generally referred to by the names of their formulators, such as "Tylor's theory," or by using some easily identifiable or quotable element of the theories advanced. For convenience, they can be placed under the three major headings—psychological, sociological, and theological, subdividing the psychological into the categories, rationalistic, emotionalistic, and psychoanalytic.[1] Both psychological and sociological considerations enter into some theories, and other hypotheses may include elements of more than one of the psychological types listed above. The classification assigned here depends upon which type of interpretation is stressed.

Psychological interpretations of the origin of religion here labeled rationalistic contain the central theme that religious ideas are the rational or cognitive attempts of primitive man to interpret and adjust to his external environment. Religious practices were created by human reason, intellectual rather than emotional in nature, and represent early and crude philosophical interpretations of the universe.

[1] See W. J. Goode, *Religion Among the Primitives*, p. 241, for a similar classification.

The best known of these theories is that of the British anthropologist E. B. Tylor.[2] Tylor held that animism, which he defined as "belief in spiritual beings," was the common denominator of religion, its irreducible minimal component. He regarded animism as the earliest form of religious behavior and saw in the various religions of primitive and civilized societies an evolutionary chain which developed as supernatural entities came to be regarded in hierarchical order of power and importance. The developmental chain proceeded from animism to monotheism, which he thought was a late development in man's history. Animism, in turn, owed its origin to early cognitive attempts to explain "several bodily and mental conditions," sleeping, waking, trance or other unconscious states, disease, life and death, and the human shapes which appear in dreams and visions. Pondering on these things, primitive philosophers developed the idea of a soul separable from the body as the source of life and the cause of sleep and unconscious states. During sleep or while unconscious, the now detached soul or souls performed the activities seen in dreams and hallucinations. The permanent loss of the soul meant sickness and death. Once man had developed the idea of separable souls or spirits as the vital force which enabled him to be a sentient being—so the reasoning continues—he extended the concept of the soul to other animals and also to plants and inanimate objects, all of which might appear in dreams and visions. On a foundation of simple animism of this kind, all of the historically known elaborations of religious belief and practice grew. Hierarchies developed among supernatural beings and the evolutionary cycle culminated in monotheistic belief.

A belief in souls is found in all societies, and in the primitive world souls do indeed often wander. One of the most common primitive conceptions of the cause of death is loss of the soul. But numerous objections have been made to Tylor's theories on other grounds. Detailed critiques appear in published form, and none will be attempted here.[3] We shall merely repeat that Tylor's theory is not susceptible to verification, and note in passing one additional criti-

[2] E. B. Tylor, *Primitive Culture.*
[3] See R. H. Lowie, *Primitive Religion;* and W. J. Goode, *op. cit.*

cism which has been offered—the contention that Tylor overstressed
the cognitive aspects of religion and neglected the nonrational, emotional elements which, according to some views, represent the vital
core of religion. Those who hold the opinion that the most important
aspect of religion is the affective or emotional argue that if religion
were truly only a crude attempt at explanation of the universe, the
growth of scientific knowledge would have wiped it out from at
least the Western World. In reply to this criticism, one might ask
if this indeed is not what is happening to one aspect of religion.
Granting that the role of religion embraces much more than interpretation of the universe, Tylor's views of one of its functions can
meet little argument. To the extent that scientific interpretations of
the universe have been offered and accepted, their supernaturalistic
counterparts have generally although often slowly been displaced.

    We may also place in the rational category the theory of Sir
James George Frazer, also a British anthropologist, who thought
that religion grew out of magic.[4] Frazer made a sharp distinction
between magic and religion, viewing magic as rational but fallacious
reasoning, the ''pseudoscience'' of primitive man by means of which
he sought to control the universe for his own ends. When man saw
that the recitation of precise formulae and other mechanical manipu-
lations of magic failed to achieve the desired ends he began, by
means which Frazer never clearly states, to engage in another kind
of behavior to help himself. This other kind of behavior, which
Frazer called religion, involved the idea of subjugation of man to
the supernatural rather than control over the supernatural by man
and replaced rote formulae and mechanical manipulation with
prayer, worship, and other forms of propitiation.

    Various other theorists whose hypotheses we may label as emo-
tionalistic have thought that religion ultimately sprang from various affective or emotional states automatically evoked in man in the
acts of daily life. A popular theory, which seems to be fairly viable
today, is that religion arose from fear and also serves the function
of allaying fear. Religion has undoubtedly often served this role,
but we have no assurance that religion arose from fear or that it
universally serves to allay fear arising from nonreligious sources.

[4] J. G. Frazer, *The Golden Bough.*

We know that it often creates rather than merely stills the emotion of fear.

The naturists of the nineteenth century, of whom Max Müller[5] is the outstanding figure, held the view that religion sprang from spontaneous emotional reactions of wonder, awe, and fear evoked in man by natural phenomena such as the sun and the moon. Impressed by these powerful and inexplicable forces of nature, primitive man reacted with the emotional attitudes and behavior to which we have given the name religion. Folklorists of the naturist school of the nineteenth century have provided us with many interpretations of mythology as ultimately reflecting nature worship, a task which was not always simple for them. The reader who plunges into naturist interpretation of mythology ignorant of the basic assumptions of naturism might easily conclude that either the writer or himself had taken leave of his senses. By ingenious rationalization, any of a great variety of mythological subjects and figures are converted into symbols for the sun or other forces of nature and the whole made to represent or spring from the worship of these natural phenomena.

It has long been abundantly clear that recourse in a causal sense to "innate" emotional reactions evoked by the phenomena of our universe leads to no satisfactory explanation of religious genesis. Rationalists have asked why should man stand in awe and fear of the most ordinary things of life, such as the sun, which he daily observes. A more weighty argument against these theories is the knowledge that no category of things universally evokes religious attitudes. What is sacred or fear-inspiring in one culture may in another be utterly commonplace or even ridiculous rather than endowed with supernatural qualities. The range of sacred and awe-inspiring objects and situations varies enormously from culture to culture, and thus the emotional reactions variously evoked appear clearly to be culturally determined rather than inherent in the situations or objects themselves. These and other shattering criticisms long ago led to the end of naturism, an end so final that mere reiteration of these theoretical weaknesses constitutes punishment of the dead.

Herbert Spencer, who accepted much of Tylor's reasoning, saw

* Max F. Müller, "Comparative Mythology." See also his later writings.

the ultimate origin of religion in the emotions of respect and fear, respect for one's elders during life, and fear of their spirits or ghosts after death.[6] He believed the earliest form of religion to be the worship of ghosts of departed ancestors, who must be propitiated out of fear.

Still other interpreters have derived religion from feelings of dissatisfaction with life or mystic emotions of religiosity held to be innate among the small percentage of emotionally unstable persons who exist in any human population and who serve as the religious formulators and innovators.[7]

Among psychoanalysts, only Freud's theory concerning the origins of religion is well known.[8] Fundamental to Freud's interpretation are the Oedipus complex and the projection into the external world of the father-child relationship of life, thereby creating a supernatural world. In an ancient time, created by Freud's imagination, the primeval sons united and slew their primeval father out of jealousy of his control over the women. In atonement, they took to worship of God the Father. Like Tylor, Freud viewed religion as unnecessary to the continued life and cultural development of man. Unlike Tylor, who implied only that religion was rendered unnecessary by another kind of rationalization, Freud clearly viewed it as a pathological illusion of immaturity from which man, for his own good, should recover.

As we shall see, ''projection'' is important to religion in the sense that the supernatural world is in one fashion or another modeled after that of ordinary life. Relations of mortal and supernatural are, however, not always patterned after the strongly hierarchical father-child relations of Freud's Europe. In other respects, Freud's theories of the origins of religion are ingenious and engrossing fiction, free of any danger of scientific verification. Out of fairness, it should be added that Freud's idea of a primeval human horde, without marriage and without regulation of sex except by personal

---

[6] H. L. Spencer, *The Principles of Sociology.*

[7] E.g., Paul Radin, *Primitive Religion.*

[8] Sigmund Freud, *Moses and Monotheism: The Future of an Illusion; Totem and Taboo.* For a brief statement of Freud's theory of the origins of religion see his introduction to *The Psychological Problem of Religion* by Theodor Reik.

preference and brute strength, came to him from nineteenth century anthropology.

Few sociologists have offered theories concerning the origins of religion, perhaps because they have seldom studied primitive societies, among which, if one follows the evolutionary reasoning of the nineteenth century, the mainsprings of religion are best discernible. The concern of sociology is, of course, with the social, and it is not surprising that the French sociologist Emile Durkheim, who has given us the single well-known sociological interpretation of religion which includes a theory of origins, should view society as its fountainhead.[9] (We may note that the chronologically much earlier theory of religious origins of the sociologist Herbert Spencer has no special sociological leanings.) Durkheim spurned the psychological, saying that social facts can never be adequately explained by recourse to psychology, and expressed the view that religion is preeminently social in nature, significance, and origin.

In looking for the social significance of religion, Durkheim saw its origins in group ritual, especially in communal ritual associated with totemism, a term applied loosely to a large variety of customs among primitive societies having the common theme of beliefs of mystic affinity with some lower animal, plant, or, much less commonly, inanimate object or natural phenomenon. "Totemistic" primitive societies are usually divided into a number of clans or other subgroups, whose members regard themselves as descended from their eponymous totems. Durkheim regarded the culture of Australian aborigines as the crudest in the world and, using it as representative of the ancient condition of mankind, he saw in Australian totemic ritual the earliest form of religion. To look for the derivation of religion in intrinsic qualities of natural phenomena, as the naturists had done, he regarded as a useless quest. He noted that the source of sacredness is manifestly not inherent in any natural phenomena and stressed instead symbolism as the key to origins. The important consideration was not the kind of things which were sacred, he stated, but what these things symbolized, and the problem was to determine the identity of symbols. Australian

[9] Emile Durkheim, *The Elementary Forms of the Religious Life.*

clan totems he regarded as symbolizing the clans themselves, and thus the collective worship of totemic ancestors represented an equation of society with religion.

Only society itself, Durkheim contended, was capable of evoking the attitude of sacredness by which he distinguished the religious from the nonreligious. He defined religion as a unified system of beliefs and practices relative to sacred things, set apart from mundane things, which served by means of communal beliefs and ritual to unite into one single moral community or church the society in question. In a curiously circular fashion, he described society as the "soul of religion," and also stated that the fundamental aspect of society was a pattern of moral-religious beliefs and sentiments. Patterns of religious behavior and sentiment observed and held by any society were thus at the same time symbolic representations of the unity of its members (that is, of society), which served to uphold and reaffirm at regular intervals through collective ritual the sentiments and values of the society (which were essentially religious).

Like all other theories of the origin of religion, Durkheim's assay has been relegated to the scholarly dustbin. Societies quite as crude culturally as those of the Australian aborigines but which entirely lack totemic beliefs and rituals are now historically well known. But this statement, most scholars of religion would agree, is mere quibbling over unimportant issues, and we hurry to say that we do not mean to brush aside all of Durkheim's theories regarding religion. Like Tylor and various other scholars of religion, he did much more than try to deal with the origins of religion, and his theories regarding the social nature and social roles of religion, as we will later note, are very much alive today in modified form.

Thus far, we have entirely omitted the most popular theory of origins: among the nonscholarly population of at least the civilized world surely the most common idea is that religion, if it be "true," has been divinely revealed. Divine revelation as an explanation of religious genesis has no place in this book, and under ordinary circumstances all theological interpretations of the origins of religion would be dismissed from consideration as irrelevant or prejudical. During the past several decades, however, theologians who are also social scientists have contributed empirical data relevant to an understanding of primitive religions and bearing directly upon theories of origin.

As we earlier noted, many of the theories of the rise of religion formulated in the late nineteenth century strongly reflect the idea of evolution, which dominated much of the scientific thought of the time in both the cultural and biological realms.[10] The religions of primitive peoples were regarded as representing the rude beginnings of theology. Evolutionary progress was toward monotheism. The culturally simpler primitive peoples, it was thought, had no conception of God and, of course, were not monotheistic. The prevalent idea, formulated first by Tylor, was that the idea of God was a late development, the slow outgrowth of an original animism or belief in a multitude of spiritual beings. The principal voice of protest raised against this line of thought was that of Andrew Lang, who stated that simple animism did not seem to be the standard for all crude societies.[11] Lang contended that some of the very simplest societies had as important figures in their religious pantheons deities endowed with very considerable power who dominated other supernatural entities, so that monolatry, if not monotheism, existed among some of the lowliest tribes.

This idea has been carried considerably further in the twentieth century by trained anthropologists who are also clerics. The objectives of these scholars, of whom Father Wilhelm Schmidt is the leading figure, differed from the scholarly interests and aims of Andrew Lang. Their chief objective was the antievolutionistic buttressing of Christian theology by attempting to demonstrate that monotheism was the original form of religion which became debased in certain societies. If evolution applied to religion, the *status quo* of Christianity was also, of course, imperiled by future evolutionary change. But the theological goals are of only incidental interest here. From the standpoint of social science, the positive contribution of the

[10] This is not to say that ideas of cultural evolution were borrowed from Darwin. Theories of both cultural and biological evolution have ancient and independent histories.

[11] Andrew Lang, *The Making of Religion*.

cleric-anthropologists lies in demonstrating fairly conclusively from data gathered in the field among the simplest primitive societies that high gods if not monotheism existed in the beliefs of some—but by no means all—peoples of crude and presumably very ancient cultures.[12]

The question of whether living primitive societies of the crudest cultural levels may be equated with the general condition of the society of primeval man remains much debated. Assuming that this equation is reasonable, it appears that early religious beliefs were quite diverse, sometimes conforming with Tylor's ideas of animism but in other societies involving hierarchically rated supernatural beings and high gods. Certainly such data as are available do not give adequate support to any general evolutionary scheme, applicable to religion as a whole, of progression from crude superstition to monotheism, although this has been the historic course for certain societies.

The sum of all these theories concerning religious origins can be presented in the simple statement that the origins remain unknown. In reviewing the lines of thought which the theories pursue, one wonders why their formulists might have searched for and expected to find a single set of circumstances which served as the initial spark for the numerous religious complexes of man. In a general sort of way, religion, as we have defined it, surely owes its existence to a single set of circumstances of a different nature, man's innate ability to think abstractly, to symbolize. We have called one kind of symbolically based thought religion or supernaturalism and the other naturalism. The origin of religion in the sense of the human anatomical structure and the physiology required for symbolic thought is, of course, unknown.

The particular bent of supernaturalistic reasoning and the super-structures of ritual and objects which have grown upon it—in other words, the development of individual religious complexes—is a very different subject. To determine the circumstances surrounding the inception of individual complexes we must look to local circum-

[12] Wilhelm Schmidt, *Der ursprung der Gottesidee.* See also writings by W. Koppers, M. Gusinde and P. Schebesta.

stances, now usually lost in antiquity. We can speculate that conditions such as those visualized by Tylor and other theorists may have been involved in the emergence of individual religions. The range of religious conceptions, as we shall see, is limited, and philosophically identical elements appear again and again in geographically widely separated cultures. It is impossible to avoid thinking that the limited range of man's religious and all other behavior reflects limited possibilities. The nature of the organism called man imposes limitations upon his behavior but nevertheless allows him a range. Coincidences and similarities of religion and other elements of culture, insofar as they are independent developments, reflect the effect of similar circumstances operating on sentient beings who are everywhere virtually the same.

Following this reasoning, the search for the origin of religion, religion in a generic sense, is a totally false problem. Who except the biologist and geneticist studying biological evolution would search among circumstances external to the human organism for factors which might have induced man to do his first symbolic thinking?

However the expression "origin of religion" is conceived, the subject remains obscured. We can say with assurance, however, that supernaturalistic beliefs and practices are ancient among man. This we know surely from the findings of archeology during the past century.

The earliest suggestions of religion are inferred from the manner of burial of the fossil man called Neanderthal Man, who lived in the Old World at a time variously estimated to have begun 50,000 to 100,000 or more years ago and to have ended perhaps 25,000 years ago. Neanderthal Man differed somewhat in physical characteristics from modern man. The bones of his skull were heavier, with protruding brow ridges and a sloping forehead. He had a large and heavy jaw but a poorly developed chin, and his head, supported by heavy neck musculature, was carried in a position thrust forward on his shoulders. All in all, his anatomy presents a picture of a short, sturdy, heavy-boned, bull-necked individual, who is thought to have walked with a stooping, somewhat bent-knee gait, but whose brain was the size of modern man's. It is clear from objects found in association with his skeletal remains that Neanderthal Man had culture. He lived principally in caves and left therein much evidence of his activities, charcoal from his fires, the bones of animals which he ate, and many stone implements which he manufactured and used.

What happened to Neanderthal Man is uncertain. His physical form may have undergone evolutionary change; he may have been wiped out by modern forms of man; or—as is suggested by finds at archeological sites in Palestine—he may have interbred with modern man and thus his offspring lost the markedly different physical characteristics by which he is distinguished from modern man.

Suggestions of religion in the culture of Neanderthal Man lie in the fact that he was not simply cast aside or abandoned upon death but was deliberately buried by his fellow men. Bodies were buried with care, sometimes with flat stones, presumably protective, placed above the heads, and stone tools such as those used in life were placed in the graves. Deliberate burial is thought to indicate beliefs in the survival of the spirit of the deceased and to represent a demonstration of respect for the spirit; the use of "grave goods" is usually interpreted to indicate a belief in an afterlife in which these objects may be useful to the spirit of the deceased. Judging from the practices of some modern primitive peoples, the objects placed with the interred bodies of Neanderthal men might also represent offerings to the now powerful spirits of the deceased. Other suggestions of the existence of supernaturalistic beliefs and practices in the culture of Neanderthal Man have also been found. The skulls and thigh bones of cave bears carefully arranged in altar-like fashion have been discovered in several European caves. One recent cave find consisted of the skull of a Neanderthal Man surrounded by a ring of small stones.

When Neanderthal Man and his culture disappeared from the world, modern man, *Homo sapiens,* became established as the only human type. Archeologically speaking, the cultural era now in question is the Upper Paleolithic or Late Old Stone Age. The time span covered by the various somewhat divergent Upper Paleolithic cultures of Europe, the area of the world archeologically best known for this period, is estimated to have been fifteen or twenty thousand years, ending approximately ten to fifteen thousand years ago. It is customary to refer to the fossilized specimens of *Homo sapiens* who were the makers of these European cultures as Cro-Magnon Man, after the name of a site in France of the early discovery of his remains. Like his predecessors, Cro-Magnon Man lived by hunting animals and gathering wild vegetable foods; and, like his predecessors he continued to use stone tools as his principal aids in gaining a livelihood.

As compared with earlier times, archeological evidence of the way of life of Cro-Magnon Man is abundant, in part because of an increase in the number of human beings and undoubtedly in part because the remains have lain in the ground a lesser time so that preservation and chance of recovery are better. Suggestions of Cro-Magnon Man's supernaturalistic beliefs and practices are numerous and varied. Deliberate burials with grave goods in the form of stone tools and the ornamental shells of molluscs were the standard practice. Cro-Magnon men were also artists, and applied their art to religion. Although not all Upper Paleolithic art is clearly or even probably religious in inspiration and nature, most descriptions of the art of Upper Paleolithic cultures of Europe are simultaneously discussions of religion. If the term art is interpreted to mean any embellishment over the utilitarian, Cro-Magnon Man practiced art in his burial practices, decorating the bodies with red ochre as well as with shells. Other and more outstanding forms of art included painting, engraving, carving in relief, sculpture, and some modeling in clay.

In the eyes of modern judges, the most outstanding form of art of Cro-Magnon Man is the paintings he laid on the walls of various caves of western Europe so that they represent veritable art galleries. Coloring matter consists principally of mineral pigments, red ochre, yellow ochre, and blue-black oxide of manganese. It is thought that burned and powdered bones were also used as a black pigment. The full range of colors—found only toward the end of the Upper Paleolithic era—is thus various shades of yellow, orange, red, brown, blue-black, and black. Animal fats are thought to have been used as a vehicle for the pigments, which were probably applied by fingers, by blowing through tubes made of hollow sections of long bones, and by means of brushes made of the various animal furs and vegetable fibers which were easily available. Preservation of cave paintings has been excellent because, barring disappearance from friction or abrasion, most of the pigments used are as imperishable as the stone walls which served as the canvases. The caves which contain these paintings were also generally long ago sealed and protected by landslides or other natural agencies, and their discovery in modern times has usually been accidental.

The subjects of the cave paintings, many of which are aesthetically very pleasing to modern eyes, were principally the now-extinct animals, prominently including bison, horses, and mammoths, which Cro-Magnon Man hunted. Man is only rarely depicted. These animals are often drawn as wounded by spears or spear cuts, bleeding, and—following the common interpretation—dying. These circumstances have led to the theory that the paintings represent supernaturalistic beliefs and practices of magic resting upon the idea, so common among historically known peoples, of sympathy or imitation : if one depicts a wounded or dying animal before going out to hunt, an animal will in fact be struck and killed by the hunter.

One of the remarkable facts about these paintings, and a strong reason for inferring magical rather than wholly decorative intent, is their location. Cro-Magnon Man used the mouths of caves as living quarters, but much of his most skillfully executed art is found in dark interiors and hard-to-reach crevices where artificial light provided by another cultural innovation, stone lamps burning animal fat, was necessary and where he appears to have gone only upon special occasions.

In discussing the question of the motives behind Upper Paleolithic art forms, the English prehistorian M. C. Burkitt makes a distinction between home art and cave art.[13] Home art consists of engrav-

---

[13] M. C. Burkitt, *The Old Stone Age.* Numerous folios present reproductions of Paleolithic art. See, for example, J. Maringer and Hans-Georg Bandi, *Art in the Ice Age.*

ings, sculptures, and paintings found at or near the places where the people lived, usually in the mouths of caves. Cave art is found only in the deep recesses of caves, in one instance a half-mile from the mouth of the cave, and in passages and crevices which can be reached only by creeping and climbing. Burkitt believes the purpose of home art was largely aesthetic or decorative, but that cave art was inspired by magico-religious beliefs and that the recessed areas which contain these examples of art were ritual chambers.

Additional features of cave paintings and other forms of art are also thought to suggest the existence of religious beliefs. One of the few anthropomorphic representations among the cave paintings has excited attention and been given the title of ''The Sorcerer'' because it depicts an indisputably male human being dressed in what appears to be ritual garb such as has been observed in use by religious practitioners among modern primitive peoples. The upper regions of the body are disguised by the head, antlers, and part of the skin of a deer. Another depicts a similarly garbed figure standing over a man lying on the ground. The two are thought to represent a medicine man and his patient. Sometimes the paintings and engravings on rock walls consist of palimpsests, figures of animals superimposed over other and presumably earlier figures. This practice has also been interpreted to indicate that the purpose of the art was magical because, to modern eyes at least, aesthetic appeal is lost by superimposition of this kind. Some scholars have thought that the pendulous abdomens of the animals depicted in paintings represent the witting portrayal of pregnancy, thus magically ensuring the increase of these animals which formed the principal sources of food. Carvings or engravings on bone, stone, antler, and ivory have also been thought to represent pregnant animals and fertility magic.

More noteworthy than engravings as suggestions of religion although far less common are models of animals in clay, found on cave floors. The deep interior of one French cave revealed the life-sized figure of a bear modeled in clay on the floor. The figure had been stabbed by spears and the earth around it was impacted. For ethnologists who have worked with living primitive peoples, it is not difficult to imagine the trampling of earth by the feet of men in a ritual dance about the bear. A similar find consisted of two bisons modeled in clay.

Sculpture, the art specialty of the early Upper Paleolithic culture called Aurignacian, is also thought to represent supernaturalistic practices in the form of fertility magic. Men of Aurignacian culture carved of sandstone, bone, and ivory small figures of human females, which modern archeologists have called Venuses because of their ample proportions. Venuses are highly stylized and nonnaturalistic representations in which parts of the female body associated with reproduction, the breasts and the abdomen, are greatly enlarged. Other parts of the body, such as the facial features, hair, and arms, are generalized or only suggested. Many scholars hold the view that the figurines represent pregnant women and suggest the presence of fertility magic based upon the idea of imitation.

As we progress to historic times among archeologically known cultures which existed after the passing of the Upper Paleolithic era of Europe, clear evidence of religion becomes abundant on all continents. Numerous discoveries have been made of many kinds of objects which could serve no obvious mundane or practical purpose and are thus assumed—or almost certainly known from comparison with similar objects in use among modern primitive societies—to represent ritual paraphernalia. Grave offerings often include food, clothing, and tools for the use of the deceased while en route to or after reaching a supernatural world. Common among grave goods are "killed" objects, a term applied to objects such as pottery containers and spear or arrow points which have been deliberately chipped, pierced, or broken before being placed in the graves. Among living primitive peoples this practice is followed with the belief that the spirits of the objects thus treated may also be released to accompany the spirit of the deceased human being. In early China and in other parts of Asia, burials of important persons involved a special kind of accompaniment: concubines, retainers, and slaves were slain and interred with their master so his wants and needs in the afterworld might be met by their spirits. Impressive remains of religious architecture, such as the famous stone ruins at Stonehenge and Avebury, England, and the great temples of the Maya in Yucatan, are well known from many parts of the world from times which antedate history.

In our discussion of the earliest evidences and suggestions of religion, we have thus far avoided any direct reference to the New World. The reason is simple. Archeological and paleontological research appears to show that the Americas knew no form of human beings until late times, perhaps 30,000 years ago. At that time modern man in the form of American Indians reached the New World by migration, probably from Asia by way of Siberia and Alaska. The cultural equipment of the migrants is generally assumed to have included supernaturalistic beliefs and practices, although archeology has as yet discovered no evidence of their existence in association with the earliest evidence of man in the New World. Later archeological sites in the Americas dating from a time at least several millennia ago, like their counterparts in other parts of the world, have revealed abundant evidence of religion.

Chapter 3. Conceptions of the Supernatural

Human beings interpret the new on the basis of previous experience, whether real or vicarious. The statement is a platitude, but it serves a purpose in leading us back to the subject of ethnocentrism as related to interpretations of exotic religions. As residents of the Western World, where Christianity and Judaism are the overwhelmingly dominant forms of religion, we are likely to visualize the supernaturalistic beliefs of all other peoples of the world after the model of these two fundamentally similar and historically connected religions.

Probably every citizen of literate nations of the world is aware of such exotic practices as witchcraft, polytheism, magic in many forms, and sacrifice, which differ from the prevailing modern religious practices of his own nation and culture. When the question arises most of us appear to assume, however, that the conceptions of the nature of the supernatural realm which might underlie these practices are everywhere the same as our own. Numerous similarities and coincidences do in fact exist among the religious complexes of the world, whether primitive or civilized; and the degree of coincidence may be described as more striking and more significant than the differences. If we examine the conditions of the not-very-distant religious past of the Western World we may find counterparts of perhaps every belief and act of supernaturalism known to the primitive world. But we may also find ideas for which there is no clear or strongly developed counterpart in modern Christianity and which scholars of the Western World during the nineteenth century, because they had little or no experience with these views, were unable to recognize as being different from the concepts of Christianity.

Since the late nineteenth century many scholars have seen among the cultures of the world two different but usually coexisting philosophies of supernaturalism and, correspondingly, two different although often intermingled kinds of religious action or ritual. Sometimes these scholars presented interpretations of religious philosophies underlying ritual acts which had the advantages of simplicity and decisive clarity, but were so rigid that the facts, as field ethnologists saw them, could not comfortably be made to fit them.

Tylor, who throughout presented an interpretation of religion, in its origins and in all its aspects and developments, as a rational kind of philosophy, saw magic as something of a very different order. Magic was for him fallacious reasoning, a pseudoscience, so distinct from religion that he separated discussion of the two by seven chapters.[1] To Tylor, magic was analogous with science and represented early and mistaken ideas of cause and effect. The presence of magic among societies with elaborate cultures he regarded as a survival from the distant past. His views of religion we know already as aggregations of belief and practice based upon the basic idea of the existence of spiritual beings with special powers.

Frazer, who was intellectually reared in the philosophy of cultural evolutionism as expounded by Tylor and other scholars of the late nineteenth century, followed Tylor in viewing magic as qualitatively different and sharply distinct from religion.[2] The fundamental conceptions which he saw as underlying the two kinds of behavior also, of course, differed markedly. Magic implied mistaken beliefs that man could control the supernatural world in the same manner that he controlled nature when he planted crops, felled trees, killed animals, and made objects for his own use. Magic was the fallacious science of primeval man which lingered among primitive societies and, less forcefully, among the civilized nations. Early man was a primitive scientist who, basing his acts upon erroneous ideas of association or of cause and effect, sought by means of prescribed recipes of magic to achieve his desired goals. Magic, as we

[1] E. B. Tylor, *Primitive Culture*.
[2] J. G. Frazer, *The Golden Bough*.

have noted, involved no attitudes of subjugation to powers greater than man, and no propitiation, humility, conciliation, or any other kind of behavior aimed at gaining ends by winning the favor of deities. Following Frazer's reasoning, these were the attitudes and techniques which characterized religion, a technique of survival which emerged and supplanted magic when man perceived that magic failed to achieve its goals.

Many criticisms have been made of Frazer's distinction between magic and religion and of his view that magic was the science of primitive man. Although they have common elements, scientific and magical acts are, of course, easily distinguishable. Both may be said to deal with cause and effect sequences. The cause and effect sequences of magic, however, are in the realm of the supernatural, which is rigidly excluded from science, and they, like the supernatural of which they are a part, are the fabrications of human minds which are neither experimentally determined nor verifiable. Primitive man also unquestionably was "scientific"; that is, he followed naturalistic behavior in hunting, gathering of roots and other vegetable foods, in raising crops, and so on. Whether primitive man himself always distinguished between his naturalistic and supernaturalistic practices is an unanswerable question, although most ethnologists appear to have assumed that he did.

A major criticism of Frazer's formulation arose from the unequivocal fact that magic and religion, as he had defined them, are often found intermingled in a single rite. This circumstance his critics of the time appear to have regarded as rendering Frazer's ideas worthless. His distinction between magic and religion is, however, far from dead. Magic has usually been distinguished from other supernaturalistic acts in descriptive accounts, and as we shall see, Frazer's conceptual distinction between the two has been revived, refined, and amplified.[3]

More recent interpretations of man's conceptions of the supernatural repeatedly present the idea that the fundamental factor in any and all religions is a belief in power of a kind which transcends the ordinary world but which may be put to practical as well as

[3] See especially, W. J. Goode, *Religion Among the Primitives,* and our chap. 4.

spiritually beneficial use in the natural world. This power is conceived in two basic fashions which may be seen to differ sharply from each other only in their extreme forms. Distinction between the two conceptions implies no necessary dichotomy, no unbridgeable border. Ideally or conceptually, sharp distinctions may be made, but in practice only the rarest case in all respects might meet the conceptual ideal. Views of the nature of the supernatural are described, in other words, as running a continuum between two theoretical poles between which no sharp line of division exists. The midpoint of the polar continuum represents equal composition of the characteristics defining each extreme. Thus individual rites which embrace both elements in equal quantity fall at midpoint, and whole religious complexes of similar ratio of composition would find the same placement. Although all known religions fall somewhere between the two poles, it is nevertheless possible and useful to speak of conceptions of the supernatural and associated religious action of a particular culture as being predominantly one or the other.

Theorists have most frequently called the two poles magic and religion. But use of these terms conflicts with our definition of religion and would exclude magic from consideration. To keep the record straight, let us repeat that our use of "religion" embraces magic, and to avoid confusion use here the terms "impersonal concept of the supernatural," and "personified concept of the supernatural," which are a slight modification of terms used by Ruth Benedict,[4] and are roughly comparable with the classifications magic and religion, respectively, of other scholars.

Benedict has given us the most succinct statement of the distinction, which has seldom in recent years been dealt with directly by other scholars but is implicitly used in many of their descriptive accounts of primitive religions. Following Benedict's writings but expanding and altering them and drawing illustrative materials from many sources, a restatement of the conceptual scheme distinguishing the two religious philosophies may be made along the lines that follow.

[4] Ruth Benedict, "Religion."

IMPERSONAL AND PERSONIFIED CONCEPTIONS
OF THE SUPERNATURAL

The impersonal pole implies a conception of the supernatural centered on impersonal power which transcends the phenomena of ordinary life. Power of this kind is not the permanent possession or inherent trait of gods or other spiritual entities but exists everywhere in man's universe or may be concentrated in certain classes of acts and material objects. Man, once he has mastered the necessary techniques, may amass and control this power in order to serve his own ends. Supernatural beings (which tend strongly to be "personified") may have at their command a greater amount of power of this kind than do mortals; they may better know how to gain and make use of the power, and they may bestow it upon man or help him to gain and use it effectively. They are not themselves, however, in this conception the ultimate sources of the power.

The impersonality of power of this sort lies in the facts that it is not an inalienable and inherent attribute of divine beings which confer it upon mortals; it may be handled like a material object; it may be gained by means impersonal and mechanical. In some religious beliefs it is given by one mortal to another, may be purchased and sold in whole or in part as a human economic transaction, and may be inherited by testamentary disposition. It may also be lost, gained, and shared with other human beings, and supernatural beings might also gain and lose it. It may work only for good in one society, and in another it may be harmful if directed to that end or if precautions are not observed in handling it.

Before we continue with discussion of views of impersonal power, it is useful here to describe briefly the criteria of the opposing pole, the personified concept of the supernatural, a subject to which we will later return for elaboration.

"Personified" means a conception of the supernatural in terms of the attributes of human beings, a projection of the self or ego so that the supernatural is viewed as being composed of and controlled by man-like beings or forces which behave as men behave. Referring to this concept of the supernatural we may aptly say that man created the supernatural world in his own image. Anthropomorphic or even zoomorphic form is not necessarily an attribute of supernatural entities found in concepts of this sort. Form may be various, but whether or not the supernatural beings have the form of men, they have other attributes of men, emotions, desires, moral codes and values. Natural phenomena such as rain, storms, the wind, or the sun and even abstract philosophic conceptions may be personified so that they have the emotions and behavior of man. These supernatural entities often have power over men, and they may use it to punish and reward. Like men, they judge, and like men they are good, bad, angry, pleased, frightful, benign, steadfast, capricious, lovable, and unlovable.

Benedict draws a distinction between impersonal and personified conceptions as being based upon analogies, on the one hand, with properties of objects, such as color and weight, and, on the other, with attributes of human beings—will, desires, emotions, and intentions. Man, states Benedict, used these two ways of thinking or interpreting the outside universe, both of them well known in his ordinary experience, and elaborated them into a creation of the supernatural world. Thus it was regarded either as a person like man himself or like the inanimate objects with which he was familiar in ordinary life.

These two kinds of religious philosophy, Benedict continues, have resulted in different kinds of behavior in the development of religion; that is, in the techniques of religion. Both philosophies are based upon mundane, commonplace experience and both represent projections of aspects of the external world into the formulation of a supernatural world. Neither has a priority, and the two philosophies and their attendant techniques of religion may coexist and cut across each other in diverse and numerous ways.

TYPES OF IMPERSONAL AND PERSONIFIED POWER

Awareness of the existence in various primitive societies of concepts of impersonal power as important components of religious beliefs did not come to the scholarly world of the West until the end of the nineteenth century. This tardiness in recognition does not appear to be entirely the result of lack of opportunity for acquaintance with the religions of primitive peoples. Published literature of the time concerning primitive religions was substantial and included many descriptions of the religions of American Indians, among whom the idea of impersonal power is particularly prevalent. But the vastly different central ideas of the well-known religions, Christianity, Judaism, and Islam, appeared to serve as a guide for interpretation and therefore also presented an obstacle in the way of understanding the beliefs of other peoples. Following the model of these faiths, the religions of primitive peoples were also generally interpreted in a personified mold, and such gods as existed in the primitive pantheon were likely to be credited with attributes similar to those of the Christian God or the Devil.

The publication, in 1891, of a work on Melanesian religion by R. H. Codrington attracted considerable scholarly attention and had important influence on subsequent interpretations of primitive religions.[5] Melanesia, with its many island groups extending from New Guinea eastward to Fiji and from the Bismarck Archipelago in the north to New Caledonia, includes a variety of cultures considerably divergent from each other. It has long been known that Codrington's description is not applicable to all Melanesian religions. As we shall later note, for example, it accords very poorly with the religion of Manus of the Bismarck Archipelago. The ideas he presented, however, appear to have inspired other students of primitive societies to examine their data from a different viewpoint, and, subsequently, primitive conceptions resembling those described for Melanesia have been reported from many other areas of the world.

Codrington's description emphasized magical practices, ancestor worship, and *mana* as the dominant elements in Melanesian religious beliefs and practices. Among these outstanding features, he regarded *mana*, an impersonal supernatural power or force, as fundamental and the others as peripheral. Melanesian religion, he stated, consisted principally of the pursuit of *mana*. Magic and, to a large extent, ancestor worship represented merely techniques for captur-

[5] R. H. Codrington, *The Melanesians*.

ing and using *mana*. Codrington described Melanesian *mana* as a force existing everywhere which acts in all ways for good and evil and which is of utmost importance for man to possess and control. Ghosts of the dead and spirits of many kinds had *mana* and it resided in numerous objects; by mechanical acts of magic and by propitiation of spirits man gained *mana* and controlled it. It was highly communicable and could be drawn from and imparted to objects and man.

Since the time of Codrington, *mana* has come to be used generically to mean impersonal supernatural power, and it is sometimes used to mean simply supernatural power whether personified or impersonal. The term itself also exists in the language of the nearby Polynesians, and a similar but not identical concept was important in the culture of aboriginal Polynesia.[6]

Polynesian *mana*, like its Melanesian relative, was highly communicable but it was much more dangerous. The Polynesian conception also differed from the Melanesian in other respects, largely in keeping with broader distinctions, especially in social organization, between the two cultures. Polynesian *mana* took on a personified flavor in the sense that it was viewed as the inherent possession of persons of high rank, and it was conferred chiefly by the impressive pantheon of powerful gods who held it in great quantity. In Melanesia one's social prestige and *mana* were gained principally by personal achievement; in most of Polynesia, society was stratified into hereditary classes and *mana* followed these lines of social class. Kings, chiefs, and the nobility, who were regarded as the descendants of the gods, had the greatest amount and commoners the least; within each class women had less than men. Rulers were sometimes so imbued with *mana* that they became almost physically immobilized by it for the reason that anything with which they came in contact became charged with *mana*, dangerous to those of lower social status who possessed and who were regarded as capable of possessing only smaller quantities. The high chiefs of aboriginal Tahiti were regarded as so laden with *mana* that they could move about outside their homes only when transported by specially

---

[6] See, for example, E. S. C. Handy, *Polynesian Religion*.

insulated bearers. The touch of their feet or hands rendered the ground and all other objects which they touched dangerous to ordinary people. *Mana* was thought to be concentrated in the head, and death was the penalty for passing anything over the head of a chief.

Thus the Polynesian concept of *mana* had a feature lacking in Melanesia, an exceedingly elaborately developed complex of taboos associated with *mana*. Some objects and acts were viewed as being permanently and irrevocably taboo because of the *mana* inherent in them. Menstruation, sickness, and death were surrounded by taboos of unsacredness. Some taboos were imposed by rulers like the promulgation of laws, and might be lifted by them, although these were often known by another name and seemed to be more secular. The aboriginal Polynesian went through life surrounded by taboos, some of them prohibitions which were trivial in the sense that they involved little watchfulness or discipline and others serving more forcefully to restrict behavior. A good number of Polynesian taboos were in effect also sumptuary laws. In Hawaii, women could not eat bananas and many other foods, and commoners of both sexes were restricted from certain foods. Occupations of prestige were often restricted to the hereditary nobility. Above all, one had to follow strict convention and many prohibitions in matters of religious ritual and contact with chiefs and royal persons. The Polynesians believed that their welfare depended upon their gods and upon their rulers as embodiments or descendants of the gods.

Mana in Polynesia could also be gained by the individual in various ways that included eating the heart or eye of an enemy slain in war. Proof of the possession of *mana*, as everywhere else where similar concepts are held, lay in one's success. The outstanding warrior, the skillful craftsman, the successful in any line of effort was looked upon as possessing *mana* beyond the ordinary.

Polynesian *mana* and Codrington's interpretation of Melanesian *mana* are the most frequently cited examples of impersonal supernatural power, and we shall linger no longer in describing them. Similar ideas are found in all parts of the globe, sometimes as subsidiary elements of religious beliefs and sometimes as dominant themes.

The *kami* of aboriginal Japan appears to have resembled Polynesian *mana* in some respects. Supernatural beings, rulers, and members of the royal lineages (who, as in most of Polynesia, were descendants of the gods), and also numerous unusual and impressive phenomena of nature—oddly shaped stones and trees, great and impressive mountains, waterfalls—were all *kami* invested with power. The ordinary person in Japan did not gain and lose *kami;* it was the attribute of those men and objects which were above and beyond ordinary man. *Kami,* in short, represented the realm of the supernatural and it implied both impersonal and personified supernatural power. The power of the emperor could, however, be transmitted to lesser persons in a harmful way. Accounts by sixteenth and seventeenth century European visitors to Japan tell us that to avoid harm to his subjects by communication of his power, the emperor took various precautions. He ate from cheap, coarse earthenware that was later destroyed to prevent the death by strangulation of others who might use them, as the food would swell in their throats.[7] When he left the imperial compound he must be carried in a palanquin or wear sandals one span in height so that his power might not make the ground dangerous to ordinary men.[8] Thoroughly harmful and quite impersonal power of another kind also existed in Japanese beliefs. Contact with blood and death resulted in harmful pollution and made the afflicted person dangerous to others and to the gods, who might incur pollution from contact. Thus Japan also had an elaborate network of taboos of somewhat different inspiration from some of those we have described for Polynesia, but resting on a similar idea of communicable power.[9]

The religious beliefs of North American Indians are particularly abundant in concepts of supernatural power of varying degree of impersonality, and for many tribal groups impersonal power has been described as a prominent element. Indian tribes of the Great Plains afford the best examples. An outstanding feature of the religious behavior of the more than thirty tribes who in aboriginal

[7] Engelbert Kaempfer, *History of Japan.*
[8] George Schurhammer (S.J.), *Shinto, The Way of the Gods in Japan.*
[9] E. Norbeck, ''Pollution and Taboo in Contemporary Japan.'' Similar ideas of pollution also existed in Polynesia.

times inhabited the great central plain of the present-day United
States and Canada consisted of attempts to gain hallucinatory
visions or revelations, which were the conventional means of gaining
power.[10] This vision quest has sometimes been described as the mainspring of Plains Indian religion. But for some tribes it seems more
appropriately regarded as peripheral to the central element of
supernatural power, as it represented only the technique for gaining
power. Visions, of and for themselves, did not constitute ultimate
goals, but they stand out so prominently among the religious acts
of the Plains Indians that they have come to be described as its
more important feature. The Plains Indian, by means of depriving
himself of food and by self-torture, sought a vision as the sign that
he had received power. Things and events which were seen in visions
were as varied as subconscious imagination might allow; the truly
important point was not so much what was seen but merely that the
visionary experience had occurred, for this was the sign of having
acquired power. Visions were interpreted, and objects or living
forms seen in these hallucinations were regarded as the visionaries'
guardian spirits, who conferred or helped gain the power and who
might be appealed to on future occasions when the recipient wished
to make special use of his grant. And again, proof of the receipt
of power—of having had a "true" vision—lay in results. The recipient of a vision who was successful, especially the man who became an outstanding warrior, had truly received power.

The numerous tribes of the Great Plains did not conceive of
power in identical fashion, but generally speaking, societal gods
were thrust to the background. Some deities, such as the Sun, were
well known, and they might be appealed to for aid in getting power,
but they themselves were not the objects of general worship. The
guardian or tutelary spirit which the individual saw in a vision was
for him the important supernatural being, and the role of the spirit
was that of personified benificent helper or bestower of lasting impersonal power rather than that of omnipotent controller. Power,
once received outright, might variously be sold, given away, or be-

[10] See, for example, Ruth Benedict, *The Concept of the Guardian Spirit in North America.*

queathed, and, in varying degree from tribe to tribe, was handled as an object or commodity, although of a very special nature. This power of the Plains Indians was sometimes like that of Polynesia in its impersonality but differed in many other respects: it did not have the electricity-like qualities of communicability and danger from physical contact with individuals who held it and, accordingly, it ordinarily involved no system of taboos. In keeping with the social scheme of Plains tribes, among which social status was generally by individual achievement rather than by birth, no individual inherently had power and any individual was eligible to receive it. Except insofar as a relative with power might give or bequeath it to one, individuals generally began life on terms of equality with respect to power.

Among the many Indian tribes of the Great Plains and other areas of North America concepts of power varied from the highly impersonal to the personified and both commonly coexisted. Both might be subsumed under a single linguistic term, best translated as supernatural.

The *wakan* of the Siouan tribes might refer directly to supernatural power of the kind we have described and it might also mean supernatural beings, objects, places, magical rites, persons of unusual eminence, or a variety of additional living forms and inanimate objects which were regarded as surpassing the ordinary. Thus *wakan* embraced all of the supernatural world and served as a generic term for it. The horse, which came to these Indians from the white man, was called "*wakan* dog" and the gun "*wakan* iron." Among the Dakota, lightning and sleight-of-hand were *wakan*— wonderful, mysterious, incomprehensible. To speak or to run unusually well were also *wakan*. A group of subaquatic, subterranean spirits called Unktehi by the Dakota could project from their bodies power that was irresistible even by the superior gods. This power was infused into fetishes.[11]

The term *manitou* of Algonquin-speaking tribes, which were concentrated chiefly in the area north and east of the central Great Plains, also comprehended all of the supernatural and embodied

[11] J. O. Dorsey, *A Study of Siouan Cults*, pp. 432-435.

concepts of supernatural power both impersonal and personal. When an Algonkian Indian referred to impersonal power, he put the term *manitou* in inanimate gender; when he referred to man-like supernatural beings the animate gender was used.[12]

In American Indian conceptions, power might be highly specialized. Among the Northern Paiute of Oregon, California and Nevada one received through visionary dreams power of various but sharply restricted kinds, including doctoring power which enabled him to cure the afflictions of others, bullet power which made him impervious to bullets, antelope power for charming and thus successfully hunting antelopes, snake power giving control over rattlesnakes and rendering them harmless to individuals, and love power with which to win desired affections.[13]

The *buha* of the White Knife Shoshoni of Nevada, neighbors of the Northern Paiute, was similar.[14] One had to have *buha* in order merely to live, but beyond the necessary minimum it was accorded to each individual in different degrees. One gained additional and specialized *buha* in unsolicited dreams and also through seeking it by remaining overnight in certain areas—caves, mountain passes, and hidden valleys—regarded as reservoirs for specific powers. Spending the night in one of these places, the suppliant received the desired power from various supernatural beings provided he had a vision or dream and followed the instructions given therein. The highly varied types of power included those known to the Northern Paiute and also various specialties within the realm of curing, wolf power to become a cunning hunter, power to control the weather, to run fast, to fight well, power which gave longevity, and even power that allowed its holders to violate certain traditional mores without supernatural punishment.

These examples of concepts of impersonal power have of course emphasized the impersonal criteria; that is, we have selected from total religious complexes certain important elements to illustrate

[12] Ruth Benedict, "Religion."

[13] W. Z. Park, *Shamanism in Western North America.*

[14] J. S. Harris, "The White Knife Shoshoni of Nevada," in Ralph Linton, ed., *Acculturation in Seven American Indian Tribes,* pp. 56-61.

the ideas set forth. This does not mean to deny that personified conceptions are absent from these religions. A brief review of our examples quickly reveals the existence of personified elements and suggests others. The vision quest of American Indians did not always or even most frequently imply impersonal power, or the existence of one kind of power to the exclusion of the other. Power was sometimes an outright gift of the guardian spirit, which, once received, could be used without further contact with the tutelary. In other Indian societies, the guardian spirit and his human ward entered a continuing relationship, whereby it was necessary to call upon the spirit whenever aid was needed. Where power came as an outright gift, it had the trait of impersonality and could be passed on to others for their use.[15] Even where highly personalized guardian spirits with supernatural power aided their human protégés, however, a tendency existed to view the power as being in some measure impersonal, vested in medicine bundles or other objectifications that might be used by others.[16]

Perhaps the best examples of strongly personified religion are Judaism, Christianity, and Islam, wherein the important and omnipotent supernatural entity is often conceived as having human form, and is consistently regarded as being sentient, as having a will, wishing, watching, judging, feeling anger and joy, and meting out punishments and beneficences in accordance with individual and group morality—in short, acting as men act. Even in these religions, however, ideas of impersonal power are included as minor elements. The Christian cross is vested with power of its own, as are talismans, holy water, and, if properly manipulated, beads. The practice of spitting on stones, bullets, arrows, and other missiles appears to be a vestige of a belief in transmitting potency, although it probably bears no relationship to Christianity. Among Moslems, the idea of *barakka*, a supernatural power which resides in religious practitioners, rulers, mountains, and children, and which may be transmitted by contact, such as in kissing the hand of a ruler, provides another example. Religious behavior among orthodox adherents to

---

[15] See Regina Flannery, ''Two Concepts of Power.''
[16] See, for example, Diamond Jenness, *The Ojibway Indians of Parry Island*.

Christianity, Judaism, and Islam is nevertheless principally a matter of conducting oneself in such a way as to win the approval of an omniscient and very man-like if exceedingly virtuous supernatural being.

The aim here is not to present a comprehensive roster of examples to illustrate the distinctions we have discussed, especially since additional examples may be drawn from materials which follow. It is instead to present and discuss the ideas of theorists of recent years who have concerned themselves with analysis or exposition of the rationale behind, or the conceptions presumably underlying, supernaturalistic behavior. It must be added that use of the phrase "recent years" is misleading; nearly all theoretically oriented anthropological writing on religion of scope so great as to attempt to comprehend the religions of man as a whole emerged two or more decades ago. Since that time, studies of religion have largely ignored these theoretical matters or have denied that they have value.

Among the ranks of anthropologists, a strongly authoritative voice, now over three decades in the past, arose in protest against the polar scheme of human conceptions of the supernatural world. Bronislaw Malinowski found it impossible to accept the idea that magic rested upon or was in any way directly connected with primitive philosophical or metaphysical conceptions of *mana*-like power pervading the universe. He offered in its place the theory that magical formulae arose from human experience of another kind, that the procedures of magic were the spontaneous formulations of individuals at times of stress when recourse to all naturalistic means known to the individual failed. At times of intense stress, he argues, some course of positive action is the "natural" response of man, and in these spontaneous acts man forecasts by word or action the results he desires. The spontaneous rite or spell which man strikes upon during the strongly emotional state of crisis—obviously effective because the crisis passes without mishap—takes on the quality of a revelation. It "seems to get hold of us from outside, and to primitive man, or to the credulous and untutored mind of all ages, the spontaneous spell, the spontaneous rite, and the spontaneous belief in their efficiency must appear as a direct revelation from some external and no doubt impersonal source.''[17] The foundations of magical practice are thus due to experiences actually lived through, from which man received the revelation of power, or magical rites, to attain his desired ends. Passed on to other members of society, these formulae become stripped of the emotion which surrounded them at their birth and are transformed into the prosaic and essentially emotionless acts which characterize most magic.

These ideas of Malinowski may be viewed in the same light as other theories of the ''origins'' of religion, as unverifiable speculation. There is merit, however, in Malinowski's contention that the theory of *mana* or impersonal power as the essence of primitive magic and religion has been ''brilliantly advocated and . . . recklessly handled.''[18] Interpreters of primitive religions have sometimes gone too far and imputed to primitive cultures far more clearly formulated and sharply outlined philosophical conceptions than knowledge of these cultures seems to warrant. Raymond Firth has called the interpretation of *mana* as pervasive impersonal power underlying magical practices a ''figment of anthropological theory.''[19] There is no doubt that scholars seeing in concepts of impersonal power the mainsprings of magic have sometimes interpreted Polynesian *mana* and similar ideas of primitive people in a way that suits their theories. The description of *mana* given in the foregoing pages certainly does not do justice to all the intricacies of this idea of the Polynesians. Yet it is impossible to avoid seeing the impersonal traits of Polynesian *mana* and many other concepts of supernatural power.

To the average man or woman of primitive society, as to many of their civilized counterparts, theology or the philosophy of supernaturalistic behavior is probably only hazily conceived and is doubtless a matter of little concern. The direct acts, the means to ends, are the things of importance and it is these upon which attention is focussed and to which rapt interest is given. Among the simplest societies, where specialists devoting full time to the practice of re-

[17] B. Malinowski, *Magic, Science, and Religion*, pp. 61-62.
[18] *Ibid.*, p. 59.
[19] Raymond Firth, *The Work of the Gods in Tikopia*, vol. 2, p. 377.

ligion are absent, the formulation of clear-cut embracive philosophies of religion of the sophisticated kind expected by civilized
scholars does not exist. The scholars themselves have in a real sense
become the religious formulators, at least the religious philosophers,
for the cultures which they describe. In their defense, it may be said
that this course of action is reasonable and even necessary, the
prerogative and special competence of scholars in order to interpret
and present their data in a comprehensible fashion. If, in the interests of simplicity and clarity, errors of interpretation or emphasis have been made, we can do nothing but await additional
information and reinterpretation.

An important consideration in connection with the conceptual
scheme presented here of the underlying philosophies of religion is
the assumption that the active religious behavior of the people of a
particular society is consistent with their concepts of the supernatural. This statement, of course, puts the case backwards; inferences about a people's ideas of the supernatural are presumably
always formed by social analysts if not by theologians from the patterns of observable behavior rather than taken directly from verbal-
ized theological ideals of dogma. It is then to actual behavior of
peoples to which we must turn for expansion and further illustration of the ideas we have attempted to set forth.

As we have implied, the analytical schemes which attempt to
classify philosophies of supernaturalism also align observable behavior, the acts of religion, with the philosophical concepts. Thus
they create the impression that the philosophies or dominant themes
were formulated first and the acts of religion later grew as locally
variant accretions always derived from distinguishable underlying
philosophies. To try to relate all forms of supernaturalistic behavior
directly and in a reasonable way to one or another of the poles or to
one or another of the categories "magic" and "religion" is not an
easy task, however.

If the writings on religion by trained observers are reviewed, it
is clear that man frequently does not sharply distinguish between
kinds of supernatural power as personified or impersonal, as we
have given meaning to these terms, and the techniques, the physical

acts, of religion accordingly may not be sharply aligned with the conceptual poles.

As much evidence from living cultures attests, magic, itself impersonal, is perfectly compatible with beliefs in personalized power which is inalienably in the hands of or in the persons of man-like entities. Where concepts of supernatural power reach heights of impersonality, such as the *maxpe* of the Crow Indians,[20] power may be gained by means other than formulae, as through a vision or through the intercession of gods with human qualities. Highly personalized techniques of propitiation of deities are also used by mortals to gain power which subsequently is impersonal in the sense that it is handled as an alienable object, and highly personalized deities may be forced to the bidding of man by mechanical procedures of magic.

The polar continuum has nonetheless been useful as a device for interpretation, classification, and exposition, and much if not all of religious behavior may be related to it. To embrace the religious acts which do not fit this scheme, it is possible to think of the supernaturalistic conceptions of man as forming a constellation of three elements:

1. A personified conception whereby supernatural power and supernatural events depend upon the wish, will, caprice, and judgment of man-like beings or powers.

2. A conception of impersonal power existing here and there or everywhere in the universe, which may be manipulated by man once he has himself gained it or learned the mechanical procedures for controlling it, and may also be treated in the same manner by supernatural beings.

3. A conception of supernatural efficiency or power inherent in certain mechanical cause and effect sequences.

The first two conceptions are recognizable as the familiar polar concept of our earlier discussion. Outside the path between these two poles but impinging upon it in many ways is the third and added element, the idea of efficiency (it is hardly power in the same sense as the other conceptions) which comes through or lies in

[20] R. H. Lowie, *Religion of the Crow Indians.*

certain sequences of events. Thus, if use is made of the adjectives "personified" and "impersonal," our added conception is impersonal; the mechanical procedures bear no direct relations to the emotions or other attributes of man, but refer to certain acts of magic. The chains of events of many magical formulas—meticulous performance of certain steps leading to a guaranteed result—are surely impersonal but it is often difficult to see them as corollaries or natural concomitants of the conceptions of pervading impersonal power, to see them as means used to control or use any reservoir or body of potent force.

Certain magical formulas are indeed used to gain lasting power, as in eating organs of the body of a human being or lower animals to gain the courage, strength, or wisdom of the living organisms; but other mechanical procedures are used differently. Power lies in these acts themselves for the moment or for a transitory and specific end, and they exist as standardized behavior in luxurious abundance in societies where pervasive and communicable power like that of *mana* is scarcely conceived. As chains of events leading to known and certain results, provided no error is made in their execution, they hold much in common with the cause and effect sequences which we call naturalism or science.

How man may have hit upon these magical rites, how he came to believe them efficacious is a matter of conjecture. Analogies in human experience conceivable as the source of this third and added conception of the supernatural are mundane acts which are seen to accomplish ends, behavior such as subjecting raw foods to heat and changing their properties, using a fire drill to produce fire, or piercing an animal with a spear to bring about its death. These are acts which, before they became the order of the day and the knowledge of all, might once have been placed in the realm of the supernatural as extraordinary and inexplicable. But we can go no further with this line of thought, which can lead only to the question of the unknown physiological factors which give man the capacity to reason or symbolize.

We may note, however, that over and over again throughout the world most of the mechanical procedures of magic are analagous with observed naturalistic events and thus manifestly represent ideas which come easily to man. The constant repetition in varied form of the same themes of imitation and contagion are due, on the one hand, to the essential identical capabilities of reasoning of all varieties of man—the "psychic unity of mankind," as we once called it—and, on the other, to diffusion of particular rites and techniques from society to society. Where the steps of magic do not reveal perceivable analogies, perceivable imitation or contagion, we may assume that rational and understandable connections between act and result may once have existed or that the formulae arose from other sources, perhaps dreams, visions, hallucinations, or circumstances such as imagined by Malinowski. Whatever the origin of magical procedures, they may be used in three ways, to gain and later to use impersonal power, to control personified deities, and, of themselves, as means of accomplishing by supernatural means highly specific ends which have no readily observable connection with conceptions of the supernatural as personified or as impersonal lasting power.

Thus, although our three conceptions of power or efficiency are logically distinguishable, the techniques or types of actual behavior which might be associated with them overlap so that none of the groups of techniques clustering about the three concepts is entirely exclusive. Personalized techniques of propitiation may win impersonal power; mechanical techniques may control the personalized deities; and mechanical acts of magic need bear no relation to either conceptions of man-like gods or *mana*-like power. To be successful, the hunter might be viewed as requiring special and lasting hunting power or the aid of supernatural beings, but the desired end may also be achieved by an otherwise powerless individual, unaided by man-like gods, provided he know and follow the supernatural cause and effect sequence or magic which is required as a preliminary before each hunt.

Chapter 4. Religious Acts

Convention has long labeled supernaturalistic acts as either magic or religion. For lack of another economical word given authority by use, we will use the term magic and divide supernaturalistic acts into the two categories magical and nonmagical. Following our earlier discussion, this two-fold classification might also be called "impersonal acts of supernaturalism" and "personalized acts of supernaturalism," but the expressions seem far too cumbersome for repeated use.

Magical acts adhere most closely to the conceptions of power we have called impersonal; nonmagical acts (those which are generally called religion) cluster principally about the personified conception. Thus we emerge with two classes of techniques associated with what we have deduced for purposes of exposition as three concepts of power. To repeat, all conceptions and types of acts may and frequently do coexist, cutting across each other in many ways.

The most recent reformulation of the distinction between the two classes of behavior is that of William J. Goode, who makes use of a polar scheme of interpretation. Magic and religion (which correspond with our "nonmagical" category) he states, represent a continuum and they are distinguished only "ideal-typically." According to Goode's formulation, the decision as toward which pole a complex of supernatural practices may be placed requires several characteristics, each of which is a variable running between the two opposing poles. He provides a useful summary of what he describes as characteristics emerging most prominently in anthropological writings as theoretical aids in distinguishing between magic and religion:

1. *Concrete specificity of goal* relates most closely to the magical complex. This overlaps toward the religious goal more than most characteristics, since religious rewards are usually to be found in this world. However, religious goals do lean more heavily in the direction of "general welfare," "health," "good weather," and eschatological occurrences.

2. The *manipulative attitude* is to be found most strongly at the magical pole, as against the supplicative, propitiatory, or cajoling, at the religious pole.

3. The *professional-client relationship* is ideally-theoretically to be found in the magical complex. The shepherd-flock, or prophet-follower, is more likely in the religious.

4. *Individual ends* are more frequently to be found toward the magical end of this continuum, as against groupal ends toward the other.

5. The magical practitioner or his "customer" *goes through his activities as a private individual,* or individuals, functioning much less as groups. At the religious extreme pole, groups carry them out, or representatives of groups.

6. With regard to the process of achieving the goal, in case of magical failure, there is more likely to be a *substitution or introduction of other techniques.* Stronger magic will be used, or magic to offset the counter-magic of enemies, or even a different magician. Since much of religious activity is less specifically instrumental, is concerned more with the intrinsic meaning of the ritual, and is expected to achieve concrete goals indirectly, by maintaining the proper continuing relationship with the gods, such a substitution is far rarer in the area of the religious pole.

7. Although the practitioner may feel cautious in handling such powerful forces, a *lesser degree of emotion* is expected at the magical end of this continuum. This may be described as *impersonality.* At the religious end, one expects a greater degree of emotion, possibly awe or worship.

8. The *practitioner decides whether* the process is to start at all, toward the magical pole. Toward the religious, the ritual *must* be carried out. That it must be done is part of the structure of the universe.

9. Similarly, the *practitioner decides when* the process is to start, in the case of magic, more often than in the case of religion. Toward the latter end of the continuum, the time relationships of rituals are fairly fixed, within rough limits, even when not calendrical.

10. Defined as instrumental by the society, magic is thought of as at least *potentially directed against the society,* or a major accepted group within it, or a respected individual in good repute with the gods. Religious

rituals are not thought of as even potentially directed against the society
or such respected people.

11. As a final, ideally distinguishing characteristic, magic is *used only
instrumentally*, i.e., *for goals*. The religious complex may be used for goals,
but at its ideal pole, the practices are ends in themselves.[1]

Although all of Goode's criteria do not bear direct relation to the
distinction we have drawn between impersonal and the personified
views of the supernatural, many of them may be seen as reflections
of the two different philosophical conceptions. Mechanical manipulation; the professional-client relationship, substitution of other
techniques when one fails, impersonality, relative lack of emotion,
and arbitrary decision as to whether rites are to be conducted are
all complementary to a view of the supernatural as being object-
like, a commodity to be handled in a certain fashion to achieve certain results. These characteristics also apply to magical cause and
effect sequences that have no relation to ideas of lasting power,
personified or impersonal. The opposing extremes of behavior are,
correspondingly, most compatible with a personified view of the
supernatural.

To bring out in sharper outline the distinctions between the two
kinds of behavior, each of them will be considered in greater detail.

IMPERSONAL OR MAGICAL TECHNIQUES

The classification of magical practices most firmly established
comes to us from Frazer,[2] who advanced the theory that all magic is
based upon the idea of sympathy between things, persons, and
events, and that magic rests upon two "principles of thought."
The first of these, which he called the Law of Similarity, is that
like produces like or that an effect resembles its cause; the second,
the Law of Contact or Contagion, is the belief that things once in
contact with each other remain forever in association even if the
contact is physically severed. Following the Law of Similarity, the
magical practitioner infers that he can produce any desired effect

[1] W. J. Goode, *Religion Among the Primitives*, pp. 53-54.
[2] J. G. Frazer, *The Golden Bough*.

by imitating it. Following the Law of Contact or Contagion he assumes that whatever he does to any material thing once in contact with a human being, a lower form of animal life, or any other material object will be communicated to the entity with which it was formerly in contact. Frazer divided magic into the two categories: contagious, resting upon the Law of Contact or Contagion; and homeopathic or imitative, based upon the Law of Similarity.

Published descriptions of magical practices are particularly abundant. Frazer alone, in *The Golden Bough*, has given us twelve volumes devoted chiefly to their description. We shall here give only minimal descriptions of the most prevalent kinds.

IMITATIVE MAGIC

A large percentage of the supernaturalistic practices of man may be placed under the category of imitative magic. These are precise formulas used to achieve specific ends by imitating them, and include both "white" or beneficial and "black" or harmful magic. Familiar examples are fertility rites to ensure or increase the growth of crops and the successful birth of animals or human beings by such acts as symbolically depicting bountiful harvests or sexual intercourse, pregnancy, and parturition. Like the cave art of the Old Stone Age or totemic rites of Australian aborigines, imitative magic may be used to ensure or increase the food supply of edible animals. Rain magic involving the imitation of falling rain or flowing water is common among primitive peoples who subsist chiefly by horticulture. The reversal of customary procedures of any form of ritual, such as the Black Mass, might also be called imitative; that is, if doing things in conventional order brings beneficial results, then inversion should result in the opposite.

One of the most striking and prevalent forms of imitation is called image magic. Images range from the highly concrete and pictorial, doll-like representations of human beings or animals to the symbolic, and in the last century have come to include photographs. The acts which one performs upon the images by imitation—most frequently evil deeds such as stabbing, mutilation, burning, searing with acid—are thought to come about in actuality. Refinements of technique to regulate the speed of death or severity of illness are well developed. Death may be brought about slowly and in lingering pain or rapidly and violently.

Recorded practices of imitative magic fill many volumes, and a complete inventory for all societies would probably reveal that the range of magical imitation omits no events or conditions which man might for any motive view as desirable.

CONTAGIOUS MAGIC

Imitation in acts of magic is usually easy to recognize. Ideas of sympathy or association involved in contagious or homeopathic magic, however, are sometimes less easily seen. At least, the nature of the associations upon which they are based must sometimes be explained before the practices may be understood as contagious magic. Supernaturalistic ideas of sympathy extend over a tremendous range, far exceeding that of mere imitation or of contagion from direct contact. Ideas of affinity may be applied to any objects, organisms, or other phenomena which share common characteristics. Thus, for example, ideas of magical affinity may be regarded as existing among related persons, among age-mates, and among members of social groups of many other kinds. Whatever good or harm befalls objects or individuals of one class also befalls other members of the class without any necessary direct contact, unless magical preventive measures are taken. Ideas such as this are easy enough to understand, but variation from society to society may be so great as to require explanation of the nature of the affinity. The scope of ideas of sympathy of this kind is unknown, but it seems safe to state that at least any logical associations, however differently they may be construed from culture to culture, may serve as the basis for contagious magic.

A common form of contagious magic is called exuvial magic, as it involves the use of human exuviae, hair combings, teeth, nail clippings, excreta, spittle, placentae, and the umbilici of new-born infants. Although the expression exuvial magic is usually limited to practices involving only organic materials such as the foregoing, many other magical rituals of essentially identical nature depend upon the use of inorganic articles such as clothing and personal possessions or other objects once in contact with a human being, and even the footprints or names of persons. Pierce a human footprint or the track of an animal with a spear and its maker will become halt; burn nail clippings or strands of hair and the individual from whom they came will suffer. Hang the skin or other part of the body of a dead animal in a tree and others of its species will be attracted for better hunting. The fear of exuvial magic may be so great that extreme care is taken to perform natural functions with great secrecy and to conceal all exuviae. Among some Melanesian societies, even leftover food, because it was once in contact with hands and lips, might be used to effect harmful magic and must be guarded.

Exuvial magic is today found chiefly among primitive societies, but magical practices at childbirth involving the placenta and the umbilicus of the new-born child are by no means limited to primitive peoples. In modern, rural Japan the placenta is still commonly buried in a traditional place, often in the dirt floor inside the entrance to the house if the child is a first-born male and outside the house if the child is female. Thus one ensures that the male child will remain home after maturity and that the female, by marrying out in normal fashion upon reaching maturity, will leave the home of her birth. The placenta may also be buried at a crossroads, where the passage of many people will dissipate little by little the danger inherent in it. Traditionally, the umbilicus, taken internally, is an effective remedy for illness which might befall the child in question later in life.

Both of these latter practices, burial of the placenta at a crossroads and ingestion of the umbilicus, involve ideas of contagion widely used in other contexts. Dissipation of harm through transference to the human beings who walk the path embodies the familiar idea of the scapegoat. Taking its name from the ancient Hebrew practice of driving into the wilds a goat laden with the sins of the community, the scapegoat has many counterparts in other societies and has, of course, also come to have derived usage in secular contexts. Supernatural beings, human beings, lower animals, or objects may serve as scapegoats and their use may involve goals as varied as expression of repressed desires by attributing forbidden behavior to supernatural beings, expulsion of sins, eradication of ceremonial pollution, and curing of disease. Rubbing with a stick, stone, or other object the body of a man stricken with disease and disposing of the new carrier of the ailment is thus the principle of the scapegoat in a somewhat different guise.

The nature of the sympathy which gives therapeutic value to ingestion of one's umbilicus is unclear, but many similar practices involve little doubt. Eating the heart of a lion may give temerity; that of a rabbit, timidity. Parts of the body—the heart, the liver, or other organ—regarded as the seat of power or emotions tend to be given special emphasis and confer the strength of the organism from which they came. Practices of this kind involve not only the consumption of lower animals and fellow men but also, in theophagy, the symbolic partaking of the bodies of supernatural beings for religious benefit.

Contagious and imitative magic are often intimately intertwined in single formulae. Image magic in pure form is imitative, and exuvial magic contagious, but they are often much alike and are sometimes hardly distinguishable. Adding to the image an article of clothing or a lock of hair from the human object in question before magical acts are performed may be a requirement or it may merely add efficacy.

MAGICAL CAUSE AND EFFECT SEQUENCES

Much of the behavior of man conventionally regarded as magic may be comfortably placed within the two foregoing categories, but a large number of common magical acts—so called because they involve mechanistic procedures and are thought to achieve or lead to results in mysterious and naturalistically unexplainable ways—fall outside them. These acts involve the idea that one event follows as the inevitable although scientifically illogical consequence of another. Referring to magical behavior of this kind, Howells and others have suggested the addition of a third classification of magic identified by the Latin phrase *post hoc, ergo propter hoc.*[3] I shall use the label "magical cause and effect sequences" as being somewhat less unwieldy.

In this form of magic no ideas of affinity or sympathy based upon imitation and contagion are apparent. Walk on cracks between floorboards, step beneath a ladder, drop a kitchen utensil, sweep scattered rice together with a broom rather than pick it up grain by grain, sweep the floor at night, whistle while in a fishing boat, or, if you are a pregnant woman of India, witness a fire or a funeral procession. Do any of these things and evil consequences of one kind or another will follow. Say abracadabra or any of thousands of other verbal formulae, rub a stone four times, or sing a special song and desired ends will come about.

Belief in these kinds of magical acts undoubtedly rests upon sympathy in the sense of some kind of association, but the basis for seeing connection or sympathy is not evident. Perhaps in some cases logical associations once existed and have been forgotten. Frazer called these acts negative magic. Many of them might also be regarded simply as a variety of taboo, belief in the inherently harmful or helpful consequences of certain acts.

DIVINATION

Like magical sequences of cause and effect, divinatory practices are not readily classifiable as imitative or contagious magic although they otherwise fit magical criteria. Divination may nevertheless often be viewed as resting upon ideas of sympathy or inherent affinity, however illogical the associations may seem from a scientific viewpoint. Events of the future or other objectives of divination are seldom seen directly; instead they are most frequently in symbolic form which must be interpreted. The two sets of events, what one sees by divination and the results it forecasts, may be regarded as inherently associated; because *a*, as seen by divination, occurs, then *b* represents the true circumstances in question or will inevitably come about. Divination differs most sharply from other

[3] W. Howells, *The Heathens,* p. 50.

forms of magic in that the diviner does not control or cause the events and conditions learned from divination but merely observes and reports.

The variety of forms of divination of which we have record is truly enormous; our dictionaries are full of "-scopies" and "-mancies." It is easily the most viable of all forms of magic, remaining common in both Europe and America in the face of a long history of discredit by science. As many observers have noted, its special appeal appears to lie in competence to predict for the individual in a manner impossible by naturalistic means. Science may predict with accuracy the percentage of a population which will survive to the age of 70, the percentage to die of lung cancer, and so on, but it cannot tell precisely which individuals will reach this age, which contract the disease, or the year, month, day and hour at which death will occur. Only divination dares to make unqualified prophecies on the outcome of a horse race.

Imitative and contagious magic appear clearly to have been practices of mankind since the Old Stone Age. The archeological record of divination is far younger. We know of its existence in the form of astrology in ancient Mesopotamia approximately five thousand years ago, but it appears safe to assume much greater antiquity. We know also, from Mesopotamia, of ancient practices of hepatoscopy or liver divination, which was elaborated to such a point that bronze and ceramic models of pig livers were used for purposes of instruction in the art of determining the future by the conformation of this organ.

Forms of divination which remain common today include, first and foremost, astrology, which is widely spread among the culturally advanced, "scientific" societies. More restricted and spotty in distribution, but still common are geomancy, haruspicy, ornithomancy, scrying or crystal gazing, casting lots, and palmistry. Geomancy divines by conformations of the earth's surface, and in East Asia is intimately allied with astrology, especially in the kind of geomancy concerned with the auspicious location of dwellings. The term geomancy includes many additional practices which involve good and bad luck, practices as diverse as reading cracks in drying mud puddles, throwing handfuls of soil into the air and determining the future from the manner in which they fall, and water-witching. Haruspicy, which takes its name from a class of Roman diviners, is divination by means of examination of the internal organs of lower animals and, less frequently, of human beings. Pigs and chickens are the animals most frequently used, and the practice remains current in the Philippines, Indonesia, Southeast Asia, and parts of Africa. As followed in the Philippines, haruspicy by examination of the internal organs of white chickens serves not only to divine the future but also to make diagnosis of human disease by noting which organs of the fowl seem discolored, malformed, or otherwise unusual. Ornithomancy, divination by the flight of birds, was practiced in ancient Greece and has today essentially the same distribution as haruspicy. This form of divination rests upon the presence or absence of certain species of birds and upon their manner of flight.

No common form of divination seems new, and many of which we have archeological or historical record have disappeared. The ancient practice of shoulder-blade divination or scapulimancy of North China, adjacent Siberia, and of some Indian tribes of northern North America is one of the many which have become extinct or are rapidly so headed. Making use of the shoulder blades of deer and sheep, and, in Shang Dynasty China (1766-1122 B.C.) of sections of the carapaces of turtles, early diviners read the future by subjecting these objects to heat and reading the cracks which formed in them. Crystal gazing and casting lots also all appear to have ancient origins among primitive peoples. Scrying, a generic term given to crystal-gazing and also to practices of divination by inspecting reflections on surfaces of water and other liquids, was known to various American Indians, who divined the future by inspecting the surface of a pool of buffalo blood poured into a skull or other container, and to many other primitive peoples. Casting lots is especially common in various forms among aboriginal African societies. Undergoing metamorphosis like the many other forms of divination which became games of chance, casting lots is the ancestor of dice.

Imagination has soared unfettered in inventing forms of divination. The Zande of Africa, probably the only people who have found a use for termites, make prophecies that depend on whether or not termites eat sticks placed in their nests.[4] The diviner among the Chibcha of Colombia stimulated a flow of mucus from his nose by snuffing irritating powder made from seeds of the Piptadenia tree. Divination rested upon whether the mucus ran straight or crooked down his upper lip, which had been carefully shaved to avoid impeding the flow.[5] The Caingang of South America gave oracular meaning to the belches of a person who had drunk *maté*.[6]

Perhaps to modern eyes the most curious and illogical form of divination is the ordeal. Intimately associated with ancient practices of law, the ordeal existed in Europe in medieval times in many forms which we view today as barbarous and brutal. In Europe and, to a lesser extent, America, the ordeal by water survived until the brink of modern times as a means of identifying witches. Based upon the idea that pure water rejects the guilty, the ordeal by water hardly conforms with modern concepts of justice. The accused but innocent person, often rendered immobile by trussing, demonstrated innocence by sinking in the water whereas the guilty failed to sink. The ordeal by water is also known to the primitive world, as are many other forms of ordeal strongly weighted toward finding accused persons guilty. Common among these are various forms of ordeal by heat or fire and, an African specialty, ordeal by poison. The defendant who emerges unscathed from thrusting his hand and arm into a vessel of boiling water to retrieve a stone or other object at the bottom is innocent, and the man who fails to die from ingesting poison is also innocent.

Descriptions of magic have often emphasized ritual directed toward harming others. No statistical weighing of the incidence of black against white magic has been made, but it seems probable that magic intended for beneficial purposes to all concerned is the more

[4] E. E. Evans-Pritchard, *Witchcraft, Oracles and Magic among the Azande.*
[5] W. T. Corlett, *The Medicine-Man of the American Indian and His Cultural Background,* p. 193.
[6] J. H. Steward, ed., *Handbook of South American Indians,* vol. 5, p. 585.

common. Even image magic, which is usually regarded as malevolently aggressive, may be used to procure offspring, facilitate childbirth, and to bring about domestic harmony. Very much of the total of recorded magical practices is directed toward the healing of the sick.

Certain forms of magic remain fairly well entrenched in our society. As we have suggested, astrology holds the lead. According to popular belief members of certain professions are more superstitious than their fellows. Traditionally, magic abounds in theatrical circles; in fact, its incidence today is probably slight. There is little doubt, however, of the existence of magic in form of taboos in American baseball circles. Jinxes are many, and the radio announcer who violates the injunction against uttering the word "no-hitter" evokes a storm of protest.

In the United States today it is probably only among children where magic is truly common, and the childhood of many of us have been rife with half-believed ideas and practices. There are the traditionally familiar dangers and safeguards, the jinxes, the crossed fingers, the lucky and unlucky numbers, but magical half-beliefs and practices of a much more individual nature patterned after the traditional are probably far more common. Much of this childhood magic seems to be a kind of divination: if I can walk to the end of the rail without falling off; if the daisy has an even number of petals; or if I count more than fifty telephone poles in the next five minutes—then I will not be punished for coming home late, will be allowed to stay up until the guests come, will get what I want for my birthday. Similar practices are doubtless common among American adults, and, as with most magic, the practitioners are ever optimistic; if one omen fails to indicate the desired result, it is abandoned in favor of a new. But this is a realm of behavior on which little information is available; few of us are willing to discuss subjective practices of this kind for fear of self-incrimination.

PERSONALIZED OR NONMAGICAL TECHNIQUES

Creating a supernatural world in his own image, man attempts to influence its events by techniques which he uses in interpersonal relations with other men. We give many names to these ways of acting. When the individual wishes to put himself in the good graces of another—especially when the other holds higher status and greater power than he—the behavior he follows is variously polite, hospitable, humble, self-debasing, and deferential. He may sometimes point out his own capabilities and sterling virtues. He respectfully requests; he entreats, cajoles, flatters, confesses misdeeds, conciliates, and placates, and he makes promises of future good conduct. He offers love, obedience, rites of honor and more material rewards, or promises them for the future. These are techniques of man vis-à-vis man in everyday life, endearing ways which often bring success, and they are all forms of behavior familiar to religions of both the primitive and the civilized worlds. Sometimes man deals with man in other and very different fashion, by force or the threat of force. This, too, is a familiar technique of religion.

Nonmagical supernaturalistic behavior has never received systematic classification, but it obviously lends itself easily to division into the two categories, propitiatory and coercive. Among the literate and "advanced" cultures of the modern world virtually all nonmagical religious behavior falls within the propitiatory range. Rituals of worship, prayers of request and of thanks, the making of offerings, conformance to codes of ethical conduct, confession of misdeeds, and expiation are the principal acts. These techniques are also common in the primitive world, although one or another is often weakly developed or absent, and magical acts may overshadow them.

Prayer in the form of suppliant appeal to supernatural beings is certainly found among primitive peoples, but it is often intermingled with magical practices and seldom stands alone, apart from other ceremony. Among the simplest primitive cultures, prayer is seldom prominent in the total complex of religious behavior and it tends more frequently than in our own society to take the form of specific requests for personal aid rather than generalized appeals for the benefit of the whole society. Prayers of thanks are often absent. Direct communion with deities is common enough and is a feature of the religion of many North American Indian societies, but, at least from reports thus far given, mystic, spiritual rapport with a supernatural being of the kind sometimes called the "religious thrill" seems to be less common in prayers of primitive folk than among members of the civilized faiths. In many primitive societies confession and prayers beseeching forgiveness for sins or aid in maintaining moral standards are both unknown and unthinkable.

One of the principal forms of propitiation among all societies is the making of offerings. Generally speaking, the magnitude of the request determines the quality and quantity of the offering. Sacrificial offerings, especially of human beings, have attracted much attention among writers of Europe and America, perhaps because such behavior has long been abandoned in the Western World and is looked upon with horror. Certain theorists of the nineteenth century regarded all forms of sacrifice as springing from a single place of origin, subsequently spreading to other societies. There is no more cogent reason to hold this view than to think that mere hospitality of man to man arose under special circumstances in one corner of the globe and spread to other men in a manner like the diffusion of tobacco. The practice of sacrifice has no doubt sometimes spread from one society to another, but it has also doubtless sprung up independently in many places, and it embodies an idea which comes to man easily. One of the ways of men to win the good will of other men is to endear themselves by valuable and, if the occasion warrants, precious gifts, and human life is often if not always precious. This statement is not, of course, to deny that sacrifice of man or lower animal may have important symbolic meanings of expiation and communion with other men and the gods.

The custom of making human sacrifice bears some relationship to the degree of cultural development of societies of the primitive world. Culturally crude and very small societies seem to provide infertile ground for the growth of this custom. This is doubtless in part because ritual is seldom well developed in these societies, but other circumstances seem also to exert influence. Human relations among the culturally simplest societies are extremely personal and face-to-face, and members of the group are united by ties of marriage and descent. Kinship in these societies is not the same as that

of the great industrial nations of the world, where the important kin
unit is usually limited to the small family. In primitive society the
scope of kinship is in every sense greater. The number of persons
who actively serve in cooperative kin roles is generally greater, including individuals whom culturally elaborate nations of the world
do not regard as relatives. Kinship is the means by which small,
primitive cultures are socially organized and in the absence of
money, specialists, policemen, judges, courts of law, social welfare
programs, and insurance policies it is one of primitive man's techniques of survival. Relations with kin are intimate, entailing many
mutual obligations and privileges, and relations with individuals of
one's own society who are not within the compass of kinship also
tend strongly to be modeled after those with relatives. It does not
seem surprising, then, that the small and culturally impoverished
societies generally lack human sacrifice. Among North American
Indians of the present-day United States and Canada, whose various
tribes at the time of the coming of the Europeans represented a
range of cultural development from the exceedingly crude to a peak
of very modest elaboration, human sacrifice of members of one's
own society was uncommon and small in scale. The culturally
simplest of these societies lacked the practice, and various other
tribes sacrificed only the occasional foreign captive of war.

We must look to culturally more elaborate and larger societies, in
both the New and Old Worlds to find sacrifice of either man or lower
animals as a flourishing practice. The peaks of pre-Columbian cultural development in the New World were represented by the
Aztecs, Maya, and Inca, and it is among these larger and more
elaborate societies in which we find the greatest development of this
custom. These words do not intend to state that any necessary or
inevitable correlation exists between human sacrifice and any prescribed degree of cultural development. Among the simpler and
smaller societies of North America the practice was discouraged.
Even among the three great Indian societies of the Americas there
is no uniformity in the incidence of human sacrifice. It existed in all
three, but it was a truly prominent feature only among the Aztecs.
Mayans made human sacrifices when new houses were built. The

Inca of Peru sacrificed some children and, less commonly, adults and—as the only society of the three with these domesticated animals—also offered the llama and the alpaca. Maya and Inca practices were dwarfed by those of the Aztecs, who in the course of a year killed in sacrifice several thousands of captives of war. It is estimated that in one year at least 2500 persons were slain in sacrifice in the Aztec capitol of Tenochtitlan alone at the time of the first Spanish contact during the early sixteenth century. Aztec sacrificial customs included very special ritual for a few individuals, especially selected for their youth and beauty. Treated as gods and given all luxuries their culture could offer for some time before their death, these young men and women were honored to meet death in this manner.[7]

In the Old World, the distribution of former customs of human sacrifice is widespread, occurring in ancient Mesopotamia, among the ancient Hebrews, ancient Crete, and echoes of the customs remained among the Greeks and Romans. To the north in Europe, the practices were established among the Vikings and Celts. The historically or archeologically known distributions of human sacrifice in the rest of the world is wide but sporadic.

Practices honoring the gods by offering the first of seasonal products are particularly common. The first-born cattle or other domestic animals and the first fruit, grain, and other vegetable products are common offerings of husbandmen. Custom among culturally simpler hunting and gathering peoples includes equivalents. Rites revolving about the first salmon taken during the annual spawning runs, for example, were well established among American Indian tribes of the Pacific coast.

Offerings need not always be made in fact but may be symbolic. A common practice of primitive society found also in Japanese Shintō is to offer food or other materials to the gods and, once honor has been paid in this manner, to put the offerings to human use. Promises of offerings upon the fulfillment of a petition, a familiar practice in some forms of Christianity, may also be made. Among some primitive peoples a conventional practice of deception of the

[7] Bernardino de Sahagun, *A History of Ancient Mexico.*

gods exists; the promise of a fine offering is made, but after the
request has been granted no offering is made or a shabby substitute
is presented.

Other forms of propitiation are as varied as are the patterns of
hospitable and endearing behavior among men. What honors and
pleases men serves to the same effect for gods. Flattery, cajolery,
praise in words as well as deeds are useful ways of influencing both
men and gods, and, like men, some supernatural beings are pleased
by dancing, singing, and other forms of entertainment, which, of
course, serves secularly at the same time to entertain men. Enter-
taining the spirits of dead ancestors by story-telling is a well established form of homage among western African societies.

As the ordinary man cleanses and tidies to make himself acceptable to an honored human guest, so must he be ceremonially clean in
approaching supernatural beings, and purification is often required
before establishing contact with them or coming into their presence.
Ceremonial or supernatural pollution seems, however, far more
serious than mundane uncleanliness, and rites of purification are
among the most widely distributed of supernaturalistic acts. These
may involve the removal of pollution from sins wittingly perpetrated
or accumulated simply from ordinary existence in the profane world.
In the primitive world purificatory rites center chiefly about pollution from impersonal sources, especially contact with blood or death.

Rites of purification are most frequently modeled after ordinary
practices of cleanliness. Water in the form of actual bathing or
various kinds of symbolic dabbling is the common purificatory agent.
In regions where water is scarce, as among the pueblo Indians who
used yucca suds, other cleansers serve. Among many Indians of the
western United States purification was had through sweating in
steam houses heated with hot stones. The use of plant emetics was
an established purificatory practice of more easterly tribes. The
sprinkling of salt and rekindling of fires, as well as lustration, are
traditional purificants of Japanese Shintō. These customs fall, of
course, within the realm of magic. They are followed to remove
dangerous pollution and also to make the suppliant acceptable and
inoffensive to the gods, and thus they represent one of the many

points at which magic and nonmagical supernaturalistic behavior conjoin.

We have no record of coercion of the gods for many societies, but this circumstance does not necessarily deny existence. Ethnologists have probably seldom looked for the custom. For the most part, coercion of the gods appears to be reported only when it in some manner struck the attention of the observer without special inquiry regarding its presence or absence. Reports are nevertheless abundant enough to indicate a wide, if scattered, distribution.

Many rites of magic compel the gods to do the bidding of the magicians, but our interest here is not with magic, which is thought automatically to achieve its end. It is instead with force in the form of threats or physical acts of hostility toward personified deities, the kind of behavior which man sometimes inflicts upon man in the ordinary world. Like all other techniques of supernaturalism, the coercive are doubtless very old, but the concrete objects which are all that remain from the preliterate cultures of long ago provide poor material for inferences of this sort. The magicians of ancient Egypt, we know from written record, claimed power over the gods and threatened them with destruction if they should fail to obey.

Inhospitable behavior of many kinds is reported for modern primitive peoples. Attempts to ingratiate oneself are customarily made first, and recourse to threats and force comes if ingratiation fails to achieve the desired results. Like propitiatory acts, the forms of coercion are conventionalized for each society in which they exist. When requests are not granted, gods may be the objects of anger and insult, or they may be subjected to physical punishment wreaked upon their images or abodes. When struck by great misfortune, the Tsimshian Indians of British Columbia might raise their eyes and hands in anger, stamp their feet, and revile their gods by calling them great slaves, the worst insult known in their society.[8] Sedna, the deity of the sea of most Eskimo groups, was harpooned to force her to release animals of the sea for the Eskimo to hunt. The East Greenland Eskimo compelled the Lord of the Wind to his bidding, making the wind blow or subside, by sticking the wind with a knife

[8] Ruth Benedict, "Religion," p. 640.

or whipping it.[9] When misfortune continued to befall the native of
Manus in the Bismarck Archipelago despite fulfillment of all conventional means of establishing rapport with his tutelary deity, an
ancestor whose skull was kept within the dwelling, coercion was
used. The ancestral spirit was threatened with the drastic punishment of abandonment, and his skull was to be thrown outside to be
drenched by the rain and scorched by the sun.[10]

Similar practices were well known until at least the end of the
nineteenth century among the culturally elaborate nations of both
West and East, particularly with reference to requests for rain. In
Japan, the image of the tutelary god who ignored requests for rain
might be thrown into the hot sun of drying rice fields, and similar
practices were common in China and Europe. The statues of Christian saints who failed to end droughts were variously immersed in
water, subjected to the hot sun, put in irons, or suffered the removal
of clothing or wings, the turning of faces to the wall, and many other
indignities and punishments. These are practices which are not
wholly dead among Christian populations. Among negroes of Brazil
who received their Christianity through the medium of the Portuguese, patron saints continue to be physically punished. When
prayers for rain, marriage, good business, or other desirables are
not granted, the images of the uncompliant saints are tied with
ribbons or are exposed to the hot sun in the middle of the fields.[11]

Probably no form of inhospitable behavior has been overlooked in
conventional approaches to supernatural beings, but prayer and
other hospitable ways of establishing rapport generally prevail.
This relative scarcity of coercive behavior may be regarded as a reflection of the patterns of behavior among men in their ordinary
interpersonal relations, and the known results of these actions. Men
ordinarily do not first use anger, threats, or punishment in relations
with other men from whom they seek to gain something. Still less do
they do so when their fellows are regarded as powerful and superior.

---

[9] E. M. Weyer, *The Eskimos,* pp. 359, 391.
[10] R. F. Fortune, *Manus Religion.*
[11] Octavio Da Costa Eduardo, *The Negro in Northern Brazil,* pp. 51-52.

Chapter 5. Supernatural Beings and Objects

The supernaturalistic beliefs and practices of man, we have said, reflect man himself and man's experiences. He has created a supernatural world derived from his knowledge of the ordinary world, expressed in it his ideals, hopes, and uncertainties, and made his handiwork usable for his own survival. In creating this world, in making it comprehensible and teachable, he has objectified his thoughts in creed, myth, ritual act, sacred object, and supernatural being. This has perhaps seldom been a fully conscious process, but it is one that has been repeated again and again.

Religions which represent purely philosophical creeds bereft of supernatural beings, sacred objects, and ceremonial have been uncommon in the history of our world. Great religions have indeed arisen as ethical or philosophical principles for the guidance of man, but once they have become the province of multitudes and have passed through many generations of adherents and interpreters they have met a common fate of objectification; that is, of being cast into concrete form so that they may be actively appreciated by the eyes, ears, or other sense organs rather than remaining only abstract ideas and beliefs. It is doubtful that any body of philosophical or ethical principles could survive in form identifiable by common agreement as religion unless it involved teachers or leaders, formal or informal, and unity among its members brought about by joint acts, in short, a church-like organization and ritual of some kind in which adherents participate.

Objectification in varying degree and form appears in all known religious complexes of primitive peoples and it has been outstanding in the religions of civilized societies. Possible exceptions—regarded

71

by some persons as philosophies rather than religions—exist in some forms of Confucianism, Buddhism, and other Eastern religions, and perhaps also in a few modern Western movements. Sometimes the great religions themselves have had strict rules against certain forms of objectification, but the concrete has usually had a luxuriant growth along other avenues. Confucianism forbids the use of depictions of Confucius for ritual purposes, but tablets engraved with his name and placed on an altar are quite acceptable. At the time of its emergence in the sixth century B.C., Buddhism appears to have been a set of ideal principles for the guidance of man. It involved no depiction in art, statuary, or ritual of its founder, Gautama Buddha, and no organized church or elaborate ritual. Subsequently Buddha came to be depicted in many ways, first by a sprig of leaves and then anthropomorphically. With the passage of time and the touch of many interpreters, Buddhist ritual became exceedingly elaborate. The mere counting of the different forms of Buddha and of subsidiary Buddhist figures depicted in statuary and painting in the later history of many Buddhist sects is a major task.

Early Christianity involved no objectification by means of paintings and statuary, but we may recall the Iconoclast Controversy of Byzantine Rome in the eighth and ninth centuries. Conservatives, holding as sacrilegious the statues and paintings which had become prevalent, demanded that they be destroyed. After waxing and waning for over a century as one Byzantine ruler approved the use of these icons and his successor banned them, the controversy ended —that is, it ceased to be an issue for dissension—after Empress Theodora again restored the use of icons in A.D. 843. Controversy over this issue has lingered much longer, however, in other areas of the Christian world, sometimes rising to the point of violence, as in the seventeenth century when the Russian priest Nicon of the Greek Orthodox Church destroyed religious paintings brought by the Russian nobility from the West.[1]

Reasons for objectification of this kind seem simple enough. Many, and perhaps most, human beings respond poorly to words or ideas alone unless they have had rich, personal experience with the things

[1] C. F. Potter, *The Story of Religion.*

and events which the words and ideas describe. Ideas expressed in unadorned words make little emotional impression on many of us. For this end we desire or need something more tangible. Man has put to use in the name of religion many forms of appeal to the senses, visual and auditory symbols of many kinds, painting, statuary, music, song, verse, mythology, stirring tales, dance, and pageantry. Whether himself a performer of the ritual or an on-looker, the individual may participate by seeing and hearing and through the vicarious experiences evoked.

Forms of art are of particular importance in objectification, and religion has often served as the chief vehicle for aesthetic expression. This is not to say that an inherent or inevitable connection exists between art and religion or that religious art is highly developed among all primitive peoples. Religion and forms of art can hardly be viewed as intimate associates in our own culture. Among primitive cultures, where art is generally much more closely allied to religion, every stage of development of aesthetics from near absence to rich elaboration may be found. If the economic base of a primitive society is adequate so that its members need not devote all of their energies toward mere survival, some development of forms of art occurs and very frequently the art is in a religious context. Among some of the culturally crudest societies which subsist meagerly by hunting and gathering wild animals and vegetable foods, little of what is conventionally called art exists or is possible, but at least objectification in the form of a modest development of mythology with strongly supernaturalistic motifs is generally found.

As Benedict has remarked, any kind of supernaturalistic theme may be developed into ceremonial, and sometimes the ceremonial grows so luxuriantly that it obscures the theme.[2] With the passage of time ritual commonly becomes highly formalized and symbolic, and whether magical or nonmagical in nature, it must be followed with absolute precision. Variation or departure from convention tends to become regarded as sacrilege. The history of Christianity reveals many episodes in addition to the Iconoclast Controversy of the most bitter acrimony over what seem today minor points of

[2] Ruth Benedict, ''Religion.''

ritual. Many of the important reforms of Nicon, for example, are small matters of ritual performance, of which perhaps the most important in arousing contention was the question of the number of fingers to be used in making the sign of the cross.

Variation from convention in the form of performing ritual in reverse order is sometimes a heinous offense. As we have noted, the reversal of normal ritual procedures also crops up for magical purposes. Reversals of a different nature are also common in ritual. Ancient folk customs of Japan, meaningless today but still observed, require the reversing of certain acts when a member of the household dies: the kimono of the deceased must be arranged so that the folds of cloth overlap in order the reverse of that used in life, and water used in funeral rites must be ladled by holding the dipper in the left rather than the right hand. These and still other forms of reversal will be discussed later.

We have noted that one of the distinctions between magic and religion is that religious acts tend to become goals in themselves. Histories of religions provide many examples of rituals rendered meaningless by the passage of time but which are nevertheless tenaciously retained. Empty of their original significance, the rites themselves have become goals which the members of society are under compulsion to reach by faithful performance. These circumstances perhaps apply most strongly to the great world religions and to other religions of culturally complex societies which have provided opportunity for the elaboration of ceremonial. It is probably true that wherever ritual has grown extremely elaborate in the hands of specialists the average citizen has anything but full knowledge of either ritual procedures or their significance. To adherents of most Buddhist sects of Japan, for example, engaging a priest to conduct a funeral is necessary not only because convention and belief so prescribe but also because the ordinary citizen neither knows all of the myriad acts required nor understands their significance.

Similar circumstances sometimes exist among primitive societies. The dairymen-priests of the Toda, a small tribe of the Nilgiri Hills of India, provide in their daily ritual an outstanding example of compulsive but essentially meaningless acts. Rivers' account of Toda dairy operations reports ritual procedures so plentiful and elaborate as to make recounting of more than a very small part of them unbearably tedious: Upon arising the dairyman-priest steps outside to greet the sun with hand to forehead; washes his hands and face in a special vessel; rinses his mouth by conveying water from right to left hand and thence to mouth; dresses his hair in priestly manner; bows before the entrance of the dairy; recites a formula as he enters the building, where he must put fire in the sacred fireplace, change his clothing to garb specified for this occasion—and then performs a continual series of prayers and other ritual acts all through the day.[3] So devoid of significance is most of the ritual behavior of both layman and priest that Rivers speaks of Toda religion as having degenerated from a higher form.

SUPERNATURAL BEINGS

A glimpse of conceptions of the nature of supernatural beings is useful in illustrating the extent to which man has fabricated the supernatural world on the image of himself. Created by man, supernatural beings may lack his form, but they unfailingly have other human attributes. They come in great variety but their types are nevertheless few. Reflecting the nature, culture, and experience of man, they too are limited in form and other attributes.

An inventory of all the supernatural beings found in the religious complexes of the world would be enormous indeed and, although based on a single common theme, it would embrace a variety of different conceptions. Souls or spirits of human beings, which exist in the beliefs of all historically known peoples, alone take many forms and have many different attributes. The individual is not always limited to one soul but may have a number of them, all different, and the forms of souls may within a single society vary with one's sex and age. Souls or spirits of the dead may be only vaguely defined in form as shadows or amorphous, ethereal substances, or they may be sharply visualized. They may be quite like the living body, or they may have the form of various flowers, birds, insects, or other animals. Less frequently, they reside in inanimate objects, such as

[3] W. H. R. Rivers, *The Todas.*

stones or other natural phenomena, figurines and other objects deliberately made by man for this purpose, and the skeletal remains of the deceased.

Souls of the dead may be punished or rewarded in various ways according to the behavior of their human possessor in the natural world, but very frequently punishment and reward are quite outside the realm of thought and all souls share the same fate. Spirits of the dead are frequently viewed as dangerous and must be placated or guarded against. Where the soul of the good man is regarded as harmless or helpful, the soul of the person who is bad in life is likely to continue to be so after death. Souls may often be offended, and they may sometimes be injured. Occasionally they take on mortality in the sense that they may be killed.

Even the locus of the soul in the body and its means of egress upon death differ widely. The soul may have a specific location in organs or regions of the body—the head, heart, and the liver are common sites—and its locus is often intimately intertwined with ideas of the seat of power and of the emotions. The location may also be generalized or unspecified. Egress, too, may be unspecified or highly specific. Most commonly it is through orifices of the body, especially the mouth, but it also may leave the body by such avenues as the whorl of hair at the back of the head, or through the big toe. A recurrent belief in primitive society adjures against sleeping with open mouth lest the soul escape. The English "God bless you!" and the German "Gesundheit!" uttered after one sneezes are said to be derived from a similar belief, archaic survivals of magic designed to prevent loss of the soul. According to a folk belief of Japan, a person's soul in the form of a ball of fire with flaming tentacles shaped like the Medusa jellyfish shoots from his body shortly before death.[4]

As variation in form is abundant among souls of the deceased, so it is among other kinds of supernatural beings. Most frequently conceived as zoomorphic, anthropomorphic, or as forces of nature, they may represent philosophical and ethical concepts, states of emotion, or anything else of cultural significance. Examples of the

[4] E. Norbeck, *Takashima*, p. 139.

philosophical are the Polynesian deity Atea (Space or Sky Father) and Te Tumu (Source or Earth Foundation), and, from the roster of approximately fifteen hundred gods of the Ifugao of the Philippine Islands, Gasp of Fear, Gentleness, Transparency, Consolation, Slamming Down Payment at Once, and Termination.[5]

The range in form of deities may be summarized by the statement that it extends from extremely vaguely defined entities and abstract concepts of many kinds through natural forces and on to concrete conceptions as plants, insects, lower animals, and man. Material objects may serve as the abodes but not the essence of these beings. A single religious complex may embrace many different kinds of supernatural beings. Perhaps the Ifugao, among whose beliefs at least forty classes of gods have been distinguished, hold virtuoso rank in this respect.

Regardless of the form of supernatural beings, however, we may say that all, even the most abstract, have human qualities. Although they may lack eyes, ears, mouths, voices or any other attributes of forms of life and inanimate objects, they invariably possess certain human qualities of behavior or personality. Although sometimes indifferent to man, they understand and can communicate with him, and their values, attitudes, and perceptions are found among the men who believe in their existence.

Goode has described supernatural beings as "anthroposocial" because of their ability, even when they lack sensory organs, to perceive what man is doing and because they communicate with man.[6] Goode has also described supernatural entities as "anthropopsychic" because relations with them are conducted as though they had mentalities like those of human members of society.[7] We shall go further and state that in the range of traits of personality they exhibit, supernatural beings are simply modeled after man. The gamut of traits of character which we commonly use to describe our fellow men are equally applicable to his gods. Gladys Reichard has classified Navaho gods as persuadable, undependable, and unper-

[5] R. F. Barton, *The Religion of the Ifugaos.*
[6] W. J. Goode, *Religion Among the Primitives,* p. 43.
[7] *Ibid.,* pp. 40-51.

suadable on the basis of their relationship to man's well-being.[8]
Gods may be wise, foolish, good, bad, or alternately wise and foolish,
good and bad. All of the undesirable as well as the desirable traits
of human beings may be found among them. They may be stupid,
lazy, dishonest, cruel, thieving, treacherous, and sexually immoral
as well as clever, industrious, kind, trustworthy, and virtuous.

Mischief makers and other beings who alternate between the good
and the bad are so common as to bear a conventional name, the
Trickster, accorded them by folklorists and other students of religion.[9] Tales of the activities of the Trickster have unusually wide
distribution and are found among the simplest cultures and among
the complex. They occur among the Chinese, Japanese, ancient
Semites, Greeks, and Norse, to mention but a few examples.

The trickster is known by various names among the Indian tribes
of central and western North America, but his acts, the tales which
are told about him, are everywhere much alike and sometimes identical. Coyote, Old Man Coyote, or Old Man as he is known among
tribes from the Great Plains on to the Pacific, is the best known of
the American tricksters. He might help man and other supernatural
beings or might deceive them. Sometimes virtuous, he is also wicked.
Many myths tell of his seduction of women, and he is capable of
such base misdeeds as incest. Supernaturally clever in a scheming,
deceptive way, he tricks his companions so that he may win races
or eat all their food; disguises himself to seduce women, tricks
mothers into eating their own children, and feigns death to catch
game. But he is also a numbskull who does such stupid things as
dive into water for reflected food which he himself is carrying,
joins the bullrushes dancing in the wind and, unwilling to stop
until they also stop, sways to and fro in an unremitting wind until
he drops of exhaustion.

Around the Great Lakes area, Manabozho or Wiskedjak is often
a helpful being about whom tales of beneficence are told, but he is
also the deceiver and the fool whose stupidities include such acts as

---

[8] G. A. Reichard, *Navaho Religion.*

[9] See, for example, Stith Thompson, *The Folktale*, and Paul Radin, *The Trickster.*

diving beneath ducks to tie their legs together only to have them all rise into the air carrying him with them. Among the tribes of the north Pacific Coast, the tricksters are called Raven, Blue Jay, or Mink, and they are credited with the same kind of behavior as Coyote, their more easterly and southerly counterpart.

The trickster has sometimes been the youngest male of a family of deities. In the beliefs of the former Kingdom of Dahomey of the Guinea Coast of Africa, the lecherous, mischievous, but sometimes humanly helpful god Legba, was the youngest of divine siblings and served as messenger for his elders.[10] In Japanese Shintō, Susanoo-no-Mikoto, is the roughly mischievous younger brother of the Sun Goddess.[11]

Within a single society or segment of a society the benevolent deity of one group of individuals might be malevolent or potentially malevolent to other individuals of the larger society. The roster of wholly harmful supernatural beings, those malevolent to all mankind, is large, but it is interesting to note that man seems to attribute to his gods beneficence, kindness, and virtue more frequently than he credits them with socially less desirable characteristics.

Quite like virtuous and helpful deities, witches and other malevolent supernatural beings may be seen as the casting into concrete form of fears and tensions variously derived. Objectification or personification through beliefs in witchcraft and malevolent spirits makes anxieties understandable, and also provides or suggests a course of action to be taken for their relief. This is a subject to which we will return for more detailed discussion.

As with their forms and personalities, variation also exists in the powers of deities. Most commonly in primitive societies, supernatural beings are profusely plural in number. No matter what the form of these beings, their powers or special competences are generally highly specific and strictly limited. Among the simplest cultures, they may or may not be hierarchical in power or authority. We have noted that high and powerful gods may be found in the primitive world, but the all-powerful is rare. Like human beings, gods

[10] M. J. Herskovits, *Dahomey*.
[11] B. H. Chamberlain, trans., *Kojiki*.

may vie with each other for power, gaining it and losing it, and the
interrelationships of god and god frequently parallel those of men,
involving the same kinds of reasoning, values, emotions, and strug-
gles. Like human beings, gods may sometimes become injured or fall
ill and die, and human religious specialists might kill them. Polynesian necromancers caught and killed souls by crushing them in their
hands or between coconut shells. They also entrapped souls in gourds
and held them for ransom.[12]

SUPERNATURAL OBJECTS

Theorists of the nineteenth century, as we will recall, entertained
the idea that certain objects and entities had inherent power to
evoke religious emotions in all mankind. But this we know is un-
true. Even natural phenomena, the class of things most frequently
credited with this characteristic by the nineteenth century scholars,
are variously regarded among the societies of man. Objects with
supernatural power are clearly so credited by arbitrary assignment
that varies from society to society.

A commonly recurrent if not universal general trend in this form
of symbolism may, however, be noted. That which is attributed with
supernatural power is often the unusual, extraordinary because of
its own qualities and rarity or given special significance by association with dreams, visions, and other events regarded as extraordinary. Selectiveness applies even within the realm of the unusual;
by no means all that is rare or extraordinary is credited with special
power. As we have noted for Japan, oddly shaped stones, trees, and
other natural phenomena, great mountains, imposing waterfalls,
and other conspicuous, imposing, or unusual phenomena of nature
may be invested with supernatural qualities. In areas where they
are rare, minerals such as rock crystal, obsidian or other stones of
unusual color, and mineral pigments with which to adorn oneself
for ritual purposes have rather often been so regarded. In the
British Isles the formerly mysterious large stone implements of man
of the Old Stone Age were once called thunderstones and stone
arrowheads were called fairy darts. Both were credited with curative

[12] E. S. C. Handy, *Polynesian Religion*, pp. 236-237.

powers. Religious value has been given to many thousands of other objects, but it is their symbolic value, not their intrinsic qualities, that gives them a special significance. A highly valued "medicine bundle," an important tribal fetish of the Mandan Indians of the Great Plains contained, in naturalistic inventory: two copper rings; one copper crescent; one large gourd rattle; six magpie tail feathers; twelve tail feathers of owls; a human scalp, said to have been taken from a Cheyenne Indian; the left arm and the skull of a grizzly bear; a tuft of long hair from a buffalo bull's lower jaw; a strip of hide from a buffalo calf's head; long hair from a buffalo's foreleg; the left horn of a buffalo; a buffalo skull; and one stuffed jack-rabbit.[13]

Compilation of an inventory of sacred objects known to the world would be a staggering and largely fruitless task. Its general nature is already amply clear: man is capable of investing with unusual powers any kind of object, act, state of being, or physical event, but he tends to select for special attention what strikes him as unusual. Even symbols created by man for other purposes have been treated as concrete objects with occult powers. Write on a piece of paper and swallow it, think or say aloud a personal name, repeat a formula three, four, seven, or any other prescribed number of times, and desired results will come about provided no error has been made in these routines.

Among all the phenomena of our universe, man has probably most frequently regarded blood and death as supernatural. Taboos against contact with flowing blood, particularly during menstruation, and childbirth, and against contact with the dead are known presently or in the past to most societies of which we have record on this subject. It is interesting to note that menstrual and childbirth taboos of societies as diverse and geographically far-flung as those of the Eskimos, Shoshone Indians of western North America, ancient Hebrews and late nineteenth century Japanese are much alike. As mysterious and potentially dangerous events, it seems reasonable that man might again and again have placed menstruation, childbirth, and death in the realm of mystery, the superna-

---

[13] A. W. Bowers, *Mandan Social and Ceremonial Organization*, pp. 302-303.

tural, something to be feared and avoided. It seems reasonable also to think that ideas of this kind have often spread from one people to another.

Sacred objects of the great civilizations differ not at all in their general nature from those of primitive societies. Protective talismans, many uses of the cross, holy water, and the sacrament may all be objectively viewed as implying power which, although interpreted as bestowed or derived from a man-like deity, become the qualities of the acts or objects themselves. Taboos against contact with blood are not wholly extinct among Christians and Jews; the Orthodox Jewish woman undergoes purification after childbirth and the disappearing Anglican ritual of "churching of women" after childbirth appears to have evolved from a rite of purification.

Chapter 6. Unusual

Psychological States

Any of the objects and events of our universe may be given supernatural significance, but we have noted some tendency in primitive society to select the unusual. This trend is most evident in interpretations of the behavior of man himself. Instances where the extraordinary in psychological states and the realm of religion touch upon each other are profuse and varied. The forms of behavior themselves have been inadequately described so that assured classification of them according to psychological or physiological criteria cannot be made. Oesterreich, who in his study of hysterical possession deals with only one of the extraordinary psychic states associated with religion, complains that ethnologists have failed to provide adequate information on even the external manifestations of these conditions of being.[1] Oesterreich's study is now old, but it is true that until very recent years few ethnologists had adequate training in medicine, psychology, or psychiatry to enable them to report the kinds of information that other specialists might desire. It is also unfortunately true that much of this information may never be gained because the traditional ways of many primitive peoples, and sometimes the peoples themselves, have disappeared.

Although clinical descriptions and information on the subjective states of the human beings concerned are rare, ethnological references to ecstatic states associated with primitive religions are plentiful. Much additional information on similar physical states among populations of civilized nations is provided by written histories and other writings. At the very least these records indicate the importance which unusual psychic states have held in religious belief and

[1] T. K. Oesterreich, *Possession*.

practice. They also often show clearly how these forms of behavior, presumably rooted in innate capabilities of man, are culturally molded by local convention into distinctive form.

Available information on the subject at hand is, in fact, too bulky for brief coverage, and discussion here will be limited to only a part of the whole. As a matter of convenience, all of the extraordinary psychic experiences associated with religion may be divided into two major classes: those which are given supernaturalistic interpretation but are not put to religious use, and those which have been religious goals or religious tools. The concern here is confined to the second category, unusual emotional states and psychic experiences which have been sought as religious or used by religion. Thus such practices as interpreting hysterical seizures, psychosis, or other illness as spirit possession will be omitted from discussion unless the cutoms also constitute religious objectives or techniques.

The psychic experiences in question have often been called the "religious thrill." These states of being vary from a vaguely described mystical rapport with the supernatural involving few external manifestations in behavior on through hallucinations, hysterical seizures, and states of trance in which observable behavior is quite abnormal. The history of the association of these unusual states with religion is long, and we can probably assume much greater antiquity. In ancient Greece, persons who could enter trance were held in regard and served as oracles and intermediaries with the gods. The subsequent history of our own culture is replete with records of emotional disturbances in connection with and sometimes as an integral part of religious experience. Seizures, trances, and visions are recorded in the scriptures of Christianity and Judaism. They appear again and again in the history of supernaturalism in Europe, sometimes reaching the proportions of epidemics. These forms of behavior have also served as outstanding features of late Christian religious movements, including the Wesleyan revival of eighteenth-century England and similar, contemporaneous developments in the United States.

The greatest upsurge in the United States of religious behavior of this kind came with the Kentucky Revival.[2] Arising at the end

[2] See E. T. Clark, *The Small Sects in America*, pp. 90-93.

of the eighteenth century and spreading widely in the Midwest, the Kentucky Revival remained vigorous for fifty years. It is remarkable from the standpoints of the violence of the bodily seizures of members of the congregations and the numbers of individuals affected. Revival camp meetings of the time impressed many observers, including Frances Trollope, then travelling through America, as orgies of madness.[3] Religious ecstasy of this kind has not entirely disappeared in the United States; generally subdued as compared with behavior characterizing the Kentucky Revival, it remains as a ritual feature of various small Christian sects.

In primitive society, states of trance occupy a position of special prominence in religion, but trance and possession do not always go hand in hand. Trance is perhaps most frequently regarded as possession by spirits, but other interpretations view it as preternatural vision or as revelatory communication with the supernatural world without intrusion of spirits into the body.

A substantial number of accounts of native Siberian and African religions tell of long periods of abnormal behavior marked by or culminating in seizures and trance as the conventional call to become a religious specialist. Once this profession has been adopted, the abnormal behavior is generally reported to cease except that controlled seizures and trance form an important part of the practitioner's ritual behavior.

Among the primitive Chukchee of eastern Siberia the future shaman of aboriginal times was said to be recognizable in his youth by listlessness, long periods of staring into space while oblivious of activities around him, mental instability, illness, emaciation, unusually long periods of sleep, and falling into trance. Individuals so afflicted must be closely watched, as they might wander about aimlessly on the tundra, exposing themselves to the hazards of starvation or death from exposure as they lay down to sleep in torpor.[4] Similar periods of lingering illness, which appears usually to be of a nervous character, have been reported for other Siberian tribes and for primitive peoples in other parts of the world as the signs of a religious calling.

[3] Frances Trollope, *Domestic Manners of the Americans*.
[4] Waldemar Bogoras, *The Chukchee—Religion*.

The events preceding the initiation of the aboriginal Amazulu diviner of Africa are much like those applying among the Siberian tribes. The future diviner becomes fussy about foods, avoiding certain kinds and eating little of others. He yawns and sneezes repeatedly, suffers pains in different parts of his body, falls to constant dreaming, and at last becomes very ill and emaciated. Sickness may continue over a period as long as several years. As the condition grows worse, the individual is given to tears and vocal crying, shouting and singing through the night, convulsions, and other abnormal behavior. These symptoms are at length recognized as indicating a "soft head"; that is, that he is impressionable or gifted with the special perceptions required of the diviner. He is then encouraged to become a diviner and, once having adopted this profession, he is again a healthy individual.[5]

Other African societies afford many additional examples of long or repeated illness, recurrent dreams, hysterical fits and trance, and other violent, abnormal behavior interpreted as spirit possession and leading to the individual's eventual emergence as a religious specialist.[6]

Examples of conventionalized practices among primitive peoples of attaching special value to nervously unstable individuals for religious duties are plentiful, but the existence of a long prelude of psychological disturbance such as we have described for Siberian and certain African tribes is not always the requirement. Many accounts which tell of the use of unusual psychic states on the part of primitive curers and diviners say little on the subject of the temperaments of these individuals and make no reference to protracted abnormal behavior (which is not, of course, equivalent to denying its existence). What the writings do tell us clearly and frequently is that falling into trance often constitutes the call to a religious vocation and that the ability to enter this state is a requirement for the specialist.

[5] Henry Callaway, *The Religious System of the Amazulu.*

[6] See for example, H. A. Junod, *The Life of a South African Tribe;* B. A. Marwick, *The Swazi;* E. E. Evans-Pritchard, *Nuer Religion;* M. J. Field, *Religion and Medicine of the Gã People;* S. F. Nadel, "A Study of Shamanism in the Nuba Mountains."

Among many North American Indian tribes trance was required of the medicine man or woman, but here, as we go from tribe to tribe, trance shades off into quite different experiences. Trance was sometimes interpreted as possession by spirits, but more commonly this state was viewed as bringing the entranced into direct communication with supernatural beings. This experience, the vision, was the immediate objective. By means of the vision the individual reached the goals of receiving a guardian spirit and supernatural power. The vision might, however, come in ways other than through trance. Although absent among the pueblo peoples in the Southwest, the vision in various forms was so widespread that Benedict has called it "the fundamental and typical religious fact of North America."[7]

The range of experiences viewed as visions was extremely great. At one extreme it consisted of convulsive seizures, catalepsy, and hallucinations, and at the other such conventionalization as to make the vision seem fictitious because it involved little that was remarkable in sensory experience. Among some tribes, dreams which the individual considered unusual, and especially repeated dreaming, constituted visionary experiences. The dreams might then take on considerable emotional coloring. In other societies, emotional and religious significance was attached by the individual to something he experienced or saw in the ordinary course of life, things which would otherwise be regarded as routine. The recipient of a vision seldom told others of what he had seen, at least not until much later in life, and it seems likely that the vision was indeed often "a later elaboration of a relatively simple psychic experience."[8]

Whether emotionally strong or weak, visions served as the basis for future actions. All, too, were strongly molded by local convention. In some tribes trance or other forms of the vision were limited to religious specialists or other restricted segments of the society and in other societies the vision was open to all with no idea of its leading to professional status. In one society only males might qualify; in another, only females, and in a third, sex imposed no

---

[7] Ruth Benedict, *The Concept of the Guardian Spirit in North America.*
[8] G. A. Pettitt, *Primitive Education in North America.*

bars. In still other societies only the descendants of professional visionaries might have visions and become professionals. Visions were deliberately sought in some societies; in others they must come unsought, in dreams or "spontaneous" trances.

Among the aboriginal tribes of California, falling into an unconscious state was frequently the requirement to become a curer, and it was a feature of the professional's performance. When this event occurred, it was mandatory to become a religious practitioner, as were the signs of the call among the Chukchee of Siberia. To ignore the call was to court serious illness or death. Taking two of the segments of a single California tribe, the northern Maidu, and their neighbors, the Shasta, we are afforded examples of the variety of custom surrounding the interpretation of these mental states. Among the Maidu of the Sacramento Valley, the call might come to anyone. The individual ". . . may see something in the woods that makes him fall down unconscious. The being or animal, whichever it is, then talks to him while he is in his trance, and tells him what he is to do. When the man recovers, he spits blood and a whitish secretion of some sort, and then feels perfectly well again. . . . After this first meeting, the same animal or being constantly appears to the man and gives him advice and help. In other cases a man dives for a fish or for shellfish, but fails to come up. He is thought to have seen something mysterious under the water, and is hunted for, and pulled out. If he revives, he is sure to become a shaman. Soon after the experience he falls sick, and has to be sung over by other shamans. . . ."[9]

Among Maidu northeast of the Sacramento Valley, the child of a shaman must follow his parent's profession or he will die. Ordinarily this comes about a short time after the parent's death. Then "Dreams come to him frequently and in these he sees numerous spirits of various sorts. This, in a short time, makes him ill; and with his illness the dreams increase, and the spirits come more often and in greater numbers. They talk and sing to him and they are the cause of his sickness. If he does not answer them, make them presents, and become friendly with them, they will kill him in revenge.

[9] R. B. Dixon, *The Northern Maidu*, p. 267.

These spirits that appear to the man or woman are those dreamed of by the parent or parents, and the same ones stay in the family for generations.''[10] Even if a shaman had many children, all sooner or later had these experiences and became shamans.

Among the Shasta Indians, where women served as curing shamans, the first symptoms of the call consisted of repeated dreams, usually frightening, and finally a dream in which yellowjackets were seen. At a later time the woman who had experienced these dreams fell to the ground unconscious and immobile and remained in this condition for several hours. During this trance the woman gained a tutelary spirit who taught her a special song to be used later in curing rites, threatening to kill her if she did not learn it. Recovery from trance was accompanied by moans and other verbal sounds and by blood oozing from the mouth. These sounds were interpreted as a repetition of the spirit's song. The oozing of blood, which usually occurred ten times in succession, indicated that she had uttered the spirit's name. Before coming a professional doctor, she must still gain the necessary power through the mediation of her tutelary spirit. Visualized as tiny and icicle-like, this power was called the ''pains,'' and it was shot from a bow in the hands of her tutelary during one of a number of trances which followed the first.

At this time the spirit appeared and told her of his intention and the woman shouted this news to her companions before entering trance. She must then be caught before falling to the ground or the power which was now in her body would kill her. If the woman survived this experience she became a curer, subsequently entering trance and making use of her power in rites of healing.[11] Here we see what may be regarded as the impersonal counterpart of spirit possession. The woman's guardian spirit at no time possessed her; instead the entry and presence in her body of the painful power appears to have been viewed as the cause of her abnormal behavior.

Among the Kwakiutl of the northwest coast of North America the vision was so highly formalized and automatic that it has been called a ''social fiction.''[12] In the socially stratified Kwakiutl society

[10] *Ibid.*, p. 274.
[11] R. B. Dixon, *The Shasta.*
[12] Ruth Benedict, *op. cit.*

the guardian spirit was a hereditary caste mark but he was nevertheless gained through a vision. For those who were socially eligible, the vision consisted of a dramatization of what constituted the customary vision quest in other societies—seclusion, the revelatory vision, and restoration to normalcy.

Similar cultural molding of ecstatic states used in religion is found in all other societies. Even motor habits associated with trance tend to be conventionalized. Convulsions, foaming at the mouth, and violent trembling are frequent features of the seizures preceding catalepsy, but we find also that certain bodily movements are characteristic of particular societies. The about-to-be possessed or entranced might sneeze repeatedly, jerk or nod the head in particular fashion, or make other patterned movements of the body. Ecstatic states of Americans during camp meetings of the Kentucky Revival included "treeing the devil," running about on all fours and emitting sounds called "holy barks." More remarkable were the "jerks," violent whip-snaps of the body which sometimes resulted in injury or, if accounts of the time are to be credited, occasionally death from a broken neck.[13]

A means of supernatural communication frequently but not universally found in association with ecstatic states has been glossolalia or talking-in-tongues. Found widely among historically known ancient civilizations of the Old World and at home in ancient Christian tradition, talking in tongues has survived here and there to modern times in the great industrialized societies. It appeared frequently among adherents to revivalistic movements during the Protestant Reformation. Early Quakers and Methodists spoke in tongues, and this phenomenon was a feature of Mormonism under the leadership of Joseph Smith. It rose again to a position of some prominence in revivalism of the twentieth century and spread among some sectors of the populations of most of the great nations of the world. Talking in tongues survives in the modern United States among some of the small sects which seek to evoke or make use of strongly emotional states and to a limited extent in modern Mormonism. Talking in tongues also has a wide but sporadic distribution among primitive

[13] E. T. Clark, *op. cit.*

societies. Primitive centers of glossolalia are Africa, Indonesia, Malaya, and Siberia. It is found among only a small number of the native tribes of Australia and North and South America.[14]

Scholars of this phenomenon describe talking in tongues as occurring while the individuals are in highly emotional, ecstatic states associated with somnambulism, hypnotism, hysteria, or cataleptic trance. The individual rarely remembers his utterances, which vary from groans and other incoherent sounds to rhythmic but unintelligible syllables, recognizable words, and even genuine foreign languages. These vocal sounds are given many interpretations, of which the most common are that they represent the voices of spirits speaking through the entranced, or repetitions by the entranced of spiritual voices audible only to him.

The cries of animals and the sounds of natural phenomena such as wind and rain may be uttered. In Africa, where ancestor worship is important, the possessed might roar like a lion, the symbol of departed kings; he might also speak his native language in a voice recognizably like that of a recently deceased ruler.

Pseudolanguages, meaningless sounds which emulate the patterns of normal speech, represent still another form of talking in tongues. Such examples of pseudolanguage as we have heard (in the United States and Japan) were rhythmically patterned so that they took on the semblance of genuine speech. This patterning seems entirely expectable, however, and its absence from the performance of the habitual glossalalist would be surprising. It is probably impossible to maintain a flow of utterances without falling into a pattern.

True foreign languages are also spoken in ecstatic vocalization. These are languages to which the individual has been exposed but which he ordinarily knows only poorly or fails to remember while fully conscious. Xenoglossia, as this phenomenon is called, is well enough known in Western society in both supernaturalistic and nonsupernaturalistic contexts. In primitive society it appears here and there in connection with states of trance. It is reported for the Americas, Siberia, India, Indonesia, and Malaya, but appears to be

[14] L. C. May, ''A Survey of Glossolalia and Related Phenomena in Non-Christian Religions.''

common only among some African tribes, where English, Swahili or
the language of a neighboring tribe has some currency as a *lingua
franca*. Possessed women among the Gã tribe of the Gold Coast
might speak one of the languages of three neighboring tribes,
tongues which they are said to be unable to speak while in a normal
state.[15]

Religious specialists among the Eskimo and various other primitive peoples employ special sacerdotal languages, learned by them
for this purpose and spoken consciously or in part consciously. Like
Christian ritual given in Latin, these are usually obsolete or archaic
forms of speech preserved by specialists and unknown to the ordinary listener.

Glossolalia in primitive society is with rare exception confined to
mediums and other religious specialists.[16] This contrasts sharply
with practices among Christian sects given to glossolalia, where any
members of the congregation may indulge in this behavior.

The use as well as the form of states of trance varies greatly from
society to society. American Indians employed them principally to
gain power for personal use and in connection with curing. They
have also been important in divination, which might be performed
by direct vision or through the intervention of supernatural beings
in contact with the entranced individual. Divination found its principal use in diagnosing illness and learning remedies for its cure.
Trance has also undoubtedly been sought for its own sake, for its
quality of transcending the mundane, although this goal is rational-
ized by interpreting the psychic state as conferring spiritual benefits
upon those who experience it.

Whether for healing, divination, or other use, where personalized
concepts of supernatural power prevail, trance appears generally
to be interpreted as possession by gods, deceased ancestors, or other
spiritual beings. Through the medium of the individual possessed,
these entities may communicate with other members of the individual's society for whatever purpose.

[15] M. J. Field, *Religion and Medicine of the Gã People*, p. 107.

[16] L. C. May, (*op. cit.*, p. 91) finds only two clear-cut examples of talking in
tongues among laymen in primitive society, the Palaung of Burma and the
Tonga of Africa.

Means employed to evoke or induce the unusual in psychic states are numerous, but most of them may be condensed under the headings of suggestion, autosuggestion, and mechanical means external to the individual which play upon and distort his auditory, visual, and other perceptions. None of these categories is, of course, exclusive. Suggestion and autosuggestion are doubtless very often important factors in conjunction with consciously used devices.

Suggestion might come from any source. Auditory and visual stimuli seem to be the most common, but it is probable that there is no form of appeal to the senses which has not been used in some society for this purpose. Music, drumming, chanting, and dancing may, of course, have independent effect upon the human organism, but they also become cues. Any acts or objects associated with rites seeking to evoke unusual psychic states may also serve this role. The elaborate trance-dancing of Bali affords a wealth of sensory appeals of this kind which, by themselves, and also as forms of suggestion, become stimuli to enter trance. Pageantry, pantomime, assembled crowds, an atmosphere of expectancy, music, incense, and religious paraphernalia of many kinds provide manifold avenues of suggestion. Add to these the stimulus of exertion from prolonged dancing by individuals who desire to become entranced and the ground is well prepared for achieving this state.[17]

The role of autosuggestion must also often enter when trance constitutes the call to take religious duties. Its role seems particularly obvious when religious practitioners are able to enter trance at prearranged times, even though the trance may be viewed by everyone concerned as voluntary. Trance or catalepsy may, of course, come to the individual without deliberate induction, but local customs which may demand "voluntary" as opposed to "induced" trance on the part of the specialist mean only that obviously artificial aids must not be employed. In inducing even these so-called voluntary states the individual may use artificial aids that are not obvious to others and which the entranced himself might not view as artifice. Control of respiration is a conscious technique in some societies; in others it may be unconsciously performed. The Balinese priest breathes alternately through each nostril by closing one nos-

[17] Jane Belo, *Bali: Rangda and Barong*.

tril with a finger, and holds his breath as long as he can.[18] Deep
breathing leading to superoxygenation, together with cramped pos-
ture and later violent motion simulating trance seizure are reported
among the Nuba of Africa as consciously planned aids which eventually bring on genuine seizure.[19] The employment of similar aids
toward reaching the desired states appears to be widespread, but
whether these are planned or unplanned is often unclear.

Obviously artificial stimuli to induce extraordinary sensory perceptions are plentiful. They include dancing and other violent physical exertion, self-torture, bodily deprivation, various forms of mental discipline, and the ingestion of narcotics and other substances.

Fasting is one of the most common of ritual requirements, familiar
in societies of all levels of cultural complexity. "Bread and meat
would have robbed the ecstatic of many an angel visit: the opening
of the refectory door must many a time have closed the gates of
heaven to his gaze."[20] The vision quest of North American Indians
frequently stressed fasting and added, in various combinations, self-
inflicted wounds, exposure to the elements, fixed staring at the sun,
steam baths followed by plunges into cold water, sexual continence,
and solitude. The most violent measures were followed by tribes of
the Great Plains, where days of fasting, torture, and intense wish-
fulness put the individual in a half-crazed state where he might
and sometimes did experience hallucinatory visions. The Crow
Indian who desired power sought a lonely place where, inadequately
clothed, he fasted for four or more days, wailing and imploring
spirits for their aid, and torturing himself. A common sacrifice was
to hack a finger joint off the left hand and hold it up as an offering
to the Sun or some other spirit for aid in gaining the vision.[21]

The account of the vision quest of the "Big Bellies, Mandanes,
and Saulteurs" written in 1806 by the fur trader Alexander Henry
describes even more violent measures (which Henry interpreted as
a form of penance and a display of courage) :

[18] W. D. Wallis, *Religion in Primitive Society*, p. 81.
[19] S. F. Nadel, "A Study of Shamanism in the Nuba Mountains," p. 35.
[20] E. B. Tylor, *Primitive Culture*, vol. 2, p. 415.
[21] R. H. Lowie, *Religion of the Crow Indians*.

When a young man has attained the age of 20 years, he generally in the depth of winter, performs his penance by setting out entirely naked and alone, with only two or three pairs of shoes, the iron barb of an arrow, and no means of making a fire. In this condition, he repairs to a certain high hill, a day's journey from the village. On this hill he must remain as many days as his strength will permit, during which time he neither eats, drinks, nor sleeps, but passes the time in dancing, bawling, howling, and lamenting. Here also he amputates a finger with the iron barb. . . . Some have been known to be absent seven days in the severest weather. . . . After several days—more or fewer—the penitent makes his appearance, coming at full speed, and as there is continually somebody upon the huts, information is instantly given of his return. He is met by a particular friend, who has kept account of the number of days he has been absent, and for every day has been prepared a bull's head, to which has been fastened 1½ fathoms of cord. The other end of this is affixed to an incision in the penitent's back or shoulders, by pinching up a fold of skin and flesh, through which is thrust the barb of an arrow; as many days as he has been absent so many must be the incisions, and the number of heads must also tally with them. He must then walk around the village, howling and bawling, with all those bulls' heads trailing on the ground; in some places, where the ground is rough, the poor fellow must pull and tug hard to get through, as the horns continually catch in uneven spots, and often fall into some of the empty corn pits, where they would hold until the skin gave way or the cord broke, were they not attended to by some children who make it their business to disengage the horns. So many days as he has been absent, so many times must he walk round the village, never ceasing to utter lamentations. Some have been known to fall senseless during this painful ordeal; but even then they only allow themselves a few moments to recover, and proceed again. Having finished the necessary rounds . . . he may then retire to his hut and take care of his wounds, as he is in a shocking condition. Some never recover, and others languish for months before they get well.[22]

The internal consumption of substances to produce derangement of the senses including hallucinatory illusions is a well-developed practice among some primitive societies. Alcohol has sometimes been consumed as a part of religious ceremonial, but extensive areas of

[22] Alexander Henry and David Thompson, *Manuscript Journals of Alexander Henry and David Thompson, 1799-1814*, vol. 1, pp. 364-365.

the primitive world including most of North America lacked knowledge of alcoholic beverages. The plant kingdom has otherwise supplied nearly all of the stimulants of this kind used in primitive
society. The list of plant drugs known to have been formerly used
or which are presently used for these purposes in the Old World
includes Indian hemp or hashish, several species of hallucinogenic
mushrooms, ivy, henbane, and the genus *Datura*.[23]

In Polynesia and some of the adjacent islands of Melanesia and
Micronesia, euphoria was sought in religious ritual, and very commonly also in secular life, by drinking the infusion called *kava* or
kava-kava. Prepared by chewing into shreds and spitting into a container roots of the shrub *Piper methysticum*, kava taken in mild
doses is said to induce a feeling of well-being. Heavier dosages result in torpor, paralysis of the senses, and finally deep sleep.

In Africa much use was made of poisons in divination, but the
employment of plant drugs to induce trance or other remarkable
psychological states in connection with religion appears to have
been uncommon.

It is among American Indians that we find the greatest use of
drugs in connection with trance.[24] American usages were often to
induce visions, and the physiological effects of various of the drugs
lent themselves well to this end. Perhaps we will not go far astray
in thinking that the relatively high incidence of use of drugs in
ritual in the Americas is in part a reflection of the importance of
the vision to American Indians. It is true that in much of aboriginal
North America where the vision was of great importance, its induction by drugs was not practiced, but suitable plant drugs appear to
have been unknown or unavailable there.

To induce trances and hallucinations, American Indians used—
and some continue to use—tobacco; peyote; mushrooms; plants of
the genera *Datura, Banisteriopsis, Rivea,* and *Piptadenia;* and various other herbs that are less well known. Only *Datura* was employed

[23] T. A. Henry, *The Plant Alkaloids;* Louis Lewin, *Phantastica: Narcotic and
Stimulating Drugs, Their Use and Abuse.*

[24] In addition to references cited later, see A. H. Gayton, *The Narcotic Plant
Datura in Aboriginal American Culture;* and W. E. Safford, "Narcotic Plants
and Stimulants of the Ancient Americans."

in both North and South America, and the use of mushrooms was confined to the Aztecs and neighboring tribes. These plant drugs were taken principally by primitive doctors for religious purposes in connection with curing rites, and with the exception of peyote (see Chapter 13), use by many or all members of a tribe or community was not common. In aboriginal times, the greatest use of plant drugs to induce visions or hallucinations seems to have occurred among tribes of Mexico, Central America, the Caribbean islands, and a large area of northern South America.

Tobacco was, of course, well known in much of aboriginal North America, where it was used in various ways secularly and in religious rites, but it appears to have been a means of gaining visions only in Central and South America. There it was variously snuffed, chewed and swallowed, drunk in infusions, and smoked to produce a state of nauseated trance. Important hallucinogens in South America included *Banisteriopsis, Piptadenia,* and *Datura.*[25] The several species of the liana *Banisteriopsis* were usually taken by infusion. These plants are reported to induce strong sensory derangement including brilliant visions in which objects are frequently surrounded by a blue aureole. Effects of the seeds of the *Piptadenia* genus of trees, ground and blown or snuffed into the nostrils, are reported to include violent excitement, auditory hallucinations, and unconsciousness.

In addition to tobacco and peyote, the ancient Aztecs used *Rivea, Datura,* and mushrooms to achieve visions and hallucinations, especially for divination. The seeds of *Rivea corymbosa,* a member of the Convulvulaceae which appears to have been the revered *ololiuhqui* of the ancient Aztecs as described by Sahagun, continue to find use in divinatory trance in modern Mexico.[26] *Teonanactl,* the "sacred mushroom" of Mexico, appears to include a number of species and genera, which are described as inducing magnificent hallucina-

[25] See J. M. Cooper, "Stimulants and Narcotics," and other works listed in bibliography.

[26] V. A. Reko, *Magische Gifte;* R. E. Schultes, "Teonanacatl: The Narcotic Mushroom of the Aztecs"; Bernardino de Sahagun, *A History of Ancient Mexico.*

tions.[27] Before the introduction of peyote, only *Datura,* the genus
to which the familiar Jimson weed of the western United States belongs, appears clearly to have been used among tribes north of
Mexico to induce visions, and its range was limited to parts of the
southwestern United States. Among the many tribes of southern
California making use of this plant, the most prominent employment was in puberty ceremonies where youths, with the aid of this
drug, were expected to have visions and thereby acquire tutelary
spirits.[28] The seeds of the shrub or small tree *Sophora secundiflora,*
variously called coral bean, red bean, and mescal (a name given to
several different plants, including peyote, and to the alcoholic drink
of Mexico prepared from maguey), were used extensively in aboriginal times in rites of numerous Indian tribes of the central and
southern Great Plains of the United States. Its physiological effects
are poorly described. Although the alkaloid sophorine in the seeds
unquestionably induces sensory derangement, it does not seem characteristically to produce hallucinations.[29]

This brief discussion does not exhaust the list of plants which
may have been used to produce states of trance and hallucinations.
Writings on this subject for South America refer to a number of
additional but often poorly described plant drugs, a recently identified genus of narcotic plants, and also the eating of the larvae of an
unidentified insect.[30] In addition, various plants with milder physiological effects were used as stimulants and euphorics in both secular
and religious ways. Notable among these is coca, the leaves of which
were formerly and are today chewed by many tribes of northwestern
South America to alleviate fatigue, pangs of hunger, and other dis-
comfort, and to create feelings of well-being. The plant is often regarded reverentially and its leaves may be chewed in religious ceremonial or given as offerings. Perhaps because the physiological

[27] V. P. Wasson and R. G. Wasson, *Mushrooms, Russia, and History.*

[28] A. L. Kroeber, *Handbook of the Indians of California.*

[29] T. A. Henry, *op. cit.;* and J. H. Howard, ''The Mescal Bean Cult of the
Central and Southern Plains.''

[30] See, for example, J. M. Cooper, *op. cit.;* and R. E. Schultes, ''A New Narcotic Genus from the Amazon Slope of the Colombian Andes.''

effects it creates do not suit it well for this purpose, however, the plant does not appear to have been used to induce trance or visions of religious significance.

Now that so much attention has been given to radical departures from normal behavior, it is useful to make some additional remarks on their importance and prevalence. Cultivation and employment of such states are extremely common in primitive religions, but they are not universal. Both the kinds of unusual states given religious significance and their importance in total religious complexes vary greatly. At least the more violent experiences have not seen use in all societies. Religious practices among most of the pueblo peoples of America, to cite one example, provide no place for trance or catalepsy. Where these states have been given religious meaning they have been most important as the capabilities of religious leaders and they seldom, perhaps never, come recurrently to all members of the social group. This is not to limit markedly ecstatic experience entirely to the religious professionals. Lay members of a good many societies also seek these states with no idea of becoming professionals. In Javanese communities, for example, trance is well established as a part of ceremonial acts, and a considerable number of otherwise seemingly ordinary persons may spontaneously enter trance. We have noted, too, that violent visionary experiences were sought by many North American Indians for entirely individual use. Hallucination, intoxication, and unconsciousness have also sometimes been obligatory, as when individuals are required to take drugs in curing rites or during ceremonies performed at puberty.

Some theorists have held that for many individuals the greatest reward which religion has to offer is the religious thrill. If we accept this statement at face value, it must be added that religious ecstasy of milder—at least, less obvious—forms than those discussed here holds an important place. Mild forms of religious emotionalism doubtless continue to be common and important in civilized societies (and some, of course, would define religion on the basis of emotional attitudes). William James and others have described religious experiences of this kind among members of the culturally elaborate societies, but for lack of information we can say little in this regard about primitive peoples.[31] Descriptions of extraordinary psychic states where external signs are not prominently displayed must, of course, depend chiefly on subjective accounts, and these are for many reasons difficult to elicit. The heavy weighting given here to states of trance and other sharp aberrations from normal behavior, in short, reflects both the importance given to these states and the inability to discuss less obvious forms of the religious thrill.

As we have repeatedly implied, ecstatic behavior is not innately religious in character. It seems apparent that a part of all human populations is capable of these experiences, and they may or may not be given religious interpretation and value. In our own society uncommon psychic experiences varying from euphoria to sharpened acuity to ecstatic self-transcendence which bear no relationship whatever to religion are often deliberately sought by such mechanical aids as alcohol and drugs. Religion has, however, often made use of individuals who are capable of surpassing the boundaries of ordinary sensory perception without these mechanical aids, and it has also employed states of transcendence when consciously induced. Religion has also frequently served as the principal or only socially approved medium whereby the ''spontaneous'' experiences may come to members of society with this potentiality. When a society places value upon unusual psychic states, the individuals capable of this behavior come to the fore. Conversely, when a society fails to value or condemns them, they are seldom evident. Cultural values serve not only to check and encourage but also, as we have seen, to determine much of the very form of these experiences. As for reasons why ecstatic states have been given religious prominence, the fact that these states stand apart as unusual suggests a partial answer. Any surpassing of ordinary sensory perception is in its own way supernatural.

[31] William James, *The Varieties of Religious Experience.*

Chapter 7. Religious

Practitioners

Many scholars have held that the first form of specialization of labor known to man was the performance of supernaturalistic rites, and this idea seems well supported by the hundreds of primitive societies in which no other kind of specialization except by sex and age exists. Specialization has more than one meaning, however, and it is also useful to remember in our discussion here that the term "primitive" covers cultures of greatly differing degrees of complexity.

Full-time religious specialists are seldom found among the culturally crudest societies, those which lack domesticated plants and animals and provide for themselves by simple hunting, fishing, and collecting edible plants. Unless the physical environment is particularly rich in easily available foods, the economic surplus provided by such crude technology seldom allows the development of large face-to-face social groups or any kind of full-time activity not directly concerned with subsistence. Holmberg has reported not only a lack of specialists among the modern Siriono of eastern Bolivia but also the very weak development of myths, magic, and all other aspects of supernaturalism.[1] Most of the time and energy of the Siriono is devoted to a pressing but not very skillful search for sufficient food to survive, and their material and nonmaterial culture, extremely threadbare in every respect, reflect this circumstance. At least a rudimentary development of religious specialization has, however, generally been found among even the very simplest societies. The specialist may be only the individual who knows and remembers religious ideas and procedures, who shows

[1] A. R. Holmberg, *Nomads of the Long Bow.*

an interest in them, and who has had apparent success in this field so that he is sought out. Part-time practitioners, persons whose acknowledged skill is called upon at times of need or upon occasions fixed by convention, are common among even the simpler societies. These men and women must rely for their subsistence or principal subsistence upon activities such as hunting and fishing which are common to all other adult members of their social groups.

Among horticultural and stock-raising societies with economic bases providing adequate surplus to allow specialization outside the quest for food, full-time experts of various kinds are found. Many Negro societies of Africa distinguish two or more kinds of religious practitioners, as do a large number of additional primitive societies of comparable or more elaborate cultural development. The societies of Polynesia commonly recognized a variety of forms of religious specialization although all were not full-time activities. The Maori of New Zealand distinguished ten classes, ranging in hierarchical order from high priests, whose duties concerned the whole of the social group, through acolytes, seers, magicians of various sorts, and on to experts in astronomy at the lowest stratum.[2] Specialization of labor was well developed among the Inca and Aztec, and this complex division of tasks extended into the realm of religious, where many individuals devoted themselves wholly to religious duties.

Religious specialties of a somewhat different sort might also be found among some of the very simplest primitive groups which lacked full-time specialists of any kind—e.g., such peoples as the Northern Paiute and Shoshone of the western United States, among which religious practitioners struggled like their lay brothers to survive by hunting and gathering foods, and served in religious capacities only at times of need. Here, where most persons had some supernatural power, the specialist was the individual who demonstrated by observable successes that he held an unusual degree of power. We may recall that the kinds of power conceived by these peoples were many and sharply limited; when the occasion demanded, the holder of extraordinary power to detect sorcerers,

[2] E. S. C. Handy, *Polynesian Religion.*

charm antelopes, cure the sick, or control the weather was called upon.

Various attempts have been made to classify systematically the kinds of religious specialists found in human societies, but, as a system, none of these has found general acceptance. Names in use are plentiful, and we have here already employed a number of them. Wach has distinguished the founder, reformer, prophet, seer, magician, diviner, saint, and priest.[3] Additional terms commonly applied to the primitive world are shaman, witch, witch doctor, sorcerer, and medicine man. Usages of these terms are not uniform; and, often, no single term of the whole roster is wholly suitable in application to the religious specialist of the simpler primitive society, where many religious roles are filled by one individual.

As a rule of thumb we may say that the terms medicine man, witch doctor, witch, sorcerer, and shaman refer to individuals whose acts emphasize mechanical techniques of magic and whose ministrations tend to be directed toward individuals rather than the social group. In popular usage, medicine men are frequently linked with the American Indian, probably in part because many Indian concepts of supernatural power were translated into English as "medicine," and because the outstanding role of the Indian specialist of the United States and Canada was curing. The medicine man of the American Indian might, however, perform many religious acts in addition to curing. "Shaman" is derived from the native name for religious specialists among Siberian tribes. Many ethnologists restrict this term to individuals who acquire supernatural power by inspiration; that is, by vision, revelation, or other direct personal experience.

Implications of the term "priest" as applied to primitive peoples generally take us to the opposite pole of religious behavior from that connoted by the foregoing terms. It usually implies large societies with centralized authority, a fairly elaborate development of culture, the existence of an organized cult with well-formulated doctrine and fixed rituals. It implies also specialists, the priests, who guide or lead in group ritual directed principally toward personi-

[3] Joachim Wach, *Sociology of Religion.*

fied supernatural beings. Thus, for example, the religious specialists of the Inca, Maya, and Aztec whose ritual acts concerned the great national gods and the society as a whole have customarily been called priests, and they are distinguished from the lesser curers, diviners, and the like of their societies. Similar specialists who lead in rites of ancestor worship among African Negro societies are customarily given this name, to distinguish them from shamans, sorcerers, witches, or diviners concerned with other forms of supernaturalism.

Members of the organized religious fraternities of the pueblo peoples of the southwestern United States are also commonly labeled as priests. Here the individual priest does not stand out as leader; instead all adult males belong to one or more of the religious societies, the members of each of which are jointly charged with specialized religious tasks to honor the ancestral gods, make rain, cure the sick, or promote the fertility of crops. These religious duties are highly formalized and elaborate. With the principal exception of curing rites, they are performed in accordance with a fixed ceremonial calendar, and are directed toward the benefit of the whole social group.

As may be seen, the distinction between priests and other categories of primitive religious specialization roughly corresponds with the distinction which has been made between religion and magic. Here again, we must repeat that although the concepts of religion and magic are logically distinguishable, as evident in actual supernaturalistic behavior, they tend to be mixed. So also with the priest and the shaman, medicine man, and diviner. The role of the primitive priest is, of course, analogous with that of the priest of our own society; that is, it emphasizes knowledge of an elaborate theology and leadership in propitiatory rites for communal benefit. The primitive priest is, however, also often a magician, and many acts which are not magic may be included among the ritual behavior of the shaman, medicine man, and diviner.

In most primitive societies religious specialists stand out prominently for a variety of reasons, and it is not surprising that ethnologists have often concerned themselves with the traits of these individuals and the means by which they came to hold office.

Religious specialists in simple primitive societies have most frequently entered their profession in response to a divine call which consists of some sort of innate trait or experience different from the ordinary. We have noted that falling into trance stands out as the most prominent form of the call, but a large variety of additional departures from the commonplace have been given the same interpretation. These might stand alone as indications of dedication to a religious profession, or the ability to enter trance might also be required. Any seemingly miraculous escape from death—recovery from snakebite or serious illness, survival after being struck by lightning, or experiencing any other near-fatal accident—has rather frequently been the sign to become a curer or even a priest.

Dreams often instruct the individual to follow a religious calling. An unusual skin color or a large variety of other extraordinary traits and experiences might be the supernatural sign. Among the Apache, albinos were thought to be specially qualified and destined for religious specialization. Among some Negro tribes of Africa, persons with a reddish skin were so regarded. The blind, hunchbacks, and other physically malformed individuals might be selected for certain kinds of religious specialization. Local convention has also sometimes fastened upon twins, persons born by breach presentation, and individuals born during thunderstorms or under other unusual circumstances. Now and then—but this qualification has usually applied only to the priest of the more elaborate primitive societies—the individual must be an outstandingly fine physical specimen with no blemish.[4]

Sexual aberration has not been overlooked as a sign of the divine call. Among some of the aboriginal Siberian tribes the highly effeminate youth frequently evinced the abnormal nervous behavior regarded as the call to become a shaman. Males in these societies customarily adopted the clothing of women once they had embarked upon a career of shamanship. Some, but not all, of these transvestites were sexual inverts who, together with the female dress, adopted the manners and roles of women, taking men as husbands or lovers. Among the Chukchee, these individuals were regarded as the most powerful and fearful of shamans. Similar customs of valuing homo-

[4] See W. D. Wallis, *Religion in Primitive Society*, chap. 4.

sexual males as religious specialists have been reported among various other primitive societies including some Eskimo groups, the Sea Dyaks of Borneo, the Bugis of the Celebes, and Indians of Patagonia.[5]

It has been contended that a close association between homosexuality and the occupations of priest and diviner is universal, but this view is not supported by the facts.[6] Male homosexuality has been reported for a great many primitive societies and female homosexuality for a relative few, but these practices do not coincide with religious specialization. Among various other primitive groups, homosexual behavior of any kind is said to be entirely absent or even unthinkable. The presence of a few socially recognized homosexual males was common among many North American Indian tribes. The *berdache* of the North American tribes assumed the roles and, very often, the clothing of women of his society. Socially, his position was comparable with that of women. If, however, we look to the traits of the religious specialists among these tribes we can find no strong correlation between this disposition and the religious calling. Berdaches were not necessarily medicine men. In a number of tribes they held special roles in certain religious ritual, but so also might women and other ordinary members of the society. Our knowledge of the whole question of the relationship between sex and religion, it should be added, is more confused than clear. With regard to primitive religion it seems clear enough, however, that homosexual individuals have indeed held special religious significance in some societies but this association is very far from universal.

Unusual traits or experiences have been the most common but not the sole avenue leading to primitive religious specialization. Many other established routes which lack the flavor of the extraordinary have also been followed. Succession to religious office may be simply hereditary, especially in the more elaborate primitive societies. Among the large and socially stratified societies such as the Inca, Aztec, Polynesians, and many African Negro kingdoms, religious specialization also follows lines of social class. Here and

[5] Edward Carpenter, *Intermediate Types among Primitive Folk.*
[6] *Ibid.*

there the established shaman might sell, give away, or bequeath his supernatural power to a petitioner. In some societies children became destined for later religious duties as the result of vows of their parents made in return for beneficences received from the gods, and children might be urged by their parents to take up the religious calling because of the advantages which will accrue to the kin group in having a practitioner in the family. Likely candidates among the youths might also be selected by established specialists to follow in their footsteps, and individuals might consciously choose the profession without divine portent directing them to do so.

A characteristic which marks the religious specialist of all societies is some degree of social separation from the rest of the population. In the occasional primitive society this distinctiveness is expressed in terms of reference for the religious professionals, "those who stand apart," and it is everywhere evident in other ways. Social separation has applied to religious personnel of the great faiths of the civilized world, and despite attempts by some of the Christian sects to narrow the gap, these circumstances continue to exist. Secular relationships between the Protestant minister and members of his congregation are not the same as those which exist among ordinary men even when the minister attempts to make them so. Much less are the relationships between Christian priest or nun and the laity like those of lay member toward lay member; but here the preservation of social distances is well-marked policy.

Neither of the sources of social aloofness implied here is exclusive to our civilization. The primitive religious professional, like the civilized cleric, stands apart because of qualities which inhere or are thought to inhere in him and in part because he has deliberately sought to make himself different from others and to create social barriers between himself and the laity. Some degree of social separation is probably characteristic of persons following any occupational specialty, but the breach between the man of religion and the rest of society is one of the widest. The dealer in the supernatural is, expectably, viewed as tinged or imbued with the supernatural; he stands apart by reason of the fear, respect, and reverence which the qualities of mystery and sanctity about him evoke. In societies with strongly ethical religions he may also stand apart as a paragon and guardian of virtue and as the symbol of divine jural authority, statuses which may not make his presence comforting in secular circumstances. The demands and nature of his office set him off in still other ways. He is often a highly intelligent and learned man, and much of his lore is unknown to others. He must often be serious when others laugh. He observes many dietary and sexual taboos followed less strictly or not at all by others, and he alone might spend long periods in solitude and self-imposed pain and privation. As paid specialists, he and others of his profession may be the only individuals who perform none of the mundane tasks by which other members of the society gain a livelihood.[7]

We have noted that the primitive religious practitioner often begins his professional career as a person set apart by virtue of remarkable psychological qualities which make him eligible for the profession. Psychological traits of a different sort have also often been pointed out as distinctively characteristic of one kind of religious specialist. The messianic prophet is frequently credited with great personal forcefulness, or, to use the terminology of Max Weber, charisma.[8] Weber introduced this expression (from the Greek, "gift of grace") to refer to power or authority held by individuals over other individuals, and he distinguishes between personal charisma and the charisma of office. The former refers to entirely personal characteristics of persuasiveness, forcefulness, and magnetism which appeal chiefly to the emotions and induce intense loyalty and obedience on a personal level. As the words suggest, charisma of office refers to the aura of authority surrounding the office rather than the man in office, and implies tempered and less emotional attitudes. Any office of prestige has its complement of charisma, and, following this reasoning, we can assume that the competent holder of religious office in primitive society is in this way accorded deference and respect. Personal charisma on the part of primitive religious leaders is, however, a subject often beclouded by lack of information. Any

---

[7] See W. T. Corlett, *The Medicine-Man of the American Indian and his Cultural Background;* and J. L. Maddox, *The Medicine Man.*

[8] H. H. Gerth and C. W. Mills, *From Max Weber: Essays in Sociology.*

prophetic leader who has attracted followers tends to be credited with personal charisma. Leadership itself implies some degree of personal force, but it does not necessarily imply strong emotional attachment to the leader. Lowie has argued that the Paiute prophet Wovoka, the founder of the Ghost Dance religion (see Chapter 13), had a colorless personality,[9] and it seems certain that the forceful personality must be backed by dissatisfaction, crisis, or other cultural circumstances favoring his cause before it meets success. Granting this, the prophet is nevertheless a leader and thus a man among men; and descriptions of primitive prophets and other religious specialists have often alluded to their outstanding qualities of personal force.

The traits of personality which set off the man of religion might often be innate, but certain features of distinction of another sort strongly suggest conscious attempts to enhance his position. His dwelling or its decor may differ, and his dress very often does so. In the simpler societies his daily garb may be undistinguished, but his sacerdotal apparel tends to be richly elaborate. The full ceremonial attire of the medicine men of many American Indian tribes is in striking contrast with the simplicity of their daily attire. Where ordinary men are clean-shaven and long-haired, the religious specialist grows a beard, shaves his head, or wears his hair in peculiar attire. Masks, body paint, and ornaments of many kinds are common symbols of office and unique to the specialist.

Whatever corner of the primitive world we look into, once an individual has become committed to the religious profession, the circumstances which follow are much the same. A long period of preliminary training is the rule, as even the primitive religious specialist has much to learn. The inspired prophet might begin at once to expound his divine message, but even these men tend to be old hands in sacerdotal matters. The usual procedure is to place oneself under the wing of an experienced professional. The priest who leads in group ritual must learn to perfection details of ritual which seem to the man of civilized society astounding feats of memory. The specialist who is priest, diviner, rain maker, and curer all

[9] R. H. Lowie, *Primitive Religions*, p. 257.

rolled in one must also learn much. It is to his advantage, of course, to know or to learn as much as possible concerning the personal traits, habits, and affairs of the members of his society. This information will be useful to him in prophesying, detecting witches, and in curing. He must also learn the pharmacopeia and the therapeutic techniques, and he must meet the ritual requirements demanded of the practitioner.

Accounts of the training of shamans and medicine men often document periods of several to many years in which the candidate experiences much physical suffering in order to befit himself spiritually for office. Common requirements are long periods of solitude for communion with supernatural beings accompanied by a program of rigid physical discipline including intermittent fasts, the avoidance of sexual relations, and the observance of many other taboos. As we have noted, self-torture is sometimes also added. Accounts of ecstatic shamanism among Siberian and Californian Indian groups tell us that individuals who have experienced the symptoms of the call are often extremely reluctant to become shamans because of the intense psychological stress which inspiration imposes. The Chukchee speak of the individual evincing the symptoms of the shamanistic calling as "doomed to inspiration," and when the command of the spirits demands a change of sex, the youthful novices are reported usually to express themselves as preferring death.[10] Where trance is a part of the specialist's ritual, he must achieve mastery over it so that it may be induced when needed and so that he is not carried away. The aspirant who has not learned to control ecstasy is useless as a shaman. Among the Tungus- and Manchu-speaking tribes of aboriginal Siberia, the individual who experienced uncontrolled seizures was merely possessed and in need of the shaman's aid; the full-fledged shaman controlled his seizures and was thought to control the spirits within him during trance.[11]

Above and beyond the psychological turmoil and adjustment which the inspirational practitioner might experience are a variety of mechanical routines which he must master with a high degree of

---

[10] Waldemar Bogoras, *The Chukchee—Religion.*
[11] S. M. Shirokogoroff, *Psychomental Complex of the Tungus.*

skill. Even such apparently simple accomplishments as drum beating and chanting might require much rehearsal, as do the various feats of legerdemain with which many primitive religious specialists impress their clients and audiences.

The beating of the drum, notwithstanding its seeming simplicity requires some skill, and the novice must spend considerable time before he can acquire the desired degree of perfection. This has reference especially to the power of endurance of the performer. The same may be said of the singing. The manifestations continue for several hours, during all which time the shaman exercises the most violent activity with scarcely a pause. After the performance he must not show any signs of fatigue, because he is supposed to be sustained by the "spirits"; and, moreover, the greater part of the exercise is asserted to be the work of the "spirits" themselves, either while entering his body, or while outside his body. The degree of endurance required for all this, and the ability to pass quickly from the highest excitement to a state of normal quietude, can, of course, be acquired only by long practice. Indeed, all the shamans I conversed with said that they had to spend a year, or even two years, before sufficient strength of hand, and freedom of voice, were given to them by the "spirits." Some asserted that during all this preparatory time they kept closely to the inner room, taking up the drum several times a day, and beating it as long as their strength would allow. . . .

Various tricks performed by the Chukchee shamans, including ventriloquism, have to be learned in the preparatory stage. However, I could obtain no detailed information on this point, since the shamans, of course, asserted that the tricks were done by "spirits," and denied having any hand whatever in proceedings of such a character.[12]

The tricks or acts of legerdemain referred to above are particularly associated with inspirational shamanism but they are also found widely in other contexts. These are mystifying performances of quite the same kind as modern parlor and stage magic, which is doubtless a heritage stemming through generations of secularization to anonymous men of religion of centuries gone by.

Tricks of primitive religious specialists include most frequently and outstandingly the mysterious production of objects or small forms of life. These are most frequently said to be sucked from the

[12] Waldemar Bogoras, *op. cit.*, p. 425.

bodies of sick clients, but objects may also be made to appear and disappear in rites not directly connected with curing. The novice of aboriginal Siberia and northern North America might also learn how to make a tent or light dwelling shake to indicate the presence of spirits. In various societies, he may learn to walk on fire, hold hot coals or hot stones in his hands or mouth, disgorge objects, swallow knives and arrows, bleed from the mouth and nose, and perform other similar feats. Houdini-like escapes from securely knotted ropes were one of the features of the demonstrations of supernatural power of the *angakok* of the Central Eskimo and of the curers of the Ojibwa.

A specialty of the Eskimo shaman was to make a "spirit flight" to the supernatural world while securely tied up. As this custom was observed among the Eskimo of the Diomede Islands, the shaman was bound with strong rawhide lines, his neck secured to his knees, hands lashed behind his back, and wrists tied to elbows. A pair of bearskin pants that served as his wings were hung from the ceiling out of his reach.

Then the seal oil lamps are all extinguished. Soon there is a flapping noise as of wings, and a swishing and whirring while the audience feels the rush of wind pass their faces. The angakok's voice seems to soar off into distant space; and he holds conference with the spirits. Upon his return to earth the lamps are relighted and the angakok is seen doubled up on the floor and bound in his original position *but with the bearskin pants on his arms and his arms bound behind his back*.[13]

Shamanistic performances of some Eskimo and Indian groups of northern North America as well as of the Siberian tribes gave an important place to ventriloquism to represent the voices of spirits. The angakok of the Central Eskimo also impressed his audience by causing a harpoon apparently to pierce his breast so that blood gushed forth.[14] This trick was accomplished by secreting an animal bladder full of blood beneath the outer clothing and piercing this container. Similar practices existed among the Chukchee and other Siberian tribes. Among some North American Indian tribes bleed-

[13] E. M. Weyer, *The Eskimos*, pp. 437-438.
[14] Franz Boas, "The Central Eskimo."

ing of the nose and mouth were elements of the shaman's performance. How this was done is not always known, although some accounts tell of practices of sucking the gums and making incisions in
the tongue.[15]

Completion of training of the primitive shaman, medicine man,
or priest was frequently marked by formal rites of initiation. Elaborate ceremonies of investiture pertain principally to the large and
settled agricultural societies, but even on a lower level of cultural
development such rites might be found. The Midewiwin society or
Grand Medicine Lodge composed of medicine men and priests of
the Ojibwa of North America recognized four degrees of membership, each requiring lengthy training and rites of initiation upon
its completion. These rites included the polished performance of
feats of legerdemain as evidence that the novice had met the requirements of office.[16]

Everywhere the ultimate test of the primitive professional has
been a record of success. Pettitt states, "Many shamans may be
quite sincere and even accurate in tracing their first intimation of
supernatural power to a psychic disturbance, but others have similar
disturbances without becoming shamans. The decision is forced by
other criteria: the will to study, and the ability to perform successfully."[17] Statistics on the number of aspiring but unsuccessful
medicine men or shamans in primitive society are, of course, not
available, but ethnological literature now and then gives revealing
glimpses which suggest that failure is not uncommon. Genuine and
spurious trances are probably distinguishable to the experienced
onlooker, and the occasional report tells us that lay members observe
the shaman's performance carefully and demand the genuine.[18]
John Tanner's description of his thirty years of captivity among
the Ojibwa during the late eighteenth and early nineteenth centuries
describes the laughter of ridicule evoked by the clumsy ventrilo-

[15] G. A. Pettitt, *Primitive Education in North America.*

[16] W. J. Hoffman, "The Midewiwin or 'Grand Medicine Society' of the
Ojibway."

[17] G. A. Pettitt, *op. cit.*, p. 150.

[18] See, for example, S. F. Nadel, "Shamanism in the Nuba Mountains."

quism and sleight-of-hand of a man claiming shamanistic power.[19]
The Copper Eskimo drove the inept shaman from his profession by
ridicule which included throwing their gloves in his face.[20] Acts of
this kind do not necessarily imply skepticism of the philosophy of
supernaturalism; they seem instead to be directed against individuals, insuring that they be well-versed in the knowledge and
skills of their profession.

More important than a polished performance of the mechanics of
ritual is success in curing, bringing rain, ensuring successful hunting, and the other objectives of that ritual. Accounts tell us rather
often that the repeatedly unsuccessful curer is driven out or killed,
and that the shaman or medicine man, as a dealer in the occult, is
more open than others to the charge of witchcraft and subsequent
punishment by death or banishment.

Now we might ask what it is that attracts individuals to the religious calling. Temperamental characteristics such as we have discussed doubtless have been and continue to be important in many
societies as unconscious motives. Individual capacities for religious
experiences of intellectual-philosophic or emotional type must surely
vary. Paul Radin has presented the interesting and plausible idea
that the field of religion in primitive society has been attractive as
the chief avenue of self-expression of individuals of philosophic
bent, the thinkers and intellectual elite who in their capacities as
religious philosophers serve for the population at large as the formulators of ideas and the interpreters of the world.[21]

Early writings on primitive religions have often expressed the
view that the religious profession is adopted with the conscious aims
of gaining material benefits. These motives have undoubtedly operated in many cases but at other times they have been absent or have
worked jointly with largely unconscious emotional and intellectual
motives. Curers, diviners, and other specialists whose services are
engaged by individuals are most frequently paid, and established

[19] John Tanner, *A Narrative of the Captivity and Adventures of John Tanner During Thirty Years of Residence Among the Indians.*
[20] Diamond Jenness, *The Life of the Copper Eskimo.*
[21] Paul Radin, *Primitive Man as a Philosopher.*

professionals under whom novices receive training may also be paid for their instruction. High fees for medical and psychiatric services are not a wholly modern innovation; the idea of charging what the traffic will bear seems anciently established. But this is not to say that the desire for wealth is paramount in the making of shamans and medicine men in all societies. Many of the shamans of aboriginal Siberia received little remuneration and were economically hard put. Those who held the statuses of clan shamans received no more than token pay for ritual performances. Among these individuals, shamanizing appears to have had the functions of maintaining psychological stability for the practitioner as well as the group.[22] To the Northern Paiute and other impoverished hunters and gatherers who moved about frequently, the accumulation of a large supply of material goods was hardly possible because of their poverty and unfeasible because of problems of transportation. The obligations of kinship and the great premium commonly placed upon generosity in these and other small primitive societies also worked strongly to prevent the accumulation of wealth by any single individual. During most of man's history he has been a hunter and gatherer living in very small groups composed principally of kin, and we have little reason to think that he entirely lacked religious specialists.

The religious profession has generally offered prestige to the man of primitive society. Occasional accounts tell of societies in which the religious specialist is accorded no special honor, but the reverse is customary and the religious leader is often also a leader in secular affairs. Chieftainship and past or present shamanship sometimes coincided in American Indian societies, or the ties between chief and shaman were close so that one supported the other. In his role as arbiter with the supernatural, the religious specialist sometimes served as a counterbalance to the excessive use of authority by the tribal ruler.[23] Dependent as it often was upon continued success, the position of the religious specialist might be precarious but his influence was generally great. The fact that his influence stemmed in part from the fear he inspired did nothing to diminish its potency.

[22] S. M. Shirokogoroff, *op. cit.*
[23] See, for example, A. H. Gayton, *Yokuts-Mono Chiefs and Shamans.*

The prestige and economic advantages which the religious calling has so often offered the primitive specialist lead to the question of his sincerity. The widespread use of sleight-of-hand, ventriloquism, and similar forms of learned deceit suggest anything but sincerity. It is interesting to note that many accounts of the nineteenth century and earlier refer to the "quackery," "mumbo-jumbo," and charlatanry of primitive men of religion. These accounts were, of course, written either by individuals dedicated to Christianity and intolerant of any other faith or by individuals who, seeing the obviously specious in acts of legerdemain, branded the whole as fraud. There is no doubt that primitive supernaturalists have sometimes capitalized on the fear of others and have created or augmented fear for their own ends. Specialists have been engaged to work harm on others, and primitive versions of shamanistic blackmail have also been recorded.[24] The modern Jivaro of South America furnish an extreme example of organized collusion on the part of tribal shamans to fleece the ordinary man. Working by prearrangement and on a split-fee basis, certain shamans induce the fear of black magic into their tribesmen and thus create clients for other shamans to cure.[25]

Even cases such as these do not necessarily belie sincerity. Power may be used to help or to hurt, but it may still be regarded with complete faith as supernatural; and there is nothing inherently non-religious about the accumulation of wealth and power on the part of the practitioner. Trance evoked on call is charlatanry only to the modern civilized mind, as an examination of the religious history of our own society should quickly reveal. Performance of sleight-of-hand and other tricks may also be compatible with a sincere belief in other tribal ideas of supernaturalism. This artifice is a dressing designed to impress the audience and it does not comprise the core of professional acts. It is difficult to imagine that a primitive shaman or medicine man might achieve lasting professional status on the basis of feats of legerdemain alone. The question of sincerity versus insincerity may be summed up, as it has been before, in the state-

---

[24] See, for example, *Ibid.*

[25] M. J. Harner, unpublished notes on field research conducted in 1956-1957.

ment that frauds exist everywhere and the number among primitive religious practitioners is very likely comparable with that found in any modern profession of prestige.

A question which we skirted in our earlier discussion of unusual psychological states is whether or not religious specialization in various primitive societies is in the hands of psychotics. (The same question has, of course, been argued in reference to some of the Christian saints.) We have already noted that in many societies nervous instability has been the mark or the requirement of the religious specialist. Out of descriptions of these societies has grown a stereotyped conception of the primitive religious specialist as a highly neurotic or even psychotic individual. Paul Radin has expressed this view in a scheme of evolution from magic to religion and medicine man to priest. According to Radin's ideas, supernaturalism began with the formulations of the emotionally unstable, and only later, when normal individuals were attracted by the material rewards which the profession offered, did supernaturalistic practices lose some of their quality of neurosis.

It has been made clear that the formulations with which he [the primitive medicine man and the later priest] operates and the techniques he uses are fundamentally rooted in the projections and behavior of individuals carefully selected on the basis of their neurotic-epileptoid mental constitution and that, however normalized these, in the course of time, may have become through the influence of the more normal individuals who entered the profession, their origin in a neurotic mentality is still clearly patent.[26]

Radin's theory goes beyond the point where it may be supported by available data. Certainly few ethnologists would be willing to use the term ''epileptoid'' in blanket reference to shamans who experience seizure and trance. Radin's most outstanding examples of abnormal behavior on the part of religious specialists have been drawn from accounts of aboriginal Siberian tribes, and these accounts also report that nervous afflictions similar to those of the shamans are common among the general populations. Much else

[26] Paul Radin, *Primitive Religion*, p. 154.

which we have already said in our discussion of unusual psychic states would also cast doubt on the theory that individuals of these dispositions were everywhere the first formulators of religious ideas and acts.

There is no doubt that the nervously unstable are selected for religious duties in some societies. Available accounts seem to describe a wide range of kinds of behavior among these candidates which at its extreme includes clinical psychosis as it is defined in our own society. Few scholars would be willing to go further, however, and state that the established practitioners are psychotic. We have noted that in the Siberian and African societies where violently abnormal behavior is the sign of inspiration, once an individual has assumed the role of religious specialist his behavior at times other than religious seances seems generally to be normal. In writing of the Siberian tribes Shirokogoroff states that shamans in states of trance stand on the very dividing line between "a normal stable state" and an "abnormal unstable state" but that among candidates "extasy usually turns into a half-delirious hysterical condition. . . . "[27] Religious specialization appears to be for these individuals a form of therapy which provides an approved channel for their nervous outbursts and brings recovery. The recorded statements of a Siberian Yakut-Tungus shaman seem to say just this:

When I was twenty years old, I became very ill and began "to see with my eyes and hear with my ears" that which others did not see or hear; nine years I struggled with myself, and I did not tell any one what was happening to me, as I was afraid that people would not believe me and would make fun of me. At last I became so seriously ill that I was on the verge of death; but when I started to shamanize I grew better; and even now when I do not shamanize for a long time I am liable to be ill.[28]

The practice of attaching special religious value to behavior which might in our society be regarded as psychopathological puts it in quite a different light. Trance and hysterical seizures, as we have noted, might also be sought by lay members of a society as

---

[27] S. M. Shirokogoroff, *op. cit.*, p. 274.
[28] M. A. Czaplicka, *Aboriginal Siberia*, p. 173.

"normal," earnestly desired religious goals regarded as rewarding in material as well as (or rather than) spiritual ways. We have noted, too, that states of trance are sometimes limited along lines of sex or hereditary right. It is also clear that many societies distinguish between the insane who chronically act deranged and those who evince the symptoms of the religious calling.[29] Benedict has referred to the kinds of abnormal behavior we have described as "border-line psychological states," and this seems to be both reasonable and cautious.[30] It seems entirely warranted, however, to say that psychological states which would be regarded as pathological if found among members of our own contemporary society are a common element of primitive religious complexes. But, of course, whether or not psychosis is involved, the religious value of these states is quite unchanged.

THE ROLE OF WOMEN

In the preceding paragraphs the male gender has been consistently used with reference to primitive religious specialists. This is, of course, imposed by the nature of our language, which lacks a singular personal pronoun clearly denoting either male or female. Coincidentally, our usage goes much of the way toward describing actual circumstances: the role of women in religion has generally been subordinate to that of men. This statement will probably surprise no one if he thinks only of the role of women as religious professionals in our own society. If, however, he considers inequalities between men and women of our society in church attendance, the circumstances are reversed. If he looks to primitive society he finds that the role of women as both lay participants and as professionals is generally subordinate to that of men.

In our society church attendance and participation in other church activities have fallen to the female side in a well-established but unrigid division of labor by the sexes. Among the laity, church attendance seems to imply spirituality and emotionality, and therefore femininity. In many opinions the manly man is not the unre-

[29] See, for example, S. F. Nadel, *op. cit.*
[30] Ruth Benedict, "Religion," p. 658.

mittingly faithful church-goer. The idea that women are more emotional and sensitive than men is open to much argument, and, as
Lowie noted long ago, an examination of the role of women in religion in the primitive world does nothing to support the view that
women are inherently more religiously minded than men.[31]

It is true that surveys of religious beliefs and practices in this
country and Great Britain show that women hold traditional religious attitudes more commonly than men.[32] This circumstance does
not necessarily, however, indicate a greater capacity for religious
experience. It suggests that conditions of their social life tend to
make them more conservative than men. We may also note that in
Western society, church affairs for lay members have long had
strongly secular aspects and these have often served as important
channels through which women, socially restricted in many ways in
the past, were provided opportunities for pleasurable association
with others. In our modern society it is women who are responsible
for much of the socialization of children, and it is also they who are
under the stronger compulsion to introduce their offspring to religion and to set examples for them by personal participation in
organized religious activities.

In 1924, reviewing the writing of the time on the place of women
in primitive religion, Lowie noted their lesser role and stated, "In
various regions women are not only ineligible for office but seem to
be shut out from all religious activity."[33] It is very doubtful that
women have in any society been totally excluded from religious
participation, and Lowie seems later to accept this view. Among
some tribes of Australia death was the penalty for women who
witnessed rites initiating males to adulthood. Similar prohibitions
involving death or severe punishment have been described for various societies of New Guinea, Melanesia, and South America. Among
these tribes women were not only barred from participation but
were sometimes also deliberately deceived and intimidated, as the
adolescent boys undergoing the rites had formerly been, by male

[31] R. H. Lowie, *op. cit.*
[32] Michael Argyle, *Religious Behavior.*
[33] R. H. Lowie, *op. cit.*, p. 205.

explanations of the activities which they might sometimes hear but never see. Noises produced during ritual by the bull-roarer, a piece of wood or other thin, flat object tied to a cord and whirled in the air, were said to be the voices of the gods. In even these extreme cases, women had rites which were exclusively female if tribally less important.[34]

The barring of women from the puberty rites of boys does not necessarily reflect the low social status of women or indicate rigid exclusion of females from religious matters. It may instead have important symbolic value. At this time boys leave the world of mothered childhood and enter the world of men. Exclusion of women from the rites may then be seen as a dramatization of the changed status and associations of the boys. Women have, however, often been barred from religious affairs which, unlike boys' rites of circumcision, were in no sense exclusively male but were instead of direct importance to the women themselves and the whole society.

Here and there, with something of a concentration in aboriginal Northern California, women have outnumbered men as specialists or the profession has been limited to females; but religious specialization in both primitive and civilized society has nevertheless been preponderantly male. Where the office is open to both sexes, ordinarily only the exceptional woman has stood out as a practitioner of high prestige. In societies where the religious personnel is stratified, only positions of low prestige tend to be allotted to women. To summarize, the severity of restrictions upon females varies a great deal, but the general rule is partial exclusion.

Various explanations have been offered to the question of why this apparent discrimination against women should occur. Lowie has emphasized the belief that menstrual blood is dangerous and polluting and that women are therefore viewed as inherently unclean and unfit for religious office. Examples may be cited of the admission of women after menopause to religious rites from which they had formerly been excluded. It seems probable, however, that multiple influencing factors are involved, and the attitude that women are unfit because of their physiological functions operates in conjunction

[34] See, for example, Phyllis Kaberry, *Aboriginal Woman, Sacred and Profane.*

with these other factors or serves as their rationalization. The religious freedom which may be accorded to aged women seems, for example, not always merely or only the result of the cessation of menstruation. Women are at this time of course freed from childbearing and the responsibilities of caring for infants. In old Japan religious participation was correlated with a traditional scheme of the division of labor by age. The performance of the many household and community rites which fell outside the province of the priest was the particular duty of the aged of both sexes, whose physical condition suited them to these light tasks.

The partial exclusion of women from the sphere of religion has also been viewed as representing "in part an extension of the social seclusion of women which characterizes most cultures."[35] The religious and the social are of course not mutually exclusive. Where the social status of women is high, prohibitions on religious participation by females tend to diminish, but this does not necessarily imply that women in these societies are strongly represented in the religious profession.

Stepping outside the primitive world for a moment, we note that the lowly social status of Mohammedan women is well reflected in the numerous religious restrictions placed upon them. In ancient Japan, women held high social status. Women of royal lineage then sometimes served as ruling empresses rather than merely as imperial wives, and women held important religious offices. As their status sank to a position much inferior to that of men, women were no longer eligible for either secular or religious positions of prominence and power in either the native Shintō religion or in Buddhism, which reached them with a long-established tradition of a male priesthood. Several Japanese religious sects arising in the eighteenth and nineteenth centuries were founded and led by women, although the status of females was at this time low. These sects, however, arose among the lower social classes of Japan, where distinctions in social prestige between male and female were the least sharp. No woman has held the position of Buddhist priest, and, since ancient times, no woman has held a high position in the traditional Shintō religion.

[35] W. D. Wallis, *op. cit.*, p. 299.

Modern trends in the United States relating to the question of women's serving in the ministry are worthy of note. The issue has arisen frequently among Protestants since about the time women were extended the franchise. Advocates of opening the ministry to women have frequently presented the argument that females are eminently suited because of their "special spiritual and emotional qualities," and this is an idea with which church leaders appear sometimes to concur even when they deny the petitions. A growing trend toward approval of women in the Protestant pulpit seems evident, and the question has become at least a live issue in the Reform branch of Judaism. In 1956, when the Northern Presbyterians ordained their first woman minister, several other Protestant sects including the Methodists had already opened the office to women. A similar trend has also risen among European Protestants, and Denmark has admitted women to the ministry since 1947, Sweden since 1958. Perhaps the first break with Jewish tradition in this respect occurred in the United States in 1955, when a woman was appointed as cantor for Rosh Hashanah rites of a Reform congregation at Oceanside, Long Island. No woman has yet served as rabbi, but the question has arisen several times since 1919 in the Reform branch. Debated at rabbinical conferences held in 1955, 1956, and 1957, the issue seems very much alive.

In view of the special qualities of spirituality imputed to women, it is interesting that actual candidates for the ministry in the United States and Europe appear to be very few. In the ten years following the opening of the pulpit to women in Denmark in 1947 only four women ministers were ordained. Agitation toward opening the clergy to females thus seems to reflect not only change in the social status of women but also to be a part of the movement toward establishing equal opportunities for women whether or not the opportunities are in fact taken.

Granting that the rush to the pulpit in the modern United States is not great for either sex, one might nevertheless expect a greater representation by women in sects which allow them. Here the weight of tradition might continue to exert influence, but still another set of circumstances which applies to both civilized and primitive society seems more important. Man is still generally the professional and the breadwinner in the human family, and it is likely that he will remain in these positions because of the limitations which the maternal role places on woman during a part of her life. Much argument has waged over innate differences of temperament and the question of inherent physiological superiority and inferiority of the sexes. Some have argued that childbirth need not inhibit women from following professional careers, and this seems reasonable enough provided the role of the mother is somehow otherwise filled. Usually this has meant that only some mothers may have professional careers as their surrogates have generally been other women.

One of the few points on the subject of sexual differences which leaves no room for argument is that only women give birth to children. In primitive society at least, they also nurse and care for young children, responsibilities which suit them poorly for hunting, waging war, or any other activities which might demand undivided attention. Most female religious practitioners of primitive society have assumed these roles as mature women without responsibility for the care of infants. The woman in advanced pregnancy and the new mother cannot always serve when they are needed for either fixed rites or emergencies. Where hysterical seizures are demanded of the religious specialist, women in these conditions of life seem particularly ill-suited to meet the strains of religious performances. Female shamans among the Siberian tribes, although customarily selected and trained during their youth, did no shamanizing during the course of pregnancy and for some time after childbirth, and were regarded as taboo during these periods.[36]

Still another matter related to the birth and care of children suggests itself. It is difficult to avoid thinking that most women, for biopsychological reasons and often also because of the cultural value placed on this role, prefer motherhood to any other time-consuming occupation which might stand in its way.

---

[36] S. M. Shirokogoroff, *op. cit.*

PART II. THE ROLE

OF RELIGION

Chapter 8. Introduction

In Western society we have come to refer to religion as belief or faith, words which often serve as markers to indicate the scientifically dubious. But validity in the sense of practical reality conforming with religious dogma has been completely irrelevant to analytical studies of the part which religion plays in human life. Ideas need have no scientifically demonstrable counterparts in the "real" world in order to be significant and even vital to man. Since religion does not spring from any recognizable biological source or physiological drive innate in man, scholars have asked why it should be found everywhere and why it should survive under circumstances of cultural change during the past several centuries that seem inimical to its existence. The answer often given is that religion is much more than ideas of supernaturalism; it is a set of beliefs with practical effect in human affairs and is at the same time a system of action and interaction among human beings with consequences important to culture, society, and the individual. Scholarly interest in religion in the social sciences has thus focused upon its significance in man's life and the "truth" of religious ideas has for most purposes been omitted from consideration.

Early anthropological interests in religion which concentrated upon the evolution of monotheism out of "cruder" and "simpler" creeds viewed religion in the same light as science, as rational, conscious ideas and acts aimed at answering questions about the universe and solving empirical problems. Analogy between the religious and the scientific or naturalistic behavior of man often breaks down, however, when the objectives of the two kinds of acts are considered. A substantial part of religious behavior cannot be seen to have what

127

we would regard as explicit, practical ends. Man's response when one of his fellows dies provides an illustration. In no society is death met in a wholly matter-of-fact manner by merely disposing of the body of the deceased. Stated reasons for conducting funeral rites may be that they render respect to the soul of the deceased, dispatch the spirit to a supernatural world, protect the living from the harm which the spirit might otherwise work, or only that they are necessary because they are customary. Funerals are a well-developed facet of most primitive religions, but no society expects that the performance of ritual will revive the dead or serve any other similar practical objective.

Various other forms of religious behavior aim at worldly goals such as successful hunting and fishing or a rich crop, but here naturalistic and supernaturalistic acts are used jointly to achieve the objectives. Malinowski has argued convincingly that primitive man distinguishes between naturalistic techniques of hunting, fishing, and husbandry and the supernaturalistic acts which he also performs as indispensable accompaniments to these activities. The primitive gardener has at his command sound "scientific" knowledge of plant husbandry which he uses hand in hand with supernaturalism, Malinowski states, but no person lays crop failure to supernaturalistic cause when it may be attributed to poor husbandry. We have already expressed doubt as to whether naturalism and supernaturalism are in every primitive society sharply distinguished by the people themselves.[1] Malinowski appears to be sound, however, in stating that much of the importance of religion applies to factors beyond the understanding and the control of man which may affect the outcome of his efforts. Given the most faithful performance of all known practical techniques of horticulture, for example, crops might still fail. Between acts of husbandry and end

[1] See, for example, F. L. K. Hsu, *Religion, Science and Human Crises*. Hsu states that in the medical practices of the people of a community in China, magic and science are intimately intertwined and not distinguished from each other.

results lies an area of uncertainty, and it is here where religion steps in.

Thus magic supplies primitive man with a number of ready-made ritual acts and beliefs, with a definite mental and practical technique which serves to bridge over the dangerous gaps in every important pursuit or critical situation. It enables man to carry out with confidence his important tasks, to maintain his poise and his mental integrity in fits of anger, in throes of hate, of unrequited love, of despair and anxiety.[2]

Clearly implied in the foregoing is the idea that the most important consequences of religious behavior are not the goals intended by the actors. The expressed objectives of ritual often seem obviously unsatisfactory to account for the ubiquity and elaboration of these acts and for their great similarity throughout the world. Native explanations of the purpose of essentially identical ceremonials differ from society to society and may be entirely nonempirical. These nonworldly goals are often assumed to have been reached once ritual has been performed. Much religious behavior has, of course, explicit worldly objectives, and these goals may or may not be reached. Regardless of the kind of goal or whether it has been attained, the fact that beliefs are held and ritual is performed is viewed by scholars as having great significance. Following this reasoning, the role of the scholar becomes one of determining the practical effects of religion which are unknown or largely unknown to its adherents.

Malinowski has been cited here to illustrate this idea, but he is not its originator. His special but not exclusive bent of theory was attention to the role of culture, including religion, with reference to the individual. Other scholars have seen the principal import of religion to be social rather than individual. Emile Durkheim, as we know, saw the chief role of religion as supporting and uniting society. By common beliefs and especially by periodic joint rituals, the important "collective sentiments" of society were upheld and reaffirmed and its members bound together into a "single moral

---

[2] B. Malinowski, *Magic, Science and Religion*, p. 70.

community."[3] Durkheim also clearly stated that the vitality of religion comes from its unintended effects:

Of the two functions which religion originally fulfilled, there is one, and only one, which tends to escape it more and more; that is its speculative function. That which science refuses to grant to religion is not its right to exist, but its right to dogmatize upon the nature of things and the special competence which it claims for itself for knowing man and the world. As a matter of fact, it does not know itself. It does not even know what it is made of, nor to what need it answers. It is itself a subject for science, so far is it from being able to make the law for science![4]

Out of a diverse background in which W. Robertson Smith, Durkheim, Malinowski, and Radcliffe-Brown stand out prominently has emerged a body of scholarly studies called "functionalist," which center upon the role of religion with reference to society and the individual, and the interrelationships between religion and other parts of culture. Functionalism has been the dominant theoretical orientation in modern analytical studies of religion among both anthropologists and sociologists. (Sociology has, as a matter of fact, made by far the greater contribution to the development of functionalist theory, and there is little beyond some attention to psychological aspects to distinguish the functionalism of anthropologists from sociological analysis.) As a preface to the chapters which follow, it is useful to know something of the basic assumptions and terminology of the studies based on these theoretical foundations.

Fundamental is the view of culture (or society, if one leans toward sociology) as a whole composed of interacting components. This system has a structure or formal arrangement of its parts, and a set of relationships or interactions among these parts. As is customary in theories which involve the idea of systems, a tendency toward equilibrium or integration of the parts is generally assumed. Each part is held to operate toward the maintenance of the whole or to be functionally compatible with other parts. Change in any important aspect implies change in others, to bring the system back into equilibrium or integration. Perhaps in part because no whole

---

[3] Emile Durkheim, *The Elementary Forms of the Religious Life*, p. 47.
[4] *Ibid.*, p. 430.

societies have been found which lacked religion, theorizing along these lines has often included the implicit or explicit assumption that religion is an indispensable part of culture.

Within this general framework, scholars have had a variety of differing theoretical orientations and lines of emphasis, and their interpretations have followed several paths. Interests have generally been weighted toward the group rather than the individual and have relied heavily upon sociological theory. Especially as followed by Malinowski and his students, functionalism has also made use of psychological concepts in relating religion to the individual. The functions of religion may then be expressed as the contributions it makes toward the integration or maintenance of either the society or the individual. Malinowski and other scholars have hypothesized certain "basic needs" of the individual and society; and the function of religion or any other item of culture is then the part they play in filling these needs.

A few scholars have held that every element of culture is indispensable and serves a positive role in meeting individual and societal "needs." Some have observed that religion as well as other traits of culture may serve as disruptive or disintegrative forces. Very commonly the view has been that although religion may contribute toward societal or individual breakdown, its positive aspects outweigh these negative or disruptive effects, for, in order to survive, every society must have functional consistency or compatible enmeshing of its institutions, and the needs of individuals must also be met. When serious incompatibility arises, change leading to consistency must follow to prevent social disintegration or psychological breakdown of the individual.

Most studies have stressed the function of ritual and belief in supporting social structure and institutionalized customs—the family and other social units, the scheme of social stratification, moral or ethical codes, institutions such as marriage, and political and economic systems. By symbolically expressing customs and social relationships and placing upon them a stamp of sacred approval, ritual and belief are held to fortify the individual element expressed and also the whole. Interpretations have also commonly emphasized the role of group ceremonies in promoting social cohesion by jointly expressing and thereby reinforcing or teaching the values of the society. Group participation in any kind of activity presumably intensifies social cohesion, but religious rites are held to be particularly effective because of the formal seal of sanctification which they give to the cultural norms they express. As Radcliffe-Brown has stated this view, society depends for its existence upon common social sentiments, and ritual acts are symbolic expressions of these sentiments which reaffirm them and maintain their intensity.[5]

A four-fold scheme of classification of types of functions has emerged in these analyses of the role of religion with reference to society and the individual. A distinction is made between positive functions, the contributions toward maintenance and support of society or the individual, and negative functions, the contributions toward disruption or disintegration. As we have implied, a distinction is also made between manifest functions, the purposes of religious acts as they exist in the thoughts of the actors, and implicit functions, the effects or consequences of the acts that are generally unclear or unknown to the members of society. The distinction between manifest and implicit functions may be made clear by a brief illustration. The expressed purpose of a rite may be to bring rain. The participants and observers may be well aware that participation in ceremonial serves such secondary purposes as providing entertainment and, perhaps, an opportunity to gain prestige by displaying wealth or standing out in some other way. They are much less likely to be aware that performance of the ritual gives them psychological assurance and promotes societal unity through joint action and common aims, effects which, following the four-fold terminology, are called positive implicit functions.[6]

Many criticisms and doubts may be expressed about interpretations resting on the theoretical foundations as outlined above. Little agreement has been reached on hypothesized societal or individual

[5] A. R. Radcliffe-Brown, "Religion and Society," in *Structure and Function in Primitive Society*.

[6] For a detailed exposition and critique of functionalist theory see R. K. Merton, *Social Theory and Social Structure*. Merton has used the term "latent" where we have used "implicit."

needs, and it is tautologous to state that unless basic requirements for group or individual survival are met no society or individual can survive. Verification of the idea that religion is necessary for society to continue can hardly be made in any conclusive way. It would depend upon observation of societies entirely lacking religion, and no such society has been known. Moreover, existence of a trait that is seen to have functional significance does not mean that the trait is indispensable. An epidemic which carries off a large part of a society or a plague of locusts that causes crop failure and famine may be seen as serving the positive roles of uniting the people by mobilizing them to joint effort against a common enemy and of contributing to their economy through such things as providing employment for undertakers and stimulating the sale of mourning clothes. Crime may be looked upon as supporting society by providing a livelihood for law enforcement officers and the numerous specialists required to feed, house, clothe, and attempt to rehabilitate criminals. Disease, locusts, and crime are, however, indispensable to society only in the sense that cultural and social conditions would not be precisely the same if they did not exist. An additional critical comment is implied here, that functionalism of this persuasion refers to static conditions and ignores change. At its worst, this theorizing seems to say only that in order for society or culture to remain precisely as they are, they must not change.

All anthropologists do not, of course, think that religion is indispensable, and functionalist theory has been accommodated to embrace cultural change. Some scholars express the view that a "functional substitute," generally unidentified, may serve in the place of religion, and the idea of societal needs is not prominent today.

Many studies have avoided the question of societal or individual needs, but they still present us with the problem of determining the validity of the evaluations they make of the functions of religion. This is perhaps inevitable since the idea of positive and negative functions brings us within or dangerously close to the boundaries of value judgment. Using the same logic in analysis, different scholars may evaluate the effects they deduce so that they differ or even oppose each other. Any established belief or custom, for example, is negative in the sense that it inhibits acceptance of other beliefs or customs which might better foster societal unity or individual well-being. Final judgment of its positive or negative value is then difficult to make. Merton has pointed out that Marxists have labeled religion (i.e., Christianity) an opiate for the masses, making them content with their lot, whereas others see only its positive aspects in supporting the social *status quo*.[7] The societally supportive and unifying effects of religion are, of course, most easily and satisfactorily deduced for small societies holding ritual in which all members participate. In large and socially segmented tribes, ceremonies which "rehearse the social order" may be seen as divisive of the whole because clan and other group social distinctions are preserved in them, or, dependent upon the interpreter's evaluation, they may be regarded as integrative of the whole for quite the same reason.

A trend of interpretation less prominent than those we have discussed but growing in recent years, has been to explain some forms of religious behavior as symbolic expressions of tensions arising from social or cultural sources. Making use of psychological concepts, these studies see religious acts as compensating for frustrations and dissatisfactions and providing channels for venting hostility which must otherwise be repressed. Ceremonial acts which seem to depart sharply from the norms of the society and have therefore resisted explanation along other avenues have often been approached in this way. Analysis of this kind has been used particularly in interpreting antisocial acts such as witchcraft, trying to account for its existence and for the variations of form it takes in different societies, and seeking in social structure for conflicts which give rise to tensions released either by acts or accusations of witchcraft.

Interpretations relating religion to tensions are difficult or impossible to verify and they often seem conjectural, but we shall reserve discussion of them for separate treatment (see Chapter 11).

It is difficult to escape the impression that the premises have shaped the conclusions of many functionalist studies. Dedication to the idea that all elements of culture are vital to support society in smooth articulation makes it imperative to see integrative functions,

[7] *Ibid.*, pp. 44-45.

and it is no surprise that scholars have tended to see chiefly the positive roles of religion. Some scholars, following Durkheim, have carried the argument of the integrative effect of ritual into a full circle: joint participation in ceremonies promotes social unity, and the ceremonies come into existence because social life emotionally compels man to conduct them.

The accusation of tautology might also be made of the much-used hypothesis holding that communal rites which rehearse the social hierarchy by giving precedence to the actors in accordance with the established system of rank thereby reaffirm the social order. Since social relations in religious acts are unquestionably a part of social life, one might well ask if the observation of ritual is not simply one of the means by which the social order is deduced. He might also question whether this reasoning states anything more than that repetition reinforces habit. In response, the argument might be repeated that the religious cloak gives a special endorsement of sanctification to the social hierarchy and any other norm it expresses.

Another criticism that may be made of functionalism of the kind we have described is that much of it seems teleological. Explanations couched in terms of purpose have long been outlawed in the physical sciences. It strikes no modern, educated person as satisfactory to "explain" the existence of the sun by means of its roles in manufacturing chlorophyll, warming the earth, melting winter snows, and so on. Anthropological studies of religion relating it to society or the individual have indeed often seemed teleological although the word "purpose" has usually been expressed in terms of human or societal needs served by religion and disguised by such substitutes as "contribution," "significance," and "meaning." One reader will see teleology in these writings and another will not. It is probable that many scholars have unwittingly been trapped into seeming teleology by the nature of our language, which often conveys the idea of purpose when the speaker or writer has no such intent.[8] Even when intentionally teleological, studies of this kind have value. Anthropocentric consideration of purpose in the physical sciences, such as the purpose of the planets or of the revolution of the earth, is both unprofitable and distracting and it has led to the formula-

[8] See A. J. Bernatowicz, "Teleology in Science Teaching."

tion of no valid scientific theories. In human affairs, however, purpose is worthy of consideration. It is when we take teleological interpretations as explanations of causes and as unquestioned reasons for the existence of cultural phenomena that they are truly dangerous.

Despite the doubts and criticisms expressed here, it may fairly be said that functionalist studies have often presented reasonable interpretations of the role of religion in supporting the social scheme and other cultural norms. No study has been able to demonstrate a precise correspondence between the norms of a society and its religion, and there is probably never a point for point correspondence unless one follows the growing trend of defining religion as the "values" or "commitments" of a society. Religion and social norms often touch or coincide, but important values may find no religious expression. Systematic research comparing religion and value systems, it must be added, has hardly begun, and it is seriously inhibited by lack of effective techniques of defining and classifying "values." Scholarly formulations of important cultural norms seem, as a matter of fact, often to have proceeded by observation of what has been expressed or sanctioned by religious beliefs and acts. This course of action naturally follows from the view, advanced by Durkheim and held by many modern scholars, that the principal significance of religion derives from its role as a social device for expressing and reinforcing the values *most vital* to societal integration.

We must add that some of our criticisms at least partially dissolve when the results of functionalist studies are examined. In actuality, interpretations have not balanced positive and negative functions against each other or related them to the maintenance of society or the individual in any systematic, thoroughgoing way. They have instead pointed out certain plausible effects of religious beliefs and practices, and they have often traced relationships between religion and other elements of culture in a useful and illuminating way.

Many recent analytic studies of somewhat different persuasion escape the charges of teleology and tautology. These are studies explicitly directed toward tracing interrelationships among elements of culture with no dedication to the idea that they are indispensable or to deducing societal or individual needs which they might serve.

The usage of the term function in these studies is familiar to all fields of scientific research. As applied in the social sciences, it has sometimes been called the mathematically derived or quasimathematical usage of this word. In the sense used here, "function" means any quality, trait or fact so related to another that it is dependent upon and varies with the other. Functional relations or covariations of this kind have been sought between and among religion, economics, social and political organization, art, and other aspects of culture which scholars have chosen for attention.

Whatever the particular bent of theory and specific goal of the scholar analyzing religion from a functionalist approach, he does not limit his study to religious beliefs but makes use of actual, observable behavior as important data. This is in sharp contrast with the practices of theologians, who have concentrated on wholly theological matters and until very recent years have hardly been concerned with religion in action. Although primitive religions usually lack well-formulated creeds, the emphasis of anthropologists upon the study of religious acts is not one of necessity imposed by this circumstance. It is instead a matter of choice, made with the conviction that much of the importance of religion may be inferred only from observation of such things as the identity of individuals and social groups involved in ceremonial, their relationships to each other, and the attitudes and values expressed in the rites.

The chapters which follow will draw materials from functionalist studies and also from others which bear on the same questions but have not worn this label. The roles of religion as seen by scholars have been varied, and no attempt will be made here to make a comprehensive survey of them. Some of the commonly hypothesized functions of religion will receive only cursory mention because they are already familiar to every reader. It would surely belabor the point, for example, to give a detailed account of how religion serves man usefully as an important form of entertainment. We have chosen for detailed treatment certain facets of primitive religions which are commonly recurrent and regarded as functionally important.

Chapter 9. Group Ritual

W. Robertson Smith, who called mythology the dogma or sacred lore of "antique religions," held that myth was derived from ritual and that ritual was obligatory whereas faith in myth was at the discretion of the worshipper. Study of ancient religions, he concluded, must therefore begin not with the myth but with ritual and traditional usage.[1] Smith's pronouncements concerning the primacy of ritual over myth by no means settled this academic issue, which is only of incidental interest here, but his insistence upon the study of religious behavior has met with the approval of his twentieth-century successors. To Durkheim and the numerous later scholars who have seen the import of religion as being primarily social, the interaction of the individuals involved in group rites has provided the best body of data to buttress hypotheses of the function of religion in unifying and supporting society. Although group ritual commonly includes elements of magic, exclusively magical rites are not often group performances and do not lend themselves well to sociological interpretation of this kind.

As we earlier noted, sacred beliefs have not been ignored in interpretation; scholars have instead added and underscored the study of religion in action as essential to an understanding of its significance. Modern expressions of their viewpoint are embodied in the statements that whatever is important in social life will receive ritual attention or that ceremonial represents symbolic expression of the beliefs and behavior patterns, arising from social interaction, which are the most highly cherished. By ritual expression these folkways or values become sanctified and are made to appear important

[1] W. Robertson Smith, *Lectures on the Religion of the Semites*, rev. ed., pp. 17-18.

and inviolable. As we have noted, no scholar has demonstrated that all which is held to be extremely important, all which is given strong emotional value, finds expression in religious action. It is nevertheless clear that cultural norms which reasonably appear to be of great importance to individual members of society and to the society as a whole are at least frequently symbolized and presumably exalted in ceremonial.

It is also significant that ceremonial acts fall into a strictly limited number of categories. Over and over again the circumstances upon which joint ritual observances center are alike. Correspondences are close among societies widely separated geographically, and neither pure accident nor diffusion satisfactorily explains all similarities.

Most group rituals may be divided into two classes, those associated with nonperiodic critical events or changes occurring in the lives of a single individual or a few individuals, and those associated with fixed, cyclic events of direct importance to all members of the society. The first of these has commonly been called crisis rites. "Rites of intensification" has been suggested as a title for the second category because they are held to maintain social equilibrium by reinforcing the habitual relations of members of the group.[2] This term has not found general acceptance, and here the expression "cyclic group rites," which does not bind us to a theory of social interaction, will be used.

Interpretation of these two classes of ceremonials has not been confined solely to their societal or total-cultural significance. Especially in analyses of crisis rites, it has frequently included hypotheses on their psychological import for the individual. The point of reference may, of course, be readily shifted from the individual to the society, as what is significant to one is also significant to the other. Many studies have included and intermingled both types of interpretation, and I shall not attempt to separate them sharply.

CRISIS RITES

Outstanding among crisis rites are ceremonials connected with the important, critical, but normally expectable events in the life cycle

[2] E. D. Chapple and C. S. Coon, *Principles of Anthropology.*

of the individual, the so-called biological crises of life, birth, sexual maturity, reproduction, and death. Rituals performed on these occasions have been called rites of passage because they involve transition from one social status to another, and this expression has also included observances that mark the initiation of individuals into warrior societies, formal age-graded groups, and other associations not directly connected with the biological crises of the lifespan. As the expression is used here, crisis rites extend beyond these ceremonials to encompass any ritual that is not calendrically fixed and cyclic. It is true that custom sometimes requires the holding of puberty rites at fixed intervals of several years for all individuals who have become eligible since ritual was last performed and, occasionally, funeral ceremonial and other rites of passage are conducted in a similar way, but these rites, of course, do not recur for the same principals.

Crisis rites are markers of special events in the life of the individual and thus differ from recurrent ritual events such as planting and harvesting ceremonies which have essentially equal meaning for many people. This is not to say that happenings such as sexual maturity, illness, or death of the individual are unimportant to the rest of society. They may be extremely important, but they affect the other members of the group only through their relations with the single individual. They are extremely important to the individual and his close relatives, and are generally of diminishing importance outside this circle. Another distinction between crisis rites and cyclic rites is that the first, as in funerals and birth rites, may involve actual loss or gain of societal members, but in the second class no change of personnel is implied except insofar as human sacrifice might be a ritual requirement.

The significance to the individual of rituals associated with the biological crises of life was first hypothesized by Arnold Van Gennep, who coined the expression "rites of passage." Van Gennep saw these rites as means by which individuals are eased through the difficulties of transition from one social role to another. He contended that all these ceremonials are divided into three consecutive elements, called in French *separation, marge* and *aggregation,* which we may translate as separation, adjustment or transition, and reintegration.[3] The individual is first severed from his old status, experiences adjustment to the new during a period of transition, and finally becomes officially established in the new position. These three steps are often clearly seen in symbolic dramatization.

The first stage is frequently a simulation of death, by which the individual is completely severed from the old way of life. Other conventional acts also point up dramatically a sharp break with conditions of the past. The persons upon whom the rites center are for a time separated socially and often physically from other members of society. The adolescent boy may be strictly separated from the company of women during rites that pass him into manhood. For the bride-to-be, social relationships of girlhood may be abruptly severed by the custom of mock capture whereby the girl is forcibly taken from her home by the kin of the groom while her own relatives offer token resistance. The new mother, pubescent boys and girls, and close relatives of a person who has died commonly undergo a period of physical isolation.

The period of adjustment or transition may be brief or months long. During this time the individual's relations with the rest of society are not those of his old status and not as yet entirely those of the new. He is under many restrictions, most of which prohibit him from following otherwise normal activities and thus point up his state of transition. Sometimes, as we noted earlier for Japanese funerals, the reversal of normal procedures symbolizes transition. Ceremonial during this period often prepares the individual for his new status by giving him instruction in matters that are common knowledge among the members of the social group he is about to join.

The third and final step ceremonially and officially restores the individual to normal social life, often with the use of a visible symbol of his new status, a tattoo, a distinctive style of hairdress, a wed-

[3] Arnold Van Gennep, *Les Rites de Passage.*

ding ring, or whatever of other insignia his society has seized upon. Where the first stage of ritual simulates death, the third stage often symbolizes a new and different life. The individual is sometimes ceremonially born, fed, talked to, and instructed as a new-born child would be; and ceremonially he is made to grow up, into the new social status.

With these introductory remarks, we will discuss at somewhat greater length the kinds of ceremonial attention given to the critical events of the normal life cycle of every individual. Although the definition of crisis rites used here includes ceremonies performed to cure the sick, this subject is set aside for separate discussion. Also to be treated separately is the group ritual in which social conventions are broken so that the normally disallowed becomes allowed.

Ritual associated with birth in primitive society customarily begins long before parturition. The pregnant woman usually observes taboos on certain foods and various otherwise normal activities. When birth seems imminent, she is often isolated and magic or other religious acts are performed to ensure an easy and successful delivery. During confinement many extraordinary rules ordinarily govern her behavior, and before she returns to her normal role in society she must undergo rites of purification. The social group participating in the various rites may be limited to the woman's immediate kin or it may extend to the whole society.

One need not, of course, go to primitive society to find examples of ritualized social attention at childbirth. In our own society, baby showers are common although entirely secular events, and the principal religious attention comes in the form of infant baptism or christening.

All elements of Van Gennep's scheme of rites of passage may be found in old Japanese practices surrounding childbirth, customs which continue to be observed with waning faith and intensity in some modern rural communities of Japan. The pregnant woman must abstain from various foods and must eat others. Some of these prescriptions are interpreted as measures to promote health of the mother and the child. Others are outright supernaturalism, and many of them today have the status of amusing superstitions. If a pregnant woman eats shrimp, her child will be a hunchback; if she eats octopus, she will give birth to a boneless child; and if she eats malformed vegetables, the child will be correspondingly misshapen.

During the fifth month of pregnancy a woman dons a pregnancy girdle, usually procured from a temple and supernaturally blessed. Relatives offer prayers in behalf of her and her child. At the time of confinement, she is isolated from all others except the women who attend her and remains apart for a fixed number of days after giving birth. This period is frequently thirty-three days, and it is divided into stages proceeding from sharp restrictions on behavior to final full resumption of normal activities. During this time the mother is regarded as polluted and dangerous to both other human beings and to supernatural beings of the Shintō pantheon. She must follow a number of dietary rules differing from those of pregnancy, and she is forbidden to engage in many normal household tasks. She may make none of the usual prayers or offerings to Shintō household gods or have any other contact with them. If, toward the end of the period of transition, it is necessary for her to step outside the dwelling, she may be required to wear something to cover her head so that her presence will not pollute the Sun Goddess. For the same reason, when her own clothing and the garments of her child are washed during the period of isolation, they must never be hung in direct sunlight but must be placed in the shadows of the eaves of the dwelling.

After locally prescribed periods of time have passed, the mother may resume the practice of taking a daily bath and again perform certain but not all of her ordinary household tasks. When the full period has passed, all restrictions are removed, and she once again takes meals with other members of the family and resumes normal relationships with other members of the community and with the Shintō gods. The end of the period of transition is also marked by the sprinkling of purifying salt on her person and the floors of the dwelling. The beginning of a new, unpolluted, and normal period is further symbolized by kindling a "new" fire in the household cooking stove. In actual fact, for decades before these customs began to wane a new fire had been made daily, but it is customary to refer in these terms to the fire kindled on the morning after the period of isolation has ended.

The child itself is the subject of less ritual observance. Some days after birth a familial name-giving ceremony is conducted. An additional rite for the newborn child is his first communication with the tutelary god of the community. When the infant has reached the prescribed but locally variable age of some weeks or months, he is taken to the shrine of the village tutelary god, to whom obeisance and some small offering are made. These acts constitute introduction of the child to the tutelary.[4]

Birth ceremonies in many primitive societies differ little in general outline from the now old-fashioned Japanese practices we have described. They are not always centered upon the mother and child, however. Among many of the simpler tribal groups a complex of customs called the *couvade* exists. In the "classic" form of the couvade the father is the focus of ritual at childbirth. He simulates lying-in and observes dietary and other restrictions.

The couvade has been interpreted as a sympathetic, symbolic stressing of the relationship between the husband and the wife's group of kin, which is instituted when the child is born.[5] Malinowski has interpreted the couvade as a means of allaying anxiety over the mother and child on the part of the father and as the establishment of "social paternity."

In the ideas, customs and social arrangements which refer to conception, pregnancy and childbirth the fact of maternity is culturally determined over and above its biological nature. Paternity is established in a symmetrical way by rules in which the father has partly to imitate the tabus, observances and rules of conduct traditionally imposed on the mother. . . . The function of couvade is the establishment of social paternity by the symbolic assimilation of the father to the mother.[6]

[4] Edward Norbeck, *Takashima, A Japanese Fishing Community.*

[5] R. Briffault, "Birth Customs," *Encyclopaedia of the Social Sciences,* vol. II, p. 566.

[6] B. Malinowski, *Magic, Science, and Religion;* and "Culture," *Encyclopaedia of the Social Sciences,* vol. IV, p. 631.

Radcliffe-Brown has called the custom a symbolic expression of concern over the welfare of the wife and mother by her husband, concern which the community *expects* him to feel whether he does so or not.[7] The particular form which the couvade and many other rites of passage take is puzzling. It is difficult to see magical aid to the mother through sympathy when she must, as we are told, almost immediately resume her normal tasks. Bettelheim has suggested that the father's acts arise from jealousy of the female role.[8]

Old ethnological writings have created a stereotype of the couvade which leaves the impression that only the father is the subject of ritual. It is extremely doubtful, however, that the mother in any society is entirely free from ritual requirements. Although the term couvade ordinarily refers to rites observed by the father, the mother might follow similar or identical procedures. Among most of the Indians of California, rules of behavior at childbirth affected both parents approximately equally. For fear of harming their child, the California Indian parents went for a fixed period of time outside their dwelling only when necessary, observed food taboos, ate apart from others, and worked and traveled as little as possible. Specific restrictions on normal activities often included prohibitions against cooking, touching tools, or the eating of meat, fish, and salt. Most of these prohibitions were observed for fear of harming the child, but others protected the parents themselves or other persons. The use by women of a stick or bone for scratching themselves was observed for fear that their nails at this time would leave permanent marks. Free intermingling in normal fashion with large groups of people and full resumption of all ordinary activities might require the passage of one or two months. During this period the parents were dangerous to others. For men, the restriction upon hunting was generally the last to be lifted.[9]

As may be easily inferred, native explanations of these rules reflect a belief of magical affinity between parent and child and many

[7] A. R. Radcliffe-Brown, *The Andaman Islanders*. See also G. C. Homans, 'Anxiety and Ritual: The Theories of Malinowski and Radcliffe-Brown.''

[8] Bruno Bettelheim, *Symbolic Wounds*.

[9] A. L. Kroeber, *Handbook of California Indians*.

of the restrictions prevent harm to the infant until it is old enough
and strong enough to ward off the dangers by itself. Conceptions of
affinity might extend to connections between the souls of the father
and offspring as among some Brazilian Indian tribes, where the
souls of children are thought to be loosely seated for some time after
birth. Such behavior as moving about to hunt or to follow other
normal pursuits might cause the baby's soul to become dislodged and
lost, and crossing rivers and bathing in deep water might result in
its drowning.[10]

In primitive society, sexual maturity approximately marks the
transition to adult status, a time of marked change in social relations. In many societies this transition is officially recognized by
ceremony initiating the child into its adult role, a process which
may be brief or continue over a period of months or years. Rites for
boys often do not coincide precisely with puberty and, exceptionally,
they may take place as much as six or eight years before or after
this event. Ritual for girls tends more commonly to be held at the
time of first menstruation. Some of the restrictions and other ritual
acts to which the pubescent girls are subjected may thenceforth be
required during all succeeding menstrual periods. The familiar
stages of rites of passage are often clear, isolation, restrictions on
behavior, a period of adjustment, and finally, formal social recognition of transition to the status of adulthood.

Ordeals to test manhood are a fairly common feature of ritual for
boys. They may be required to perform successfully feats of hunting
or other adult male activities, and be subjected to hazing and genital
or other operations on the body. Both sexes sometimes undergo
physical ordeals. Lengthy fasting and sitting motionless in a prescribed position for long periods of time are common forms. Others
were more violent. Both boys and girls of a number of tribes of
South America were subjected to whipping and to the bites of
stinging ants or wasps.[11]

Physical suffering often comes in the form of mutilations of the
body that serve as permanent markers of maturity and are fre-

[10] Alfred Métraux, "The Couvade."
[11] Ibid.

quently also regarded as enhancements of beauty. Tattooing, accomplished by pricking in soot with thorns or other sharp objects,
is a common insignia among light-skinned people. When skins are
dark so that tattoos are not prominently visible, the body may be
scarified in designs. Soil or other foreign matter is rubbed into incisions in the skin which heal to form patterns in relief. Circumcision of boys is prevalent in many societies, as a mark of adult
status. Among some Australian groups it was accompanied by subincision, slitting the under side of the penis to the urethra. Clitori-
dectomy or other counterparts of male circumcision are performed
on adolescent girls among a smaller number of societies, including
some Arab societies of North Africa. Other common bodily mutilations, observed at puberty or marriage, require the removal of one
or more front teeth, filing the teeth to points, piercing the nasal
septum and piercing and enormously stretching the tissue of the
ears and the lower lip for the insertion of ornaments. Many additional forms of ornamentation, including distinctive clothing, hairdress, bracelets, and necklaces also signify membership in the adult
groups. The social importance attached to these insignia is commonly great; to lack them is unthinkable, a disgrace.

Accounts of puberty ceremonies have often emphasized their role
in instructing adolescents in religious knowledge thus far concealed
from them and, especially, in teaching them the behavior appropriate for adults. It is probable that fasts, ordeals, and taboos engender
an atmosphere of intense seriousness. Frightening religious ceremonial involving masked figures, as is conducted in the puberty rites
of some societies, might well serve to impress upon adolescents the
importance of following such injunctions as their elders might pass
on to them at the time. In various African societies where the period
of transition from childhood to adulthood entails ceremonial and
instruction over periods of months or years, the educative aspects
might be of considerable importance. Outside of religious lore first
imparted to young people at this time it seems unlikely, however,
that the didactic worth of puberty ceremonies in most societies could
be great. The ritual period is generally short, and by the time
adolescence is reached the individual has undoubtedly become so

well immersed in tribal culture that little remains that is wholly new. The principal value of puberty rites in this respect is probably in reinforcing customs and values already learned.

In primitive society, marriage ceremonies generally are the simplest of all rites connected with events in the life cycle of the individual, and they may include no religious elements. An exchange of gifts between the two families involved is, however, a common feature, and in the more complex societies, whether the ceremony is secular or religious, use is made of distinctive clothing, hairdress, or other symbols indicative of marriage.

Classic features of rites of crisis are often most clearly evident in funeral ceremonies. The bereaved refrain from many normal acts; they perform various rites of mourning for prescribed periods, and finally, the funeral and their personal grief now formally ended, they are ritually brought back to normal social relationships.

The assumption has often been made that the greater the importance to the whole society of the critical change in the life of the individual, the greater the elaboration of the ceremonial and the larger the number of persons involved. Many examples may be cited to support this statement, which will doubtless strike most readers as a commonplace. Funeral ceremonial for a very old and economically nonproductive person whose death has long been expected tends to be simple. Children, who are not full-fledged members of society, are often accorded simpler obsequies than adults; and the very young might be buried in a different manner and different place. The death of a ruler or other socially important person has bearing on the lives of many individuals and becomes the occasion for extreme elaboration of ritual. In the aboriginal west African kingdom of Dahomey, the death of the king called for a ceremony called the Grand Custom which included as one of its features the slaying of hundreds of human beings.[12] And the death of historically known khans of Asia were followed by observances entailing the sacrifice of many thousands of victims. Marriage among the politically and socially elect, is of course, an important event to many individuals, and ceremonies tend to be accordingly elaborate. Where the social

[12] M. J. Herskovits, *Dahomey.*

status of males is markedly higher than that of females, the birth
of a son and heir might prompt greater celebration than the birth
of a daughter, although, as we shall see, social status as determined
by sex may be overridden by other considerations.

As Chapple and Coon explain quantitative differences among
crisis rites, they "depend upon the magnitude of change in the
relationships involved and this in turn depends upon the ramifica-
tions of the relationships of the individual causing the social disturbance."[13] Judgment of the relative importance of different kinds
of rites and the events upon which they center is, however, often
difficult to make. No convenient measure is available for cross-
cultural comparison of the importance of any given type of rite,
especially since ritual is influenced by economic and other considerations that inhibit or encourage its development.

Comparison of different types of rites within a single culture is
also difficult. How, for example, might we appraise the social significance of death versus marriage in, let us say, nineteenth-century
Japan, where funeral rites and subsequent memorial services extended over several decades for every adult but the traditional marriage ceremony, which involved extremely elaborate ritualized action over a much shorter period of time, had no direct relation to
religious beliefs and was not regarded as a religious event? From
our own cultures many additional examples, including baby and
bridal showers, the charivari, the honeymoon, graduation, initiation,
and inaugural ceremonies, may be given of observances which celebrate important events and have many of the features of sacred rites
but involve no supernaturalism and are not regarded as religious
events. This suggests that religion is not the fundamental matter,
that important events evoke ritualized action, but it may be either
secular or religious. In primitive society, where supernaturalistic
philosophy is more pervasive, social happenings of importance tend
far more to be given religious interpretation. Even there, however,
all of the presumably important events in the life of the individual
are not occasions for religious observances.

Religious rites at birth, puberty, marriage, and death vary greatly

13 E. D. Chapple and C. S. Coon, *op. cit.*, p. 486.

in length and elaboration. Puberty rites may be held for one sex only, for both, or for neither. Among the simpler tribes marriage may receive little social attention, and we have noted that the formalities of entering marriage frequently have no obvious religious aspects. It is probable that social structure may account for many differences in ritual emphasis from society to society, but analyses of this kind have been offered in only a few cases. Marriage may in fact be socially less significant than other changes in the individual's social life, but we are hard put to provide conclusive support for this statement as a generalization.

The absence or near absence of wedding ritual seems consistent with social organization like that of the Zuni Indians, which provides that the bride and groom reside with the kin group of the bride. Descent among the Zuni is traced through females, and thus the important social affiliation of the children is with the mother and her consanguineal relatives, male and female. Even if marriages should fall asunder, matrilineal descent and matrilocal residence assure approved social identification and a suitable home for children and at the same time, of course, assure continuance of Zuni social groups since they are based upon these rules of descent and residence. From these standpoints at least, the sanctification of the marriage union is not a vital issue. It is interesting to note that the incidence of divorce is reported to be higher in matrilineal than in patrilineal societies.

Attempts to correlate the presence, absence, or degree of elaboration of marriage and other rites of crisis with social structure must give consideration to many influencing factors in addition to rules of residence after marriage and customs of tracing descent. These include differences in social status of males and females, patterns of authority, and rules governing property and inheritance. Following the reasoning outlined in the preceding paragraph, the sacralization of marriage is not vital to the social identification of children and the continuation of lineages, clans, and other functioning social groups in patrilineal and patrilocal societies. But many factors beyond rules of descent and residence may make lasting unions vitally important. Cementing the social bond between kin of the husband

and wife may be highly desired for various reasons. In order to survive, infants in primitive society must ordinarily be cared for by their mothers until they have been weaned. Where marriage involves the transfer of property, the maintenance of lasting unions becomes an important matter to the relatives of both bride and groom. In many African negro societies, for example, marriage requires the transfer of cattle or other valuable goods to the relatives of the bride. This custom encourages lasting marriages because divorce usually means that the bridal gift must be returned.

In societies such as our own, where married couples ordinarily reside apart from their parents and the only important kin group is the small family of spouses and offspring, the sanctification of marriage should be highly important to establish stable unions and provide for the welfare of children. Marriage in our society must have social and legal recognition, but we may note that sanction in the form of a religious ceremony of marriage is neither required nor always sought. It may nevertheless be true that the couple united by the full complement of bell, book, and candle is the more firmly wed.

Observations such as these on the importance of the sanctification of marriage may be made for many societies, and they seem to be reasonable. They do not, however, provide a sound basis for the statement that religious behavior of this or any other kind exists or must exist because it appears to be important in the ways we can deduce. The apparent functional importance of religious rites is not an adequate explanation of their genesis.

In societies which favor one sex against the other in customs of descent, postnuptial residence, and control of property it seems reasonable to think that not only marriage but all of the crisis rites will be more elaborate for the members of the favored sex. Comparative studies would undoubtedly reveal many correlations of this kind, but, as with marriage, the issue is complicated by additional conditioning factors. Rules of matrilocal residence, matrilineal descent, and matrilineal inheritance of property do not, for example, necessarily indicate the social ascendancy of females over males. Political authority is generally in the hands of males even in matrilineal societies; that is, the greatest authority is held by brothers or other male consanguineal relatives of the women who form the core of lineages, clans, and other social groups.

The problem of correlating ritual with social organization becomes, then, very complex. Comparative research on the subject has hardly begun, perhaps in part because many scholars have taken, as demonstrated the assumption that ritual observances will appear in all cultures where the activities and relationships they celebrate seem essential to the support of the individual and the group.

A recent study by J. M. Whiting and others combines sociological and psychoanalytic theory in an attempt to explain why male initiation ceremonies are conducted in some societies and not in others. The hypothesis is presented that puberty rites for boys tend to be held in those societies in which the boys are particularly hostile toward their fathers and dependent upon their mothers.[14] Harsh treatment, sometimes including genital operations, is thought "to prevent open and violent revolt against parental authority at a time when physical maturity would make such revolt dangerous and socially disruptive." Isolation from women and tests of manhood are thought "to break an excessively strong dependence upon the mother and to ensure identification with adult males and acceptance of the male role."[15] Although rivalry between father and son are not viewed as exclusively Oedipal, it is assumed that a long and exclusive relationship between mother and son provides conditions that should lead to an exceptionally strong dependence upon the mother. It is further assumed that if the father terminates this relationship and replaces the son, strong envy and hostility will be engendered in the boy which may be dangerous at the onset of puberty unless measures (puberty rites) are taken to prevent it.

A test of these hypotheses on fifty-six selected societies reports a high correlation between the presence of harsh male puberty rites, on the one hand, and, on the other, customs of long postpartum sex

[14] J. M. Whiting and others, "The Function of Male Initiation Ceremonies at Puberty."

[15] *Ibid.*, p. 361.

taboos between spouses and a long period when mother and son
sleep together to the exclusion of the husband and father. Puberty
rites are divided into three elements, hazing, genital operations, and
tests of manhood; the presence of one or more of these elements
places a society in the category of those having puberty rites.
Throughout the study it is clearly implied that the rites constitute
harsh treatment.

We are not certain that the psychoanalytically derived elements
in this interesting interpretation contribute to an understanding of
why the rites are held in some societies and not in others. It seems
reasonable to think that male puberty rites are most likely to be
conducted in societies in which boys are identified with females
until their maturity, societies in which they do not fully enter the
world of males until this time. Thus the rites mark a social or cultural transition. Of the societies in the sample without puberty rites,
we are not told when boys enter the male world. In all of the sample
cases, mother and father resume sexual relations many years before
the sexual maturity of their son, and the idea is open to doubt that
resentment of the father because of sexual jealousy rises to critical
proportions at puberty. We are given no assurance that this hostility
exists in fact, and surely the degree of sexual freedom allowed the
young among themselves is an important conditioning factor.

The interpretation of data on individual societies in this study
seems sometimes questionable. Samoa is included among the societies
having puberty rites, with the implication that treatment of pubescent boys is harsh. A seemingly mild genital operation, subincision
of the foreskin, was the custom. According to Handy, however, this
did not constitute puberty ritual, which he reports to be of little
importance or absent entirely in Polynesia:

The absence of anything that might be called initiation rites that ushered
boys into manhood is due to the fact that in Polynesia a boy left the company of women and was accepted into association with men at weaning,
when the food tabu that required men to eat apart from women was laid
upon him. The Polynesian boy became a man when he began to eat the
food of men, not at adolescence. In all the main Polynesian groups with

the exception of New Zealand, subincision of the foreskin of boys was the custom; but this operation was performed at any time from infancy to full manhood.[16]

On the other hand, rites of the Ojibwa, one of the societies of the sample that is exceptional in having puberty ritual but lacking the correlates, are held by Whiting to be mild even though the Ojibwa boy ". . . generally when he is 11 or 12 years old . . . goes alone into the forest where he stays often for several days without food, water, and generally without sleep until he either has a vision or returns home to recuperate before trying again."[17]

Also open to question is the validity of including in the sample France, Japan, and "Homestead" United States. All are elaborate societies with a strong development of scientific philosophy that discourages rites of the kinds in question, and in at least the United States attitudes toward sex would probably serve as an additional inhibitory factor.

Theories concerning the principal functions of ritual have been stated in general terms in our introduction, and it is not necessary to repeat them. To give a clearer idea of how scholars have used these theories, however, we will summarize in greater detail two interpretations of rites of crisis. Both are modern studies deriving from a large backlog of social and psychological theorizing; both make use of hypotheses common to numerous other analyses of group ritual, and they may be regarded as representative.

THE CHISUNGU

Audrey Richards' account[18] of the series of rites called the *chisungu* of the Bemba tribe of Northern Rhodesia describes it as a female initiation ceremony. Traditionally preceding marriage, the chisungu is an integral part of a series of observances by which a bridegroom is united with the family group of the bride. It consists of a long and elaborate succession of ceremonies which include singing, dancing, miming, and much use of sacred paraphernalia.

[16] E. S. C. Handy, *Polynesian Religion*, p. 223.

[17] *Ibid.*, p. 367.

[18] A. I. Richards, *Chisungu*. This report rests upon field research done in 1931.

The Bemba number about 150,000 persons widely dispersed in villages of thirty to fifty huts. Subsistence is gained principally from horticulture, in which women have the greatest responsibility. When the soil is exhausted after an interval of several years, new land is broken and the village moves. Economic efforts produce little above minimal requirements for subsistence. Land is held communally, and virtually no form of inheritable property or wealth exists. The Bemba are politically united under a paramount chief or king with much authority over his subjects. Below him are a group of territorial chiefs or princes with considerable power over the residents of their domains. Under these subchiefs are headmen of villages.

The principal social affiliations of the individual are the family and the matrilineal clan, whose members reckon descent from a common ancestress. Great emphasis is laid on the principle of matrilineal descent. The most important relationships of the Bemba family are the ties between mothers and daughters. Bonds between a woman and her brother, who are members of the same matrilineal lineage, are also close and the brother has much to say in the affairs of his sister and her children.

The traditional Bemba marriage was contracted over a period of years beginning in childhood by many steps, generally marked by ritual, which culminate in rites forming part of the chisungu. Girls marry immediately after puberty, usually taking husbands from outside villages. A young man who marries goes to live for at least several years in his wife's village, where he builds himself a hut near the natal dwelling of his wife and becomes part of her family, for which he performs labor service for several years under the direction of his father-in-law.

For the new Bemba husband, marriage is a source of tension arising from clashes of interest. Bound by ties of loyalty to his own matrilineal descent group in another village, he is an outsider in the family and the village of his wife. He is economically dependent upon his wife and her relatives, persons who are outside his own lineage, and he must share authority over his own children with his brother-in-law, who is the recognized legal guardian of the children.

Despite the disadvantages to males which the kinship system imposes and the relatively high status of females, Bemba society is dominated by men, and women are taught to be submissive to their husbands. After some years of successful marriage and the growth of a family, the husband comes to hold a position of prestige and authority. He may then move with his family to his ancestral village if his wife is willing.

In addition to rites connected with marriage, the chisungu contains many other elements. In the performance observed by Miss Richards, eighteen separate ceremonies, each divisible into a number of simpler rites, were observed over a period of about a month. Some are secret rites observed only by a girl and adult female ceremonial leaders, and others are public performances in which the whole village participates. Rites are conducted by mature females of whom one woman of prestige in these matters serves as mistress of ceremonies. The chisungu is preceded by a brief puberty ceremony, conducted when a girl first menstruates. When convenient thereafter, the chisungu is conducted, perhaps for two or three girls simultaneously. As in the earlier puberty rite proper, the stages of separation, transition, and reintegration are evident. The girls are isolated except when actually participating in a rite; they wear old and shabby clothes and abstain from many usual pursuits; they are not allowed to wash themselves, and their food is cooked over a separate fire. Customary behavior is resumed by degrees and the transition to normality is marked by symbolism including new fires and the return of freedom to cook and offer food to others.

The series of rituals is extremely elaborate, involving much symbolism, and only bare mention of some of the elements will be made here. Mimicry, dancing, and many other symbolic acts outstandingly depict the woman's proper role in society, expressing her economic and social obligations and privileges with reference to husband, children, the ruler, other members of society, and her matrilineal ancestors. The bridegroom holds a prominent symbolic position in certain rites and participates in person in ritual whereby he claims the bride. Included also are ceremonies to promote agricultural and human fertility, and various ordeals. The girl is subjected to teasing and tests of maturity whereby she must catch water insects with her mouth and kill a tethered chicken by sitting on its head, rising and sitting repeatedly until the bird is dead. Final rites consist of bathing the girl, dressing her in new clothes, and ceremonially presenting her to the community as a full-fledged adult. A wedding ceremony, distinct from the chisungu, quickly follows.

The Bemba themselves see the person of the chisungu in a different light according to their sex. Men usually state that the rites are necessary because no man would want to marry a girl for whom they have not been performed. Without the chisungu she would be a piece of rubbish, an uncultivated weed, an unfired pot, or just a fool. Women, who hold the principal roles as conductors of ritual and better understand its symbolism, hold that the chisungu makes a girl grow by means of the magic it employs, teaches her, and transforms her into a woman. Fresh knowledge imparted by the "teaching" is limited principally to some ritual matters, as a girl at this point in life has long known the social obligations of a wife and mother which are expressed in the ceremonies. Chisungu ritual also explicitly "teaches" the Bemba social hierarchy constantly in various ways. Adult women perform acts in order of precedence or rank; a song referring to Bemba social ranking, "The armpit is not higher than the shoulder," is sung over and over again; the girl is reminded to be submissive to her elders; dances are explicitly performed as a mark of respect to others, and much additional symbolism emphasizes the hierarchy of rank.

The Bemba are aware of a number of incidental motives for the chisungu. It provides entertainment and an opportunity for the pleasurable meeting of friends and relatives. Food is as plentiful as circumstances allow, and much beer is drunk. A well-run ceremony conveys prestige on the woman in charge of its performance, upon the girl and her family, and also upon the village.

Miss Richards' analysis suggests many additional functions of the chisungu of which the Bemba are less conscious or unaware. Among these are the reinforcement for all participants of the numerous tribal values. Most outstandingly expressed in the rites is the social structure of the whole society. Patterns of authority and rules of descent, marriage and the family, village groupings, and social groups as determined by age and other considerations are all given sanction by numerous and varied ritual acts. Essentially the whole social hierarchy including maternal ancestral spirits is expressed symbolically by ritual objects and by song, dance, mime and other acts. Specific examples of ritual expression include the use of clay images of a brother and sister, which express their intimacy, and images of husband and wife performing domestic duties. Mimicry of respect to superiors is expressed by the girl's offering food to her elders, singing songs about the chiefs and the king, and making obeisances before each house in the village.

The value of the chisungu in reinforcing tribal values comes in part from its intimate association with two other important series of tribal ceremonies, the funeral of a ruler and rites installing his successor, and a series of economic observances when clearing land, planting, and harvesting. Many tribal values expressed in these latter rites are also given expression in the chisungu. Much of Bemba dogma promising security and supernatural blessings through observance of traditional relations with kin, ruler, ancestors, and fellow villagers finds, in fact, its best expression in the chisungu. According to Miss Richards, it is for this reason that the chisungu is so important.

Other emphases of the rites are upon human fertility and the supply of food. Miss Richards suggests that the importance accorded to fertility, which is not ritualized in many African tribes with similar social structures, may be linked with the lack of any form of permanent possessions in the Bemba culture and also with matrilineal descent. Bemba rationalize matrilineal descent in the belief that a child is formed entirely from the physical contribution of the mother. Since children belong legally to the mother's family, it is to the advantage of the mother's kin if she bears many children.

Clan and lineage find little ritual expression in the chisungu; it is the family instead which is emphasized. Unlike many other African societies, Bemba clans and lineages except those of the ruler have no political functions as corporate groups. The family is, however, extremely important in Bemba society, and the maintenance of a stable family group is difficult because of the customs of descent and residence and the lack of permanent and inheritable property. The bride's desire to stay in her own village is opposed to that of the groom. If her husband, after completing his marriage labor service in her village, elects to return to his native community she may be unwilling to accompany him. No effective economic links bind the family to either village. These circumstances, it is suggested, may account for the stress in the chisungu upon the wife's duties of submissiveness and obligations to please her husband and the honor given the groom by ritual offerings of food and other acts of deference toward him.

With reference to the individual, chisungu ritual is interpreted as resolving the fears of the girl and easing her into the new status of married adulthood. Contributions toward the well-being of the husband come in the form of ritual attention to him, welcoming him to the family and community, and perhaps thereby compensating for the tensions he faces as a new husband, torn from his own matrilineal relatives, subservient to his father-in-law, and holding no legal authority over his own children.

The contradiction between the masterful male and the submissive son-in-law, between the secure young married woman backed by her own relatives and the submissive kneeling wife, is one which struck me forcibly in the course of the chisungu ceremony. This contradiction, I think, finds expression and perhaps resolution in the chisungu, which might be regarded as an extreme expression of the dilemma of a matrilineal society in which men are dominant but the line goes through the woman.[19]

THE KOTA DRY FUNERAL

David Mandelbaum has given us a description and analysis of a funeral among the Kota of southern India.[20] A small, primitive tribe of about twelve hundred persons, the Kota live in seven small villages of the Nilgiri Hills, where they are surrounded by three neighboring tribes with whom they live in symbiotic economic relationship.

[19] *Ibid.*, pp. 50-51.
[20] D. G. Mandelbaum, ''Form, Variation, and Meaning of a Ceremony.''

When a Kota dies, two funeral ceremonies are conducted. The first, called the Green Funeral, is performed shortly after death. The second, a series of rites called the Dry Funeral, is held at intervals of a year or two for all deaths that have occurred since the last performance of these rites. Terms for the ceremonies are derived from analogies with vegetation, green when it is first cut and later dry.

According to Kota belief, the dead have not left the world of the living until the Dry Funeral has been conducted. A widow continues to be her deceased husband's wife until this second ceremony, and if she becomes pregnant in the interval between funerals, the child is his and shares in his property. The stated purpose of the Dry Funeral is to dispatch to the other world the spirit of the deceased which, if left to linger in this world, is a source of harmful pollution to the living. This objective is always assumed to have been successfully accomplished once the ritual has been performed.

Participants in the Dry Funeral include the relatives of the deceased and all other members of his community, representatives of the six other Kota villages, and also representatives of the neighboring tribes. Men take the most active parts, and women, whose social status is much inferior to that of men, rarely initiate or carry through any of the rites.

Much of the activity focuses upon the close relatives of the dead person, whose mourning roles vary according to their relationship to the deceased. During the ritual period most of these relatives wear old and dirty clothes, dress their hair in a fashion that is not customary, abstain from participation in much of the ritual except as observers, do not bathe, and observe other taboos. During the first two days the close relatives and especially the women, who have little to do with ceremonial preparations and thus have more time for this activity, spend much of their time in loud wailing to show their excessive grief. Mourning roles of the relatives of the dead person vary considerably. A widow or widower is subject to the greatest number of taboos and ritual prescriptions. Roles of bereaved siblings are lighter, those of children still lighter. Curiously, no special mourning roles are given to parents or any relatives of ascending generations whose grief might be keen but who do not even observe the mourning taboos.

In the funeral processions a widow must be carried by her brothers as though she were too stricken by grief to walk, and a widower must be supported by his brother. The widow's earrings and other jewelry are formally removed during the course of the rites, as are the ornaments worn by a widower. Throughout most of the observances, the widow or widower of the deceased, and certain of the other close relatives keep apart from other persons, witnessing but not directly participating in dancing and singing.

Members of the community who are not related to the deceased hold many special ritual offices. These include the priest, bell boys who ring a bell continuously and perform other acts, diviners, various minor officers, and a secular official charged with responsibility for funds expended and for keeping participants informed of the time and sequence of events. Fellow villagers contribute funds to meet expenses of the funeral feast and aid in preparing it. As well as participating in many public ritual acts, they observe taboos against eating after sunset. Visitors from other Kota villages and representatives of the neighboring tribes hold minor posts in the ceremonies. As guests, the funeral is to them a festive occasion. Free of any obligations of preparing food or of onerous office, they may wear fine clothes and indulge freely in chatting and ceremonial dancing. At two points in the course of the ritual, however, representatives of all villages formally participate.

The complete series of rites extends over eleven days. After a day of preliminary ritual, mourning taboos are observed for a week and dancing is held nightly. Then follows a highlight of the ceremony, an elaborate funeral procession to the cremation grounds outside the village where the relics, a bit of bone of each of the deceased preserved from the Green Funeral, are again cremated. After spending most of the night at the cremation grounds, the procession returns to the village. A ceremonial meal is then served to the principal mourners and the bell boys as the first of a number of steps of transition to normalcy from the critical state of pollution these persons are in.

On the following day the cremation grounds is the scene for a lavish feast, which concludes at nightfall with the climax of the festivities. At the signal of a smashed pot, all persons run to the village without looking behind them—and the spirits of the deceased have been dispatched to the other world. As a part of the transition to normalcy, on this evening widows and widowers are freed from the taboo against sexual intercourse placed upon them. A widow may have sexual relations with a brother of her deceased husband, and a widower with a brother's wife. During the final two days rites are conducted to purify the village; ornaments are formally returned to the widow or widower, and they participate in village dancing as persons fully restored to normal life. After a final day of singing by women of the community, the visitors leave and everyone settles down to normal activities.

For the Kota, the Dry Funeral has sent off the spirit of the deceased, removed the pollution incurred by his death, and restored everyone to a condition of purity and of proper relations with the supernatural world. The Kota are also well aware of certain incidental effects of the Dry Funeral. Prestige is conferred by lavish giving for the funeral feast, and personal satisfaction may be gained through skilled performance as a leader in ritual. For many persons, the festivities are opportunities for rest, entertainment, conviviality, and the partaking of rich foods. For the young, the funeral celebration provides an opportunity for greater sexual freedom than is otherwise allowed.

Mandelbaum's analysis sees in the Dry Funeral other effects that are not so readily obvious and are not stated by the Kota themselves as its purposes. Restoration of order applies not only to the relations between man and the supernatural but also to the relations among human beings. The social order, disturbed by the loss of a member, has officially been reinstated by ritual demands that mourning cease and normal social relationships prevail. The effect of ritual acts is also seen as a ''reaffirmation of the social order.'' The place of the individual Kota in his society is portrayed in the course of ritual. His roles with respect to his family, the larger body of his kin, the clan, the village, the Kota tribe, and neighboring tribes are reenacted and thereby reinforced. The Dry Funeral provides an occasion for many people to come together and renew relationships; at the same time, it makes use of the normal social groupings in its organization. Familial members and the clan, for example, are recognizably distinct units in certain ritual acts. All members of the village of the deceased participate, and they are set apart from the members of other Kota villages by their roles as hosts. Dates of the Dry Funerals in the various villages are arranged so that they do not overlap, and they therefore provide an opportunity for representatives of all Kota communities to attend and reestablish social links. Members of the neighboring tribes also have roles to perform. As with all other social groups, the roles of the neighbors are distinctive, so that they are set apart; at the same time, their traditional links with the Kota are given symbolic expression.

Like Richards in her interpretation of the chisungu, Mandelbaum sees the Dry Funeral as an enactment of the total Kota social scheme, reminding each participant of his obligations and privileges, his part in the whole. A sense of the social whole is also seen as being reinforced by the various acts involving everyone, the two processions, the series of dances, and the feast. Of these joint festivities, the communal feast has special import; to eat signifies social unity that overrides or puts aside any discord.

Hierarchical relationships of ordinary life among the people are also expressed in the performance of ritual. Men come before women, officials and elders before others, the priest before the diviners, and all other social priorities are strictly observed. Even the dead who are being mourned are socially ranked. Before the cremation, relics of the deceased are arranged in the order of social precedence they held in life, and the mourners pay respects to them following this order and in their own proper social turn.

For the individual Kota, Mandelbaum sees the Dry Funeral as a means of assuaging grief and of achieving personal reorientation. The rites provide a clear-cut course of action for the bereaved in handling their sorrow. The pain of grief is again evoked and it becomes a point of emphasis during the ceremonial period. It is then sharply terminated, and the bereaved are formally returned to normal status with all grief and personal distress officially put behind them.

As with other similar studies, Mandelbaum's interpretation leaves unanswered questions. If we grant that ritual serves importantly to assuage grief, it is impossible to avoid wondering at the Kota assignment of roles of mourning among the relatives of the deceased, for which no explanation is offered. Bereaved parents observe little formal mourning, and therefore presumably receive little aid from this source in overcoming their sorrows. If, as some theorists have held, human beings "must" have some means of meeting grief, Kota parents then find it outside of ritual.

CYCLIC GROUP RITES

Fixed, recurrent group rites that have nearly equal significance for all or most members of the social group in which they are performed range from familial ceremonies to those which apply to whole societies. The time of their observance tends strongly to be correlated with rhythmic changes of nature. Many follow the cycles of the sun and moon and the seasons of the year, and observances may be daily, weekly, monthly, seasonal, or annual. Calendrical fixing of the ceremonies, in turn, has often depended upon changes in the physical environment that are important to man. Winter, spring, summer, and fall represent times of change in vegetation and in the number and habits of forms of animal life, and mark either the beginning or the end of periods of heightened economic activity. These are times, varying in accordance with his interpretation of the universe, when primitive man by means of magical ritual assures himself of success in the agriculture, hunting, fishing, and the gathering of fruits and nuts which will follow, or asks for supernatural aid and offers thanks for it in these enterprises.

Among peoples subsisting by agriculture, planting, first fruits, and harvest rites are particularly common. The clearing of ground before planting, as we noted for the Bemba, and any of a large number of similar agricultural activities of importance to the group may also become the occasions for ritual observances. Among the Indians of northern California, who practiced no agriculture, the great tribal rites came in the spring and the early fall and marked the beginning of the spawning migrations of salmon and the maturation of acorns, foods of great importance to these tribes. Similar linkages with seasonal activities may be noted again and again for other primitive tribes. It is probable that most cyclic rituals of the primitive world receiving society-wide observance may be shown to be connected with the seasons and thus also with climatic changes.

Among the culturally elaborate societies, where technological control over nature is much greater, man's activities are less intimately associated with the physical environment and less subject to seasonal change. But many cyclic religious observances of the civilized nations of the world, now changed in form, find their roots in annual changes in agricultural activities as formerly observed and thus are also linked with climatic changes. Village festivals of rural Japan, today often lacking any direct reference to agriculture, are customarily held at the beginning and end of the planting season, and many other ceremonies coincide with seasonal changes. The important ceremonial occasions of Christianity are linked with the annual cycle of agricultural activities of the Mediterranean area in which Christianity arose.

This is not to say that all major cyclic rites of primitive society consist of explicit supernaturalistic safeguards to ensure economic success or to offer thanks for beneficences received. The human roles in forthcoming economic enterprises are indeed frequently mimed, and rites to bring rain or otherwise to ensure abundant crops and flocks are performed. In other instances, however, rituals conducted at times of seasonal changes have little or no manifest connection with economic matters in the activities they express. Like many important ceremonials of African groups, they might stress in their symbolism tribal relations between the sexes, between ruler and subject, or other interrelationships of the social scheme. Attempts to interpret rites of these kinds have sometimes tried to trace the probable intellectual paths of the tribesmen, seeking thereby to find the link between the ritual symbolism and the changes of physical environment important to man. Frazer, for example, saw the numerous classical myths of the annual death and resurrection of gods as a personified dramatization of the annual decay and revival of life.[21] Rites performed to help the dying gods were acts designed to ensure the continuation of the growth of animal and plant life.

Modern inquiry has been less concerned with patterns of thought which might have led to the development of these rites. It has instead stressed the identity of persons and social groups involved in ceremonial and the relations expressed among them. The question of why rites not connected with subsistence should take place at planting, first fruits, harvest and other important occasions in the annual round of work has, however, not been abandoned. The completion of harvest provides food in abundance for celebration, of course, and this and certain other junctures in the work routine are times when man may have a minimum of demands on his time. Since these cyclic events in subsistence activities are also correlated with annual changes in nature, they provide a convenient and obvious calendrical scheme upon which to organize all kinds of activities. These are circumstances which encourage the selection of the certain points in time for ceremonial observances, although they fail to explain the significance of rites that have no ostensible bearing on the economic events with which they coincide.

A current interpretation of cyclic group rites of these and all other kinds including secular observances sees them as mechanisms for smoothing over social disruptions. According to this reasoning they come at times when the social equilibrium of the group is disturbed by changing patterns of social interaction. As activities concerned with subsistence slacken, heighten, and change, the relationships among the members of society change, and the old, ordered sets of relations are abandoned for new and less immediately familiar sets. It is following this reasoning that Chapple and Coon have called these ceremonials rites of intensification. The acting out of the habitual relationships "has the effect of reinforcing or intensifying their habitual relations, and thus serves to maintain their conditioned responses. . . . In the technical (physiological) sense, the performance of these rites prevents the extinction of habits . . .

[21] J. G. Frazer, *The Golden Bough.*

to which the individual has been trained.''[22] All ritualized actions involving groups including those conventionally regarded as secular are included by Chapple and Coon among the rites of intensification. The idea that these festivities might give authority and approval to both new and established sets of relations seems reasonable enough. It is impossible, however, to see in the circumstances surrounding fixed patriotic celebrations, meetings of social and professional societies, and numerous other "secular" rituals that social equilibrium has been actively disrupted in any way except by the lack or the threat of a lack of an "habitual" in-group feeling brought by the absence of joint action since the last meeting.

On the question of why rites with political and other nonagricultural themes should take place at first fruits, harvest, and other times of importance in the agricultural routine, Gluckman uses essentially the same reasoning as Chapple and Coon. He suggests that socially disruptive forces are at work during these seasons.[23] Social relationships as required for the prosecution of agricultural duties change at these times. First fruits and harvest come in some of these societies after a period of want and hunger, and a successful harvest puts an end to uncertainty so that the atmosphere is charged with emotion. We may note, however, that in many of the tribes no ceremony is held if crops are poor, even though these are presumably the times of the greatest emotional stress and the most urgent need for release.

Still another hypothesis has been offered to explain how political ceremonies are associated with new crops in African negro cultures. Fortes and Evans-Pritchard suggest that the political structure becomes associated with food because it is the political structure which guarantees the peace and order necessary to allow the successful growing and harvesting of crops.[24] This is an idea which one must accept on faith; it can never be supported in any conclusive way. It is clear, however, that in many societies the welfare of the people

[22] E. D. Chapple and C. S. Coon, *op. cit.*, p. 507.
[23] Max Gluckman, *Rituals of Rebellion in South-East Africa*, p. 21.
[24] M. Fortes and E. E. Evans-Pritchard, *African Political Systems*, p. 16 ff.

and the land is regarded as indissolubly linked with or dependent upon the welfare of the rulers.

Whether cyclic rites are familial, clan, or tribal, whether they deal directly with planting, first fruits, harvest, the increase of totemic animals, or activities of other kinds, they are customarily analyzed along the same lines as we have noted for crisis rites. Going beyond the manifest goals as visualized by the actors, scholars have probed further to deduce effects of greater significance that are unknown to the participants.

Chapter 10. Religion and

Social Control

Basing his statements upon accounts of primitive religions available in the nineteenth century, Tylor told us long ago that no necessary relationship exists between religion and ethics: "Savage animism is almost devoid of that ethical element which to the educated modern mind is the very mainspring of practical religion. Not . . . that morality is absent from the life of the lower races. But these ethical laws stand on their own ground of tradition and public opinion, comparatively independent of the animistic beliefs and rites which exist beside them."[1] The close association of ethical codes and religion that Tylor noted for the civilized world he viewed as having only its rudiments in primitive religions, and the coalescence of the two represented an innovation of the final stage of religious development, monotheism.

Tylor's evolutionary scheme of religion, as we have noted, has not survived the accumulation of ethnographic reports on primitive societies, and thus it is not surprising that his view of the relationship between religion and ethics appears hardly to have reached even the scholarly world beyond the confines of anthropology. Perhaps because their field of study has emphasized societies adhering to the historically related and ethical religions of Christianity, Judaism, and Islam, sociologists tend to see a close connection between the morality or ethics (terms which are here equated) and religion. MacIver and Page, for example, state that "Religion and morals are very closely interwoven."[2] Yinger finds four logically possible

[1] E. B. Tylor, *Primitive Culture,* vol. 2, p. 360.
[2] R. M. MacIver and C. H. Page, *Society, an Introductory Analysis,* p. 318.

relationships between religion and morals: morality as an insepa-
rable but subsidiary part of religion; an intimate relationship between the two with morality as the senior partner; morality and
religion not only intimately related but identical; and religion and
morality separate and quite unrelated.[3] Yinger adds that each of
these conceptions "mixes statements of value with statements of
fact." Religion and morality, he states, may be studied separately,
but "it is vastly clear that they are interdependent in most times
and places."[4]

Popular and understandably ethnocentric opinion among the
populations of Christian and Jewish nations leans strongly toward
ideas of close association or identity of religion and ethics. Both
religions are frequently defined today as "a way of life" or "a
guidepost for living," expressions carrying the common meaning
that the religions are preeminently ethical or moral codes. To be
un-Christian is to be unethical or immoral, and we are familiar with
the curious anomaly of the nonbeliever who is "more Christian than
most Christians." To many modern adherents of Christianity, ethics
appears to constitute its principal or only meaning, and the loss of
religion implies the disruption or even destruction of society
through loss of morality. Popular and theological opinion both frequently implicitly include the idea that religions *should* incorporate
codes of ethics and that those failing to do so are not really religions
at all.

However apt a definition of religion in terms of morality might
be as applied to the religions of the West, it applies only poorly to
many others. Ethical or moral codes—that is, rules of conduct for
man in his relations with other human beings—exist in all societies,
as they must for man to survive. Allowed the license to satisfy in
direct animal fashion all needs, desires, and whims on a level unfettered by culture, man could not have survived in his present form
and with his present capacities. Such unrestrained behavior is, of
course, beyond imagination; to be human implies culture, and culture inevitably includes as one of its prominent aspects ideal modes

[3] J. M. Yinger, *Religion, Society, and the Individual*, pp. 23-28.
[4] *Ibid.*, p. 28.

of behavior and standardized means of ensuring that these conventions are fairly well followed. Conceptions of the proper and improper in interpersonal relations found among the societies of the world vary in many or few respects, but they all define patterns of obligation and privilege among societal members, locally modified along lines of sex, age, social status, in-group and out-group.

In societies adhering to the great religions of the world, rules of ethical or moral conduct are ideally fortified by religion. If one leads the good life, he receives supernatural reward; if his conduct is bad, he receives supernatural punishment. We see here religion acting as a form of social control, punishing and rewarding, and at the same time reinforcing ideas of what is socially acceptable conduct. In a vast number of the small primitive societies of the world this manner of connection between ethics and religion is only weakly developed so that the two realms touch only here and there rather than in a thoroughgoing fashion. Giving equal weight to each historically known society of the world regardless of its size, a statistical balancing of the number of societies in which religion and ethics are closely associated versus those in which the two have little connection would result in the scales tipping steeply toward the latter circumstance. If man's conceptions of the supernatural beings are considered, it seems altogether in keeping that human morality in many societies bear little relation to the supernatural. Among societies which credit their gods with all the weaknesses and vices as well as the virtues of humanity, and whose pantheons and world views represent no war between good and evil, it is reasonable that religion lacks ethical significance. Where manipulable impersonal power rather than gods is a central idea, ethics and religion may find little to draw them together.

Discussion of the relationship between ethics and religion is simultaneously, of course, a consideration of religious sanctions, the forms of supernatural punishment and reward which influence human behavior. Many ethnologists have stated that in the primitive societies of their investigation ethics and religion are essentially divorced; others have reported some degree of association, and a few have found a close identification. It is possible that the relative scarcity of reported supernatural sanctions for ethical behavior in the beliefs of primitive peoples reflects in some degree failure on the part of ethnologists to inquire into every aspect of supernaturalism. The Wallises find, for example, a belief among several Indian tribes of the Great Plains that sickness may be caused by sins of one's ancestors, a concept of disease not recorded for this area in earlier accounts.[5] LaBarre reports that the custom of confession, previously said to be rare in North America, is in fact fairly widespread.[6] In even these two instances, however, it is impossible to identify the religions in question as strongly ethical. Confession among North American Indians applied to a limited number of acts, often ritual sins of omission or commission, and did not embrace the whole complex of behavior regarded as proper in interpersonal relations. Among the Dakota, the wrong-doing of a greatgrandfather, grandfather, grandmother, or parent resulting in disease among descendants consisted of a strictly limited range of both ritual and moral offenses:

Sins that cause illness in descendants are of at least three types: ritual transgressions, torture or mockery of animals, crimes against a person or against the group. The eight informants mentioned a total of fourteen cases: eight sins were ritual; three were against animals; three were social. All of the ritual sins named were positive: warriors participated in a ceremony or went on a raid while sexually incontinent, or left bloody knives around the house to contaminate children; menstruous women broke taboos by touching, or stepping over, object or person. One ancestor had tortured an animal, and two women who had mocked at animals had defective offspring; two progenitors were murderers; a third, single-handed, started the Minnesota uprising.[7]

Where ancestor worship is a prominent feature of religion, as in many African Negro societies, it may operate indirectly as a force toward conformance with ideals of behavior. Although explicit

[5] R. S. Wallis and W. D. Wallis, "The Sins of the Fathers: A Concept of Disease Among the Canadian Dakota."

[6] Weston LaBarre, "Primitive Psychotherapy in Native American Cultures: Peyotism and Confession."

[7] R. S. Wallis and W. D. Wallis, op. cit., pp. 432-433.

supernatural sanctions for ethical behavior may be lacking, any departure from norms might be regarded as meeting with the disapproval of the ancestral spirits, and, sometimes, the consequent withdrawal of their favor. Schapera points out a "fundamental" difference between the approaches of Bantu peoples of Africa and ourselves to the problem of moral goodness: "The Bantu demand moral behaviour within the family and tribe rather than moral behaviour in general. And this is in complete harmony with their ancestor worship, for the common ancestor must of necessity resent any action by one of his descendants likely to harm another descendant and incidentally to upset the social order within the group."[8]

Religion might also work in other ways indirectly to give support or partial support to moral codes. Where the welfare of society is viewed as intimately linked with that of the rulers as embodiments of the gods or guardians of social propriety, supernaturalistic beliefs may support the laws the rulers promulgate and the customs they uphold. We are told of the Nupe of Africa:

As for the realm of ethics, Nupe doctrine is altogether silent. It upholds no ideal man, nor condemns his antithesis. There is no eschatology, no mythology exemplifying rights and wrongs, crime and retribution, and no promise of reward to the law-abiding. Nor is the formulated doctrine concerned with norms of action of more common currency, the simple rights and wrongs of everyday morality. . . .

Only two explicit ethical commands occur in the whole range of Nupe rituals. They refer to filial obedience . . . and to the blessedness of fecundity. . . . On the balance, then, Nupe religion is amoral.

. . . Religion plays a part only indirectly, through sanctioning the persons—kings, chiefs, executioners—who act as guardians of the accepted good. . . . But let us note that these men guard no real morality but only that part of it which has solidified in the form of politically enforced law. Differently expressed, Nupe society knows mainly crimes and few 'sins,' and only lawful, not saintly behaviour. On occasion religion abandons even this indirect support for the conventions of morality; for certain rituals deny these conventions, as in the sexual license of the *gunnu* and *gani* or in the condonation of violence in the *navũ* [ceremonies].[9]

[8] I. Schapera, ed., *The Bantu-speaking Tribes of South Africa*, p. 270.
[9] S. F. Nadel, *Nupe Religion*, p. 268.

Although we lack the required data to make a positive statement, it seems highly probable that at least a few supernatural sanctions for specific violations of ethical rules exist in all societies. Supernatural sanctions are, to be sure, extremely plentiful in primitive religious beliefs, but the offenses involved are frequently acts which we find it impossible to view as ethical transgressions and often they are acts which are given no moral significance by primitive peoples themselves. The tremendous list of taboos known to the primitive world all, of course, involve supernatural sanctions; violation of the taboos brings unpleasant consequences of supernatural cause, whether as the result of punishment by supernatural beings or as automatic consequences. The acts themselves, however, are frequently far removed from our ordinary conception of the province of ethics; that is, they often have no bearing on the relations of man with his fellow men. In this class are numerous sanctions against the eating of certain foods and many ritual offenses of omission, commission, and misperformance. Other isolated acts which are supernaturally sanctioned in primitive societies come closer to our conception of ethics. Incest is frequently punishable supernaturally, but in the same societies sexual intercourse with socially approved partners may also be punished supernaturally if indulged in during periods of ritual celibacy, as before making war or during established periods of religious observances. Murder, adultery, theft, and similar social offenses considered extremely serious by the peoples concerned may go quite unpunished by supernatural agency.

Supernatural sanctions are sometimes invoked in primitive society in the form of the oath or conditional curse whereby the individual enters a contract with the supernatural, and these may concern ethical matters. Certain of the tribes of the Great Plains required oaths of truthfulness bringing calamity upon their heads for dissembling before they could recite and receive social recognition for their feats in battle; similar forms of the oath are known in other areas of the primitive world. Under other circumstances, however, lying was not supernaturally punished.

The supernatural punishments of primitive society are most frequently sickness, death, or deprivation of foods and other necessities of life. The withholding of rewards after death—that is, the consignment of the sinner to an afterworld or afterlife less desirable than that granted to the blameless—is much less common, even though punishments are more strongly emphasized than rewards. The afterworld may differ from the world of life in no respect connected with the individual's comfort and well-being. Where the afterworld is conceived as a desirable place, everyone may meet a common fate upon death, and virtue or lack of virtue in life serve to bar no one from admission. The disposition of one's soul may depend simply on his social status in life, the souls of the elite going to a finer place than those of the common herd. It may even depend directly on the nature of the funeral; a lavish funeral may be the requirement for admission to a favored afterworld.

Manner of death rather than mortal character is sometimes the key to the fate of the individual's spirit. Among the Aztec, the souls of men who died in war and of male captives of war who were slain in sacrifice to the Aztec gods went to the most desirable of several afterworlds; the souls of women dying in childbirth, the female equivalent of death in battle, were destined to another but equally desirable place. Spirits of persons dying from drowning, lightning, dropsy, or leprosy went to a third afterworld, and those of persons dying through sickness, old age, or in other undistinguished fashion were consigned to still another.

Among the Aztec a large list of acts considered crimes met with harsh punishment at the hands of mortals. Certain of these crimes, including adultery, were also sins against specific gods but many of the serious offenses punishable by death were under no supernatural sanction. Crimes which were also sins were in fact less threatening to the welfare of the transgressor than offenses regarded only as crimes. The penalties of known crimes could not be avoided but sins could be absolved and temporal punishment could be escaped by confession—allowed only once in a lifetime—of the misdeeds to the priests.[10]

Other characteristics of supernatural sanctions among primitive

[10] Bernardino de Sahagun, *A History of Ancient Mexico.*

folk present ideas of morality quite different from those of our society. Penalties are often the same whether violations and sins of omission are deliberate or unwitting, and the penalties may be imposed upon persons other than the wrong-doer, even upon individuals who are unrelated to him and whom we would regard as being sinned against.

Techniques for avoiding supernatural punishment after offenses have been committed are as varied as the techniques of supernaturalism. Sometimes no countermeasures exist and the unwelcome consequences are thought inevitably to follow. More frequently, recourse is taken to one or more of the techniques of the range of magical and nonmagical behavior which local convention has fastened upon to control or influence the supernatural. Since most supernatural punishments of the primitive world are of an automatic sort involving little conception of divine justice or the actions of supernatural beings, techniques of evasion run strongly to the magical. No class of behavior known to the great world religions, however, is entirely unrepresented.

The custom of confession which we noted among North American Indians and the Aztecs is also known to other primitive societies as a device to avoid divine punishment, although it is far from being universal or broadly embracive of whole ethical codes. Confession most commonly applies to only a few offenses, with or without ethical import, which are thought to result in punishment for the transgressor or for other members of his society. Where supernatural punishment may strike any member of society for the acts of one of its members, public confession—in effect if not in principle to one's human associates rather than to the gods—and expiation in the form of penance, offerings, or the payment of fines may be the requirement. Even among the primitive societies where rules of morality are under strong supernatural sanction, appeals to the gods for aid in following the path of propriety are not characteristic.

A clearer idea of the nature of the relationship between ethics and religion in primitive society may be gained from a closer look at actual cases. For this purpose we have chosen four societies, widely separated geographically and of varying degree of cultural complexity, in which the relationship between ethics and religion ranges from the tenuous to an extreme of intimacy.

THE ESKIMO

Weyer's succinct summary of the relationship between ethics and religion in Eskimo culture tells us:

Religions of more advanced peoples commonly regulate social relations by sanctioning the code of laws. Not so with the Eskimo religion. The requirements which it imposes constitute a distinct system of duties and taboos, quite apart from the code of justice. The morality of the Eskimos in purely mundane matters, on the other hand, is influenced by religion only in one way: by the fear that the spirits of the ancestors might be offended if the traditional code of justice were not adhered to. Whether the soul of a person after death will go to a happy or an unhappy place depends scarcely at all upon whether he has been law-abiding according to the civilized code. Actions involving worldly morality are rarely specified as entailing punishment in the after world. Only in isolated instances are theft and homicide, for instance, taken into account in this connection; and it seems that adultery never is. Thus, the regulative force of religion operates chiefly in a different way among the Eskimos than among civilized peoples. The greatest importance is attached to the manner in which a person dies and to the extent to which he has observed the religious taboos. Strict compliance with these taboos is regarded as a moral duty, however; for the violation of them will anger the spirits and bring calamity upon *the whole group*. Confession in the event of breaking them is required. But they seem to a civilized person, at least on first sight, largely arbitrary and extraneous to the well-being of the group or of the individual in his after life. Hence it must be concluded that the folkways of the Eskimos do not appear to embrace in any broad sense enforcement of worldly morality through religion.[11]

THE LUISEÑO

The aboriginal religion of the Luiseño Indians of southern California appears to represent something of an extreme among California tribes in the degree of coincidence of ethics and supernatural beliefs, but the relationship remains far from close, and acts which

[11] E. M. Weyer, *The Eskimos*, pp. 230-231.

we would regard as mere manners or customs with no ethical significance are included among supernaturally sanctioned behavior.
Kroeber reports that to the Luiseño supernatural punishments are
inevitable facts and that their beliefs contain no allusion to the will
or pleasure of any deity and no direct references to his anger.

Despite the existence of a powerful supernatural being,

> There is no concept of any law, nothing that we should call a principle,
> only an inexorable causality manifest in innumerable specific but endlessly
> varying instances. One does not reason about this sequence nor stop to
> bow before an omnipotent personality behind it. One merely adjusts him-
> self to events as to the stress of nature, and takes measures for a wise
> arrangement of life instead of a series of troubles, in the same spirit as
> one might provide against storm or starvation. . . . On the purely ethical
> side, one trait stands out which is also a general American rather than a
> tribal characteristic. There is no provision against theft, assault, rape,
> witchcraft, or murder, nor any mention of them. Such violent extremes
> are too obvious for condemnation, as incest was to the ancient Aryans. . . .
> The Indian, beyond taboos and cult observances, centers his attention on
> the trivial but unremitting factors of personal intercourse: affability, lib-
> erality, restraint of anger and jealousy, politeness. He . . . sets up an open,
> even, unruffled, slow, and pleasant existence as his ideal. He preaches a
> code of manners rather than morals. He thinks of character, of its ex-
> pression in the innumerable but little relations of daily life, not as right
> or wrong in our sense. It is significant that these words do not exist in his
> language.[12]

Counsel in the form of a "sermon" given to Luiseño girls during
ceremonies held at their puberty gives an explicit statement of the
acts supernaturally punished and rewarded, omitting behavior
which Luiseño sentiment regards as particularly reprehensible and
which Christian sentiment would judge as much more worthy of
inclusion:

> See, these [things depicted in a sand painting: bear, mountain lion,
> raven, earth, sky, and wood mountain] are alive; these will think well of
> you if you believe; and if you do not believe, they are going to kill you;
> if you are heedless, a dissembler, or stingy. You must not look sideways,

---

[12] A. L. Kroeber, *Handbook of the Indians of California*, pp. 683-684.

you must not receive a person in your house with anger; it is not proper. You will drink hot water when you menstruate, and when you are pregnant you will drink bitter medicine.

This will cause you to have your child quickly, as your inside will be clean. And you will roast yourself at the fire [after childbirth], and then your son or daughter will grow up quickly, and sickness will not approach you. But if you are heedless you will not bear your child quickly and people will speak of your heedlessness.

Your elder relatives you must think well of; you will also welcome your daughters-in-law and your brothers-in-law when they arrive at your house. Pay heed to this speech, and at some future time you will go to their house, and they are going to welcome you politely at their house. Do not rob food of overnight; if you have a child it will make him costive; it is also going to make your stomach swell; your eyes are also going to granulate, and people will know by your eyes what you have done. And as your son or daughter will grow up, you will bathe in water, and your hair will grow long, and you will not feel cold, and you will be fat, if you bathe in water. And after the adolescence rite you will not scratch yourself with your hands; you will scratch yourself with a stick; your body will have pimples if you scratch yourself with your hands. Do not neglect to paint yourself, and people will see, and you will grow old, if you pay attention to this speech, and you will see your sons and daughters.

See these old men and women; they are those who paid attention to this counsel, which is of the grown-up people, and they have already reached old age. Do not forget this that I am telling you; pay heed to this speech, and when you are old like these old people, you will counsel your sons and daughters in like manner, and you will die old. And your spirit will rise northwards to the sky, like the stars, moon, and sun. Perhaps they will speak of you and will blow [three times] and [thereby] cause to rise your spirit and soul to the sky.[13]

THE NUER

Evans-Pritchard's description and analysis of the religion of the Nuer, a Negroid people of the Anglo-Egyptian Sudan, provides a wealth of information seldom reported for any primitive society. Nuer conceptions of "faults" draw no hard and fast distinctions between sins punishable by supernatural means and offenses other-

[13] *Ibid.*, p. 685.

wise sanctioned. Any fault *may* lead to ill results of supernatural
cause and many serious faults are thought always to do so, but the
Nuer conception of sin (offenses regarded as consistently resulting
in divine punishment) is vastly different from that of Europeans.
Sins to the Nuer are not bad because of intrinsic qualities; they are
bad because the punishment they incur is bad. They include, moreover, many acts which Europeans would regard as utterly unrelated
to ethics.

In using the word "sin" to refer to the ideas I have been discussing we
have to be more than usually on guard against thinking into Nuer thought
what may be in our own and is alien to theirs. From our point of view
the ethical content of what the Nuer regard as grave faults may appear
to be highly variable, and even altogether absent. A fault of inadvertence,
though it may not have such serious consequences as a deliberate fault,
may nevertheless . . . entail grave consequences; and most of the acts Nuer
class as *nueer* [a term whose meanings include grave sin and contamina-
tion] would seldom, if ever, be committed deliberately. Moreover, the sin-
ful act may bring misfortune not only to the persons who committed it
but also to persons who are, as we think of it, in no way responsible. It is
not the adulterer but the injured husband who is likely to be sick, or it
may be some person with a sore who is quite unrelated to either who suffers. It is not the husband or his nursing wife who suffers if he has congress with her but their child, and possibly also children of other parents.
Likewise, incest may harm relations of the partners to the sin who are
not even cognizant of it . . .
    It is difficult also for the European observer to understand why Nuer
regard as grave faults, or even as faults at all, what seem to him rather
trivial actions. That incest and adultery are regarded as faults and, in the
sense we have given to the word, sins, he can understand, but not a man
milking his cow and drinking the milk, or a man eating with persons with
whom his kin are at blood-feud. I can only say that these rules make sense
when viewed in the total context of Nuer social life as interdictions arising
out of basic social relations. . . . Nuer can give no reasons for the acts
being bad other than that God punishes them. Consequently also, sins do
not arouse indignation, as some quite minor fault may do. The consequences
of incest may arouse hostility on the grounds of damage, but I have only
heard Nuer express indignation about incest as such when it is with the
closest kinswomen, and even then they condemn the man's folly rather than

the man. Acts of the kind they call *nueer,* with the exception of the suckling interdiction, are . . . almost invariably unwitting offences. Nuer do not, therefore, though they fear the consequences, blame the man. They are sorry for him. In cases of incest with distant relatives and of intercourse with a suckling mother they tend to take the view that it is scarcely for them to censure a man whose desires have got the better of him. When there is adultery, the husband may be indignant and demand compensation for the injury done to him, but Nuer do not become indignant at the idea of adultery. The essential point is that such faults as we are considering are, wholly or in part, conceived of as offences against God, and Nuer think that it is he who punishes them. It is God's *cuong,* right, rather than, or as well as, man's that has been violated. The man who commits them, therefore, places himself, and possibly others too, in danger by having done something which brings Spirit into action in the affairs of men.

This danger is a condition which to some extent appears to be regarded as physical, the threatening misfortune, usually sickness, which results and is the outward manifestation of the sin being already in the man before it manifests itself. He is contaminated by his act. This is why medicines, aspersions, fumigations, and other modes of expulsion and cleansing are used in addition to the atoning act of sacrifice. This is more than mimicry. The pollution is substantival. That the sin is felt to be attached to the man is further expressed by two words of great significance, *dop* and *woc.* *Dop* means to catch alight, the spreading of a flame or fire. It is also used to describe a man catching a disease, yaws for example, from another and the spreading of an epidemic or murrain, such as smallpox or rinderpest; . . . and it can likewise refer to anything spreading, as a fight developing out of a quarrel and people other than the principals becoming involved in it. The general idea is that of a person catching something from another, an infection, whether it be a disease, a quarrel, or a bad habit. In our present context the word means that the uncleanness which results from sins may pass to others closely related to those who are directly concerned in them. They are also in danger. *Woc* is used in a number of contexts in which the sense is getting rid of something especially by wiping it out. . . . Sacrifice is said to *woc,* wipe out . . . any . . . fault. . . . We have in the words *dop* and *woc* two ideas which throw much light on the way Nuer regard since and sacrifices made in consequence of them. Sin, as has been noted, is something which destroys and which tracks down. Two other characteristics of it are now revealed. It can spread and it can be wiped out by sacrifice. But though sin is regarded as bringing about a condition of the person which is contagious, the uncleanness is not simply a physical impurity which can be washed or purged away. It is also a spiritual state which can only be changed by sacrifice; and not even sacrifice is sufficient by itself to change it, only sacrifice which carries with it the will and desire of the sinner. What gives emphasis to the physical quality of the condition is the fact that the consequences of sin, which in a sense form part of it, are physical. This brings us to a very important matter, the identification of disease with sin.

Nuer may speak, as we have seen, of the consequences of a sin by the same word . . . as they use when they speak of the sin itself. *Rual* is incest, and it is also syphilis and yaws. *Nueer* is a breach of certain interdictions, and it is also the violent sickness which follows the breach. *Thiang* is a breach of the weaning interdiction, and it is also the dysentery the breach causes . . . if the sin which brought the sickness about is known it is spoken of by the name of the sin. . . . Even when there has been no breach of a specific interdiction . . . any sickness tends to be regarded as the operation of Spirit on account of some fault on the part of the sick person or of someone closely related to him. . . . No attempt may be made to discover whether there has been a fault or not or what the fault, if any, was, but Nuer think that a man would not be sick if there had been no error. . . . This, then, is a further characteristic of sin. It causes physical misfortune, usually sickness, which is identified with it, so that the healing of the sickness is felt to be also the wiping out of the sin.[14]

THE MANUS

Probably the most extreme example among primitive societies of the intimate association of ethics and religion comes to us from the Manus, a Melanesian fisher people inhabiting several islands of the Bismarck Archipelago. Fortune's account of their aboriginal religion emphasizes as its central element an extremely puritanical code of morals under strong supernatural sanction.[15]

The most important supernatural being of the Manus is the spirit of the father of the male head of the household, which becomes the tutelary god of the household and supervises the behavior of its members. Spirits of the newly dead are regarded as the most powerful, and when the head of a household dies the old tutelary is dis-

[14] E. E. Evans-Pritchard, *Nuer Religion*, pp. 188-192.
[15] R. F. Fortune, *Manus Religion*.

carded. The defleshed skull of the man is placed above the entrance to the dwelling on the inner side, where it may watch the conduct of all within. Each family thus has its guardian spirit, which rewards members for good conduct by bringing wealth and long life, preventing mishaps, and providing protection against the potentially malign influences of the guardian spirits of other families. An equally important role of the tutelary is to punish family members for unethical conduct by taking from them soul stuff, in small or large quantities, for short periods or permanently. Loss of soul stuff results in illness for the individual upon whom the punishment is inflicted; if it continues to be withheld the invalid grows sicker and finally dies.

Breaches of conduct punishable by the tutelary are many. Although the Manus have never explicitly formulated a code of commandments, Fortune reports sixteen as implicit. The most serious of these is loose sexual conduct, which includes almost any sort of behavior having to do with sexual relations except ordinary intercourse between man and wife. Obscenity between spouses and even seeing the sex organs of an individual of opposite sex accidentally exposed while he is sleeping are included among the sex offenses. Other commandments inveigh against laziness, failure to meet economic obligations of many kinds including the holding of funerary rites for relatives, selfish use of wealth, theft, disobedience to elders, and the remarriage of widows with children. One must also keep his house in repair, observe traditional food taboos, avoid places where the blood of his ancestors was shed, report all infractions of the rules, and make no false charges of misconduct.

If an offense involves more than one family, illness may strike any member of the families concerned. (Punishments other than illness or death also occur, especially for offenses which are not sexual, and the deaths of infants and of the aged are usually attributed to outside malevolent forces.) When someone in the community falls sick, it is usually first assumed that the cause lies in a sexual transgression and suspicion mounts. Relatives of the stricken individual consult a diviner, who fastens guilt upon some person or persons. Accusations appear usually to be based upon observations

of furtive or unusual behavior during the recent past and to represent community consensus. Because sickness may be caused by anyone in the community, its occurrence is a matter of concern to all,
and the divination is made public. The accused must then make
public confession and pay fines of goods to the guardian spirits
of all households directly concerned (actually to the families themselves, who make use of the goods). Immoral conduct involving a
member of a second household and taking place in the dwelling or
on the grounds of a third household requires expiatory payment to
two guardian spirits.

Mere innocence is no protection. The accused who claims innocence is regarded by the public as a murderer if the stricken person
dies. Had he confessed and made expiation, the soul stuff would be
returned and death averted. Serious as it is, the social stigma of
confessing a misdeed is much less than that of being regarded as a
murderer. Any moral transgression is thus the concern of everyone
and the compulsion to follow the code is strong. Public accusation of
guilt, confession, and expiation also bring shame and loss of social
prestige and serve to strengthen the supernatural sanctions.

Fortune states that Manus religion stands out in sharp contrast
with that of most primitive societies including neighbors of the
Manus. Avoiding concentration on direct attention to the supernatural, it embodies the belief that the right in human relations sets
men at right with the supernatural and exemplifies in a society of
crude cultural development the "thoroughgoing coalescence of religion and morality that has been characteristic also of the Christian
religion."[16]

The examples we have cited here give evidence that the disasso-
ciation of ethics and religion is not an inherent characteristic of
primitive culture. If, however, we review a large body of data on
primitive religions we are forced to a conclusion little different from
that of Tylor: any degree of identification is possible but a tenuous
association is the most common. Thus the definition of religion in
terms of ethics leaves many societies with little or no religion.

This discussion suggests a question. If moral standards are neces-

[16] *Ibid.*, p. 357.

sary for group survival, what are the mechanisms which serve to keep primitive peoples with nonethical religions on the paths of moral rectitude? The same question may well be applied to the non-religious members of our own society and also to adherents of certain subsects of Zen Buddhism that emphasize mystical enlightenment rather than morality and require no acts of worship or atonement.

We must note in the first place that the question credits religion with greater force than actual circumstances seem to warrant. Religion probably rarely if ever stands entirely alone as a force toward conformance with ethical codes, if purely ritual offenses and taboos which do not involve human interrelationships are excluded from the scope of ethics. Multiple sanctions operating in conjunction are customary, and even ritual offenses and violations of taboos may involve more than supernatural sanctions as a pressure toward avoidance. These conditions apply, of course, to positive sanctions as well as to negative; that is, to forms of reward as well as punishment. A serious breach of morality is likely to be punished by law, loss of prestige, verbal censure, avoidance, ostracism, and ridicule, and it may also be punished supernaturally. Conversely, conformance with ideals of moral behavior may win praise, prestige, and affection as well as supernatural reward and immunity from supernatural punishment.

Sanctions, of whatever kind, need not of course be exercised, or even threatened, to be effective. They may become highly internalized so that the individual serves as his own monitor, so that one's conscience serves as his guide. Much has been written on this subject. We have heard the opinion that Americans are becoming "other-directed" rather than "inner-directed," that is, that the most effective control over their behavior lies in sanctions imposed by others rather than in conscience or internalized social sanctions.[17] Essentially the same idea has been used in labeling certain cultures as "guilt cultures" and others as "shame cultures."

The question of primacy of sanctions is one that cannot be answered except in a general way. Intersocietal variation in emphasis is great, and within a single society different kinds of acts

[17] David Riesman, *The Lonely Crowd.*

are by convention associated with different complexes or weightings of sanctions. We may repeat, however, that a network of sanctions variably large or small serves to support and reinforce social norms whenever they are seriously violated.

Referring to examples close at hand, we may compare the ethical codes of Christians and agnostics in the population of the United States. Except insofar as exclusively religious obligations such as attendance at church might be included in individual conceptions of ethical acts, the codes of ethics of the religious and the nonreligious, their degree of conformance to these codes, and the social sanctions which ensure conformance appear to be much alike. It seems reasonable to believe that devoutly religious individuals might conform more closely to ethical ideals because an added sanction impels them to do so but there is not clear evidence to support such a statement.

Various sociological surveys have reported on attitudes toward sex and marriage of the devout and the nondevout, but they say little about morality. In both the United States and England, for example, a larger proportion of the devout is reported to disapprove of premarital sexual intercourse.[18] This does not assure us that the devout have higher moral standards; it seems to say only that standards of sexual morality differ. For offenses such as murder, homicide, and theft, information is inadequate to make comparison. The trend in both countries, however, seems to be toward a growing secularization of life so that the traditional sanctions of Christianity have less and less weight.

It is possible to argue that the beliefs, the ethics of Christianity have penetrated everywhere into our culture so that the individual without religious faith is also affected by them. This is undoubtedly in some measure true. Except to the considerable extent that it has expanded or changed to conform with conceptions of the proper in human relations as derived from other sources since the time of the emergence of Christianity, however, the Christian code of ethics surely represents incorporation into that religion of moral values extant before its formulation. Rather than being a mainspring of

[18] Michael Argyle, *Religious Behavior,* chap. 10.

moral principles, religion takes the primary role in social control of supporting and reinforcing these cultural values. As we have seen, this role is essentially denied to it in many primitive societies and it appears to be increasingly weakly performed in our own society.

In this discussion we have dealt chiefly with sanctions implying personalized conceptions of the supernatural, punishments inflicted by man-like beings. We have also referred briefly to violations of taboos with automatically harmful or unpleasant consequences, at least some of which concern matters of ethics. Supernaturalistic beliefs and practices of primitive peoples work in still another fashion to help maintain propriety in interpersonal relations—specifically, through witchcraft, a subject set aside for separate discussion in the following chapter.

Chapter 11. Witchcraft
and Ritual Rebellion

As the preceding pages have stated, psychological stress placed upon the members of society has often been the central point in attempts to explain the significance of supernaturalistic behavior. We have noted that definitions of religion frequently describe it as a means of resolving uncertainty and anxiety arising from man's relationship to his physical environment and to other men. We have seen, too, that theorists have emphasized the positive role of religion to the minimizing of its negative effects. The obviously disruptive effects of witchcraft might seem to put it in a special category of supernaturalism that is not amenable to this kind of analysis. The term instantly brings to mind communities full of suspicion, jealousy, hatred, accusations, cruel punishments, and retaliation that could serve no easily apparent end except to create anxiety and set community members at odds with one another. Perhaps until recent times no scholar sought or expected to find in it anything but the symptoms or the seeds of social disruption and personal distress. During the past two decades, however, hypotheses concerning socially positive effects of witchcraft have become common. Their formulation makes use of psychoanalytic theories concerning projection, displacement, and compensation, and these are often linked with sociological and ethnological theories concerning social structure, especially the idea that any element of culture plays a part in the maintenance of society.

But let us pause to make the subject of discussion clear. Witchcraft, as used here, means any acts of magic and the employment of supernatural power to work harm on one's fellow men. In some societies lower forms of animal life and, occasionally, natural phenomena may bewitch one, but witches are generally human beings and this discussion is limited to human witches. Where beliefs in more than one distinctive form of harmful supernaturalism exist and native terminology makes a distinction between the types, it has been useful for scholars to give them different labels, and such terms as sorcery and wizardry have been used for this purpose. Evans-Pritchard, for example, distinguishes witchcraft from sorcery in describing customs of the Azande and other people of Africa. In Azande belief, witchcraft power is a substance in the stomach of certain people. Only wicked persons, the quarrelsome, greedy, spiteful, and bad-tempered, have and use it; their wicked feelings constitute witchcraft. It is then a psychic act. Persons with no innate wickedness may work harm on others by means of magical spells; these acts are called by a different name, which Evans-Pritchard translates as "sorcery."[1] Among the Gã of the Gold Coast, witchcraft is "simply projected at will from the mind of the witch. . . . Witches are people mentally afflicted with the obsession that they have the power to harm others by thinking them harm."[2]

Convention varies. In some societies witchcraft is performed only by conscious projection of thoughts; the witch knows himself to be a witch. In others it may be done unconsciously or only by following magical formulas, and in some societies the witch may practice his craft either by projecting thoughts or by performing mechanical acts. As a matter of convenience, the single word witchcraft is used here to comprehend all forms of supernaturalism intended to harm fellow human beings.

Even where witchcraft is performed by mechanical acts, ethnologists have often reported an abundance of accusations of witchcraft but little or no evidence of its actual practice. Kluckhohn reports that no white person has ever actually seen witchcraft performed by the Navaho, although he himself over a period of years recorded 222 cases of persons accused of practicing it.[3] Secrecy is, of course, essential if the witch wishes to escape detection and punishment, but

[1] E. E. Evans-Pritchard, *Witchcraft, Oracles and Magic Among the Azande.*
[2] M. J. Field, *Religion and Medicine of the Gã People*, p. 137.
[3] Clyde Kluckhohn, *Navaho Witchcraft.*

there is ample reason to think that in many societies accusations far outnumber practices. We have noted that witchcraft does not require any physical act; a witch may project harm consciously or unconsciously. Where spells or other formulas are required, they need not, of course, be performed in order to set witchcraft at work. Merely the belief that one is bewitched is all that is required.

The potency of beliefs in witchcraft depends in large part upon interpretations of the genesis of illness. In the natural course of events, men fall ill and sometimes die of diseases and injuries. Belief that witches have caused these misfortunes provides an explanation of their cause in the absence of other explanations, and at the same time it suggests a course of action for cure. Naturalistic interpretation of the causes of disease, injury, and death is sometimes quite compatible with beliefs in witchcraft. Among African tribes that from aboriginal times have held naturalistic views of the genesis of some illnesses and among tribal peoples in other areas of the world which have recently accepted the scientific view, beliefs linking witchcraft with disease may remain strong. By fastening blame on enemies of the afflicted, the theory of witchcraft explains why rather than how the particular person suffered misfortune. The witch has caused the disease to strike his victim.

The question of whether witchcraft and other supernaturalistic beliefs can lead to sickness and death has been answered long ago by trained scientists observing the physiological reactions of men of primitive society who have thought themselves supernaturally stricken. The victim of witchcraft, who must either know or think that magic is being worked against him, is killed by his own nervous system. Dr. Walter B. Cannon has given us a description of the physiological processes that culminate in death.[4] Under the stimulus of fright, the sympathetic nervous system supplies the body with unusual amounts of adrenalin and causes other physiological changes to meet the emergency. Continued stimulus from fright and continued response of the nervous system without any physical action to

---

[4] W. B. Cannon, ''The 'Voodoo' Death.'' See also Hutton Webster, *Taboo*, p. 24 ff.; and E. H. Ackerknecht, ''Psychopathology, Primitive Medicine, and Culture.''

relieve the bodily state of emergency results in multiple harmful effects including lowered blood pressure, deterioration of the heart, and serious disturbance of normal circulation of the blood. Loss of appetite follows, making the condition more acute, and finally the individual is unable to carry on normal and necessary metabolic processes.

Newspapers and *Time* magazine in 1956 carried the account of a 19-year-old native of Australia's Arnhem Land who became paralyzed in the arms and legs and could scarcely breathe as the result of sorcery performed by his mother-in-law. Taken to a hospital in Darwin, he was examined by four white physicians. "A thorough examination showed no sign of polio. X-rays revealed nothing. There seemed to be nothing wrong with Charlie's heart or nervous system. Yet his breathing and swallowing were labored. So the doctors put him in an iron lung. Bit by bit the explanation came out: Charlie's mother-in-law had become angry with him, evidently wanted him out of the way so her daughter could marry a Groote Island aborigine. So, Charlie gasped from his iron lung: "I bin sung." Explained a fellow tribesman, acting as interpreter: "Him bin sung song of dreamtime snake. When you sung snake song, snake coils around legs and arms and chest, and you no longer breathe. If I bin sung, snake get around me, and I bin finished."[5] In this instance, white man's magic in the form of intravenous feeding and psychotherapy appear to have effected a cure.

The accused witch who is quite innocent of any overt act of magic but who himself believes in witchcraft may also be convinced that he has unconsciously bewitched another, as seems often to have happened in the history of American and European witchcraft. The borderline between witchcraft, divination, and the mere harboring of aggressive thoughts is sometimes very thin. The Northern Paiute of Harney Valley, Oregon are capable of practicing witchcraft by dreaming or wishing ill fortune for another.[6] Reports on neighboring Northern Paiute groups of Nevada tell us that individuals may dream of the illness or death of any person and may also dream

---

[5] *Time*, May 7, 1956, p. 90.
[6] B. B. Whiting, *Paiute Sorcery*.

portentously of other kinds of events which come true. Park describes anger and the expressed desire to kill a friendly guest who fell asleep at the table after the noon meal and on awakening told of seeing in a dream the death of the young daughter of his hosts. Feeling arose when the girl fell sick a few hours later, and witchcraft was suspected. But among these Indian groups anyone might also see in dreams things to come, events of any kind, and these visions seemed to imply no witchcraft unless they foretold misfortune to some individual.[7]

Individual motives for performing witchcraft or accusing others of doing so prominently include vengeance, jealousy, a desire for power when other avenues are difficult or have resulted in failure, and compensation for the bewitched in the form of the sympathy and attention of one's fellows. Much evidence from accounts of European witchcraft and—probably because this subject has had less investigation there—a smaller amount from studies of primitive society indicates that the lowly, those to whom prestige has otherwise been denied, stand out prominently among the sufferers from witchcraft.[8] Frequently, either the fear of witchcraft or of being accused of performing it serve as checks against the excessive accumulation of wealth and authority.

Like many other ideas of supernaturalism, the belief in witchcraft is itself a source of anxiety, but scholars have seen its principal significance as an expression of anxiety arising from numerous sources. Witches are seen as projections, the casting of anxieties into concrete form so that they may be easily understood and dealt with by familiar forms of behavior, or the acts of witches are seen as the expression in phantasy of desires which custom prohibits. Beliefs and practices of witchcraft, then are a means of expression and control of repressed desires, anxiety, and hostility. Relieved of tension, social relations are smoothed and the social order maintained.

Dependent upon the particular conformation of beliefs in witchcraft, societal integration is variously affected. If witches are con-

---

[7] W. Z. Park, *Shamanism in Western North America.*

[8] See Montague Summers, *The Geography of Witchcraft;* and Clyde Kluckhohn, *op. cit.*

ceived as members of social groups other than one's own or are entirely supernatural creatures rather than human beings, feelings of hostility or frustration, however engendered, may be expressed against them or, by phantasy, through them, with no harm to social relations. Joint acts against witches of this kind may be seen as societally unifying. When the scapegoats, those accused of witchcraft, are members of one's own society, social relations between individuals are disrupted but, so a prevalent line of reasoning goes, integration of the total society is less seriously damaged than if aggressive feelings were allowed no conventional outlet.

When witches are conceived as remote or unidentifiable persons outside one's society they become functionally indistinguishable from scapegoats of other kinds, including the malevolent and, unlike most witches, entirely supernatural beings that exist in the beliefs of numerous primitive peoples. Analyses of the positive value for the individual and society of beliefs in malevolent spirits have followed much the same course of reasoning as used in studies of witchcraft. Spiro's study of the people of the Micronesian coral atoll of Ifaluk may be taken as representative, although it is remarkable in including in its title the words "teleological functionalism."[9]

The 250 Ifaluk, whose everyday domain is one-half square mile of land and one square mile of lagoon, are notable for cooperation, mutual helpfulness, sharing and a lack of aggression toward one another. As with other peoples who live in cramped quarters in constant face-to-face contact, it is vital for the perpetuation of the society that in-group aggression be suppressed, or deflected into less harmful channels. Among the important elements of Ifaluk religion is a belief in malevolent ghosts, the souls of people who were bad in temporal life. These bad ghosts cause illness and every kind of immoral or abnormal behavior among the living, and are therefore intensely hated. Much of the ceremonial life of the Ifaluk consists of techniques for controlling or curtailing the activities of these spirits.

Beliefs and practices centered upon the bad ghosts are seen, on the manifest level, as explaining disease and abnormal people and

[9] M. E. Spiro, "Ghosts, Ifaluk, and Teleological Functionalism."

providing techniques to deal with these problems. Anxiety is thereby minimized, but at the same time the beliefs create anxiety as well as sickness and death, and thereby "threaten to destroy" Ifaluk society. From the viewpoint of the people, it would be better if there were no bad ghosts. Thus, the negative effects might seem to outweigh the positive. Why then, Spiro asks, do these beliefs survive, and he offers in answer the interpretation that the bad ghosts, as scapegoats, serve functions unknown to the Ifaluk. For survival under their condition of life, the Ifaluk can allow little aggression among themselves. The belief in bad ghosts and joint rites centered on them allow individually helpful and societally harmless expression of hostility, and, at the same time, common belief and a joint front of antagonism strengthen bonds of group solidarity. The absence of this belief or some functional equivalent, Spiro states, would be disastrous because aggressive drives "demand expression" or the result is disintegration of the personality.

Returning now to the subject of witchcraft, sources of tensions or conflicts it expresses are seen as various. They may come from the physical environment in the form of epidemics of disease, drouth, flood, plagues of insects, or any other threat to the food supply and welfare of the human society concerned. They may come from the social environment, from conflicts of interest engendered by social living, and it is in this area where scholars have looked most frequently in seeking an understanding of witchcraft. Like religious movements, the existence of beliefs and practices of witchcraft are viewed as indicative of stress in the social structure and corresponding tension for the individual. The spread of witchcraft among African societies that formerly lacked it and increases in the number of accusations of witchcraft among native African tribes, for example, have been interpreted as indicating social disturbance brought on by acculturative pressure; that is, conflict between European and native custom.[10] The amount of anxiety expressed by witchcraft is held to be a function of both the intensity of social conflict and the degree of repression through other channels.

[10] A. I. Richards, "A Modern Movement of Witch-Finders"; M. G. Marwick, "Another Modern Anti-Witchcraft Movement in East Central Africa."

But even the scholar most blindly dedicated to the idea that any enduring supernaturalistic custom contributes toward the maintenance of society can hardly fail to see the negative effects of witchcraft in creating tensions and disrupting social relations. To escape this more or less tight corner, a customary hypothesis has been that witchcraft provides a way of relieving hostility when other means are prohibited or inadequate. Beliefs in witchcraft are then seen as less costly to society or the individual than such acts as open physical aggression.

Clues to sources of conflict in social organization are afforded by examination of the relations between the accused, the accusers, and the victims. Accusations of witchcraft are not made indiscriminately against all persons whom one dislikes or envies. In every society accusations follow patterns. Persons who hold social status much higher than the bewitched seem rarely or never to be accused, and it is probably unthinkable that accusations might be made against them. A great social gap, such as between noble and commoner, gives little encouragement to the growth of truly personal conflict. Moreover, where the social breach is great, the superior in one way or another holds power over the inferior, and they do not vie with each other. Accusations against close genetic kin are not common, although the witch of the Northern Paiute of Harney Valley was thought to work harm first against members of his own family, and in certain African societies brother might accuse brother of witchcraft and mothers might bewitch their children.[11] The strength of emotional ties between parent and child seems generally to override such friction as might arise. Perhaps a relatively free expression and release of tension is encouraged or allowed among very close kin simply because of the binding force of emotional ties and the strength of the idea that their relationship cannot be ended.

It is clear that the ordering of society exerts strong influence on beliefs in witchcraft. Often it sets against each other certain persons who are related by marriage. In the occasional society where witchcraft is practiced against one's children, brothers, or other close genetic kin, circumstances which encourage this practice may

[11] B. B. Whiting, *op. cit.;* and Max Gluckman, *Custom and Conflict in Africa.*

usually be seen in social rules that create conflict between the relatives concerned.

In polygynous societies of Africa, co-wives compete with each other for favors from their husbands for both themselves and their children, and accusations of witchcraft against rival wives are common. Among Kluckhohn's Navaho cases, the largest single category of accusations were those made by women against their fathers-in-law. This is seen to be in keeping with a social rule requiring that a woman upon marriage leave the psychological security of her own kin group and take up residence with her husband and parents-in-law, where, as an outsider, she is subjected to considerable strain. The high proportion of accusations of witchcraft made between brothers among the Yao of the Lake Nyasa area of Africa is explained as arising from tribal social organization, which places them in competition for social prestige derived from the right to care for their sisters.[12] Among the Mesakin tribesmen of the Nuba Mountains in the Sudan, a man's mother's brother is most commonly suspected of witchcraft. This circumstance is explained as arising from the Mesakin social organization, which creates ties between a man and his sister's son but also creates conflict over their relative roles and over inheritance.[13]

In his study of the Cewa, a people of Northern Rhodesia who trace their descent through females and take their important social affiliations through these matrilineal connections, Marwick reports a tendency to accuse one's own matrilineal relatives. Using the same sort of reasoning Kluckhohn applies to the Navaho, where accusations are often against a woman's father-in-law but also often against people living far away, Marwick states that face-to-face living groups of the Cewa are not so isolated, small, or vital for subsistence as those of the Navaho. For this reason tensions arising among them in competition for social status may be released against the members of one's own society. Marwick notes that the Cewa themselves recognize the danger of repressing hostility. Tribesmen

[12] J. C. Mitchell, ''The Yao of Southern Nyasaland,'' in E. Colson and M. Gluckman, eds., *Seven Tribes of British Central Africa*, pp. 322-323.
[13] S. F. Nadel, ''Witchcraft in Four African Societies.''

stated that members of the same matrilineal kin group tend to practice witchcraft against one another because when they quarrel they
are inclined, out of loyalty to their kin, "to leave unspoken words
of speech with one another."[14]

Among the Azande of Africa in aboriginal times a man never
accused paternal kinsmen of witchcraft, although friction between
these relatives might be great. This male kin group formed a social
unit of great importance and beliefs of witchcraft operated in such
a way as to avoid the threat of dissension over witchcraft within the
group. Witchcraft power was thought to descend through male lines
from father to son. To accuse a paternal relative of witchcraft was
equivalent to accusing oneself and all his male relatives of having
witchcraft power in his stomach, and of being wicked.[15]

Circumstances that might foster antagonism between the sexes
have been sought to explain why the sex of persons accused of witchcraft are predominantly or exclusively male in some societies and
female in others. African witches are generally female, and resemble in this respect European witches of the past. It is possible
that this and many other African beliefs of witchcraft are derived
from a common source. Similarity to European witches is not limited
to beliefs concerning sex; specific acts and attributes of the witches
are frequently the same or closely similar. They often fly at night,
taking the form of birds or other animals; they hold witches' con-
gresses at which victims are eaten or their blood sucked, and witchcraft is often held to be hereditary, through female lines of descent.
The idea of diffusion of these beliefs is, however, rarely considered
by most ethnologists writing on Africa, who instead look to the social
order of particular societies for conditions that might lead to sex
antagonism.

Nadel reports that the Nupe of Northern Nigeria invariably accuse women of witchcraft despite a tradition allowing witches to be
of either sex, whereas the Gwari, a neighboring people, accuse individuals of either sex.[16] He attributes the difference to the fact that

---

[14] M. G. Marwick, "The Social Context of Cewa Witchcraft Beliefs."
[15] E. E. Evans-Pritchard, *op. cit.*
[16] S. F. Nadel, *op. cit.*, and *Nupe Religion.*

Nupe marriage is full of stress and Gwari marriage is relatively free of tensions. Nadel describes the Nupe conception of a witch as "The enemy of men and of male authority; she seeks to dominate men; her evilness is somehow bound up with the married state and occasionally old age, that is, age beyond child bearing; and her evilness is often directed against a husband and kin. . . . So that the witchcraft beliefs and fears paraphrase a true state of affairs and the anxieties and frustrations arising from it."[17] Stress in Nupe unions springs from conflict between ideal and actual behavior. Ideally, males dominate females and wives are faithful women. In actuality, women who assume the established feminine role of traders are often unfaithful, willfully independent of their husbands, and, through the economic advantage gained from their position as traders, they may usurp the husband's role as head of the family. Nadel regards witchcraft as a poor solution to the problem of venting aggression. He suggests that the reason for its existence among the Nupe is that the amoral nature of their gods provides no supernaturalistic concepts that provide a framework for moral indignation and action in relation to everyday activities, and beliefs in witchcraft fill this gap.

Other scholars interested in the social context of witchcraft have seen anxieties arising from such circumstances as widely extended incest rules that provide limited opportunities for sexual relations and from practices of rearing children.[18]

Of somewhat different orientation from the foregoing studies are interpretations that link types of society with the presence or absence of beliefs in witchcraft. These studies made no direct use of theories concerning the release of tensions, but are instead attempts to correlate this form of supernaturalism with the manner of ordering whole societies. A correlation is held to exist between the presence of witchcraft and societies with "atomized" social structure; that is, "unorganized" and "individualistic" societies in which institutions and social groups demanding intense cooperation and

[17] S. F. Nadel, *Nupe Religion*, p. 174.
[18] See, for example, Monica Wilson, "Witch Beliefs and Social Structures"; and J. M. Whiting and Irvin L. Child, *Child Training and Personality*.

hierarchical chains of authority are poorly developed or absent. Instances of the coexistence of loose social organization of this kind and witchcraft as an important explanation of illness have been noted among many North American Indian groups and primitive peoples in various other parts of the world. Coincidence is so frequent as to put in serious doubt the idea that the association is accidental, and the question of a cause and effect relationship has arisen. Does the presence of witchcraft bring about social "atomism"; does an atomized society merely provide an atmosphere that encourages the growth of witchcraft; or are the two things merely compatible and derived from other sources? The questions remain open.

Referring to the Ojibwa Indians, Barnouw states that the fear of sorcery serves to perpetuate the isolation of the individual.[19] Hallowell has gone further along the same line: "This [i.e., witchcraft] is the psychological explanation, it seems to me, of the 'atomism' or individualism of the Ojibwa society and of Indians with comparable cultures in the past. It is impossible for people to get together when their outlook is colored by the possibility of malevolence, particularly when there are no social institutions that demand a high degree of cooperation."[20]

Although it does not deal with witchcraft, Miller's study of the Fox Indians, one of the tribes labeled as atomistic, is of interest here.[21] The Fox and other Algonquin-speaking tribes of Wisconsin, Illinois, and Indiana had been extremely puzzling to colonial whites of the seventeenth century, who called these Indians insubordinate, and observed that they seemed to conduct war and all other social activities with no recognizable sort of authority. They were said to have "no visible form of government." No one was superior to anyone else; no orders were given by chiefs to subordinates, or by parents to children. Orders were insults.

In attempting to understand how the Fox had maintained themselves as a social group, Miller examines their religious beliefs and

[19] Victor Barnouw, *Acculturation and Personality among the Wisconsin Chippewa.*

[20] A. I. Hallowell, "Some Psychological Characteristics of the Northeastern Indians," in F. Johnson, ed., *Man in Northeastern North America,* p. 222.

[21] W. B. Miller, "Two Concepts of Authority."

finds the same lack of hierarchy among the gods and between gods and men. Relations with gods were reciprocal; there was no adulation and no supreme deity. The term used by a man in addressing Wisakeya, one of the important gods, was "my nephew," and the uncle-nephew relationship was one of equality. Punishment for those who lived a bad life was consignment after death to a supernatural world where they must ask permission of the supernatural beings before undertaking any action.

According to Miller's interesting interpretation, social action among the Fox was coordinated by each individual's following directly the small body of procedural rules that governed every activity. The Fox related himself directly to supernatural power, and in daily life he related himself directly to the rules governing collective actions such as waging war, religious ceremonials, and council meetings. He deemed it his inviolable right to respond directly to these rules without control from above, and although there was intense resentment of control there was also intense internalization of the rules. Following Miller's interpretation, the term "atomistic" seems hardly appropriate for Fox society, which he regards as having a type of authority that differs from our ordinary hierarchical structure.

The most ambitious attempt to link witchcraft and features of social organization is Beatrice Whiting's comparison of fifty societies, a study which has direct reference to the question of a relationship between atomized societies and witchcraft.[22] She reports that in 60 percent of her societies, witchcraft is "important" as an explanation of disease, and superordinate punishment (individuals with authority to give punishment for offenses between families) is lacking. In 24 percent of her cases, witchcraft is unimportant as an explanation of disease and superordinate punishment exists. Not all of the societies comprising the 60 percent may be called "atomized," but exceptions are limited chiefly to African groups in which there are individuals with authority over others who judge innocence or guilt, leaving actual punishment in the hands of kin of the injured. Whiting's study is interesting and should stimulate further in-

[22] B. B. Whiting, *op. cit.*

vestigation, but many questions may be asked about the data on which the correlations are based. One wonders, for example, why Japan should be included among a group of much simpler primitive societies, especially since European countries that saw much witchcraft are excluded. Japan and other elaborate civilizations essentially lack witchcraft, and one can easily see reasons for its absence that have no bearing on patterns of authority. The development of our great cultures has depended importantly upon scientific knowledge in applied form, and the emergence and acceptance of scientific knowledge renders belief in witchcraft untenable. Whiting also suggests that a correlation exists between the presence of witchcraft, as important, and societies structurally based upon kinship and personal ties. This idea seems hardly surprising for the reasons stated above. Societies in which kinship plays the smallest part are the great civilizations built upon the growth of scientific knowledge, the effects of which include the creation of an intellectual atmosphere that deals a lethal blow to beliefs of supernaturalism of this kind.

Whiting's study of correlations between features of social organization and the presence of witchcraft arose from an investigation of witchcraft among the Northern Paiute Indians of Harney Valley, Oregon in which she presents another major hypothesis, that beliefs in witchcraft serve as a mechanism of social control. This idea, together with the theory that witchcraft serves to release tensions, constitute the principal positive functions of witchcraft that scholars have deduced.

Ethnological studies of the functions of witchcraft have emphasized two avenues by which it becomes an agency of social control, fear of the supernaturally wrought consequences of witchcraft worked against one, and fear of the accusation of sorcery with its attendant worldly punishment by one's fellows. The key toward understanding the effectiveness of beliefs in witchcraft to control behavior lie in the events which are thought to inspire its performance and in the attributes of the witch. In briefest statement, both are simply antisocial behavior. The bewitched might, in the eyes of the community, be an innocent man who has become the target of magic because of jealousy or desire for gain derived from his illness or death. But he is frequently an individual who has committed aggressive or improper acts that arouse the resentment of another and make him the target of vengeance by witchcraft.

Studies of witchcraft among American Indian tribes tell us repeatedly that the individuals most likely to be suspected or charged with sorcery are those who do not conform with ideal patterns of behavior. Among the people of the pueblo of San Ildefonso, New Mexico, "Certain types of individuals were more likely to be suspected of witchcraft than others. Men or women who were aggressive, who spoke out in public, who expressed jealousy or resentment were frequently thought to be dealing in witchcraft . . . any individual who did not conform to pueblo ideals."[23] Jenness reports that for fear of witchcraft the Wisconsin Ojibwa "strives to avoid malice and ill-will by hiding his emotions and by carefully weighing his words lest he give vent to some angry or ill-timed remark."[24] Again and again studies of other American Indians—the Hupa, Hopi, Navaho, Paiute, Menomini, and still other groups—report that beliefs in sorcery operate in similar fashion to inhibit antisocial behavior or other departures from social norms. Among primitive peoples of other continents (where fewer studies of this kind have been made) the same motifs are repeated often enough in ethnologists' accounts. Among the Azande of Africa, expressions of jealousy, envy, hatred, or greed "may be regarded as diagnostic of witchcraft in a person and a man who wishes to avoid suspicion of witchcraft must refrain from displaying ill-will toward his neighbors."[25]

The Harney Valley Paiute of Whiting's study conceive supernatural power as being specialized and receive it through recurrent, unsolicited dreams. "Good" specialties are in several forms, including doctoring power to diagnose and cure disease. Bad power consists only of the supernatural ability to injure others; that is,

---

[23] William Whitman, "The San Ildefonso of New Mexico," in Ralph Linton, ed., *Acculturation in Seven American Indian Tribes*, p. 418.

[24] Diamond Jenness, *The Ojibway Indians of Parry Island*, p. 88.

[25] E. E. Evans-Pritchard, *op. cit.*, p. 419.

ability to perform witchcraft. Disease is largely attributed to supernatural cause, which includes witchcraft. To inject bad power into
the body of another the witch has several techniques; he might place
the power into a person by hitting him with a stone or stick, by
biting or spitting into his food, by thinking mean thoughts and wishing someone dead, and even by dreaming of killing an individual
or of telling him to die. When someone falls sick, diagnosis is likely
to be witchcraft as the cause if there has been recent dissension
among members of the camp. The individual with good doctoring
power may then be called in to determine the identity of the witch,
and he, as appears generally to be the case in societies where guilt
is determined by divination, makes a charge that is in accord with
the weight of public opinion. The accused then suffers the penalty
of social ostracism, a severe form of punishment, and usually takes
flight. In former times, it appears that the accused was killed.

The hallmark of the Paiute sorcerer is antisocial behavior. Those
who use aggressive and antagonistic behavior, the cranky, ill-tem-
pered, critical, and mean looking and acting are thought to have bad
power. Other evidence may also enter, including fearfulness on the
part of the accused. Remedies, performed by an individual with
doctoring power, consist of acts to induce the sorcerer to recall the
bad power, exorcism by song, and sucking the afflicted part of the
body.

As in many other societies, beliefs in witchcraft among the
Harney Valley Paiute serve as a form of discipline for children.
They are given intensive training from early childhood to prevent
aggressive behavior, especially fighting. If a fight occurs, children
are hustled from the scene, as bad power may be thrown about and
enter the children. Children are also frequently exposed to parents'
discussions of the fear of sorcery and of aggression. They are told
never to laugh or deride others for fear of witchcraft and are repeatedly admonished always to be polite and speak pleasantly. The
fear of aggression extends to fear of its unconscious expression. It is
believed that a sorcerer will first kill members of his own family. If
one has aggressive dreams about family members, he undergoes
ritual to purify himself.

The constant fear of loss of help and support, in a society where the individual is dependent on his family economically and for protection, serves to strengthen the training in the control of aggression. As a result of the childhood training the mechanisms of control are highly internalized and may be said to function primarily as a part of the conscience. They are maintained, however, by the constant threat of aggression from people outside the family.[26]

By way of caution, it is useful to add that witchcraft is claimed by no scholar as the primary or sole means of social control, and, because of its role in creating tensions, probably few would contend that it is in this respect an efficient device. A glance at the record of European witchcraft casts serious doubt on the validity of any pansocietal generalization that witchcraft is a relatively harmless way of releasing internal hostilities. It is impossible to see social harmony in the imprisonment, torture, and killing of many thousands of people.

Like witchcraft, ritual that expresses open rebellion against conventional behavior and cultural ideals has resisted interpretation that gives it a positive value. These are rites, taking many local forms, in which persons in authority are mocked and reviled; those to whom one is normally polite and deferential are ridiculed or calumnified in song or pantomime; serious acts of ritual are mocked by buffoons; obscenity and sexual license meet with social approval; women who are normally weak, submissive, and virtuous assume masculine roles to become rude, domineering, shouting braggarts or parody wanton lewdness; and valued conventions are flouted in other ways.

Institutionalized behavior of this kind has a wide distribution in the primitive world, but it has been the focus of little analytical attention by anthropologists. From a psychological viewpoint, these rites are seen as safety valves, socially approved expressions of hostility and other emotions which, for the maintenance and welfare of the society, must ordinarily be repressed. In this respect, the rites hold much in common with beliefs in witchcraft and malevolent spirits or the expression in mythology of behavior that is customarily forbidden.

[26] B. B. Whiting, *op. cit.*, p. 74.

At the turn of the century the German ethnologist Heinrich Schurtz discussed customs of this kind at some length, referring to their role as mechanisms for the expression of repressed emotions.[27] Various other ethnologists have casually referred to them in a similar way. Max Gluckman has recently given us the lone detailed interpretation that attempts to relate the rites to sources of tension in the social order. His study concerns negro societies of Africa, in which ritualized expressions of rebellion against authority and antagonism between the sexes appear to be common. He has given the title "rituals of rebellion" to these and other institutionalized ceremonies that flout convention. Adapting ideas earlier advanced by Georg Simmel and others, Gluckman regards the rites as illustrations of the positive role of conflict in maintaining the social order. The acting out of conflicts of interest that are inevitable in human society is seen as a form of catharsis that banishes the threat of disunity imposed by the conflicts.

But customs may be defied and burlesqued, and social superiors mocked, reviled, and threatened in only certain kinds of societies. Gluckman holds that institutionalized rebellious rites occur only within an established and unchallenged social order, and that our modern civilized society has no place for them because our social order itself is questioned. "The acceptance of the established order as right and good, and even sacred, seems to allow unbridled excess, very rituals of rebellion, for the order itself keeps this rebellion within bounds."[28] He points out that Bantu peoples among which these rites exist have never questioned the system of institutions, and that women of these societies who ritually abandon their normal feminine roles to act lewdly and burlesque the actions of males accept the social order without other organized protest.

Although societies having these rites are stable, fundamental social conflicts are said to exist within them. The interests of the individual in economic and other matters do not coincide with those of the society at large as personified by the ruler, but the needs of the individual cannot be met unless he follows the legal and moral

[27] Heinrich Schurtz, *Altersklassen und Männerbünde.*
[28] Max Gluckman, *Rituals of Rebellion in South-East Africa,* p. 21. See also his *Custom and Conflict in Africa.*

mandates of his society so that peace and order prevail. When kings are ritually reviled and rejected, it is the individual ruler who is the target of hate; although kinship as an institution may be resented, the aim of the ritual is never to subvert the institution. As they are observed among the Swazi of Southeast Africa, rites of rebellion are led by members of the royal family. Thus, "Rebellion confirms that family's title to the kingship" and, for fear of his rivals, the incumbent ruler is put on his mettle to become a good ruler. The Swazi themselves say that the rites "strengthen kingship," even though traditional songs sung at this time explicitly express hatred of the king.[29]

Ritual burlesque and reversal of normal behavior are very common among Indians of the Americas. In North America, the ceremonial buffoon was especially prominent in the Southwest, California, the Great Plains, and the northwest coast.[30] In many societies one or more persons—in the Southwest, frequently the members of a religious society—served as clowns during religious ceremonial. "Reversals" by these performers differ in a number of respects from those emphasized in reports on African tribes, and their clownish acts include behavior that implies no contradiction or reversal of the normal except insofar as burlesque itself is not customary.

In discussing American Indian humor, Steward classifies the acts of the clowns into four major categories based upon themes he states are regarded as humorous by all peoples: ridicule and burlesque of sacred ceremonies, folkways, and mores "essential to the smooth functioning of society," including the ridicule and burlesque of persons; ritual obscenity; themes based on "sickness, sorrow, misfortune, etc., and important activities in daily life"; and the caricature and burlesque of foreigners.[31]

[29] Hilda Kuper, *An African Aristocracy: Rank Among the Swazi*.
[30] See J. H. Steward, "The Ceremonial Buffoon of the American Indian"; E. C. Parsons and R. L. Beals, "The Sacred Clowns of the Pueblo and Mayo-Yaqui Indians"; and V. F. Ray, "The Contrary Behavior Pattern in American Indian Ceremonialism."
[31] J. H. Steward, *op. cit.*, p. 189.

Performances of the Indian clowns included many acts and mimes that flouted important conventions. Serious ceremonial acts were frequently parodied, and society members of various rank were sometimes imitated and ridiculed. Among the pueblo Indians, the buffoons burlesqued the serious dancers, stumbling, falling, dancing out of time, grimacing, and doing many things that are ordinarily strictly forbidden. Clowning frequently centered on sexual and other forms of obscenity, including the handling and consumption of urine and excrement. Sexual license on the part of buffoons was generally limited to burlesquing erotic activities in full view of fellow tribesmen.

As the lecher, the glutton, and the lazy-bones, the clown amused and at the same time he pointed up by reverse action the proper mode. Satire directed toward individuals reduced their status for the moment and might point out social failings. Ritual reversals of the American Indians emphasize humor, and in this respect differ conspicuously from the African rites to which we have referred. Many acts seem to have been planned first and foremost for their comic effect, although this statement is not to deny them social significance. The pueblo clown might continue dancing after the serious performers have ceased and until he "discovers" his mistake, and he indulges in much similar behavior, outright buffoonery that represents no violation of custom except the convention that one does not ordinarily act the fool deliberately. A clown society of the Zuni once devised an imitation telephone through which they pretended to talk with the gods, even though Zuni gods do not speak.[32]

Pueblo clowns also present acts that seem little different from the performances of comedians of our own society, social satires of poverty and misfortune, and of hunting, fishing, farming and other activities of daily life. Like Chaplin, the Indian clown may be poverty-stricken, woebegone, and ludicrous. The Indian burlesque of strangers—people of neighboring tribes and, in historic times, the white man—is, of course, also a comic motif well established in

[32] *Ibid.*, p. 190.

our own society. A fiesta of Santa Clara pueblo depicted drunken
United States troops arriving in a covered wagon, their losing fight
with the Navaho, and, finally, their rescue when the Utes came to
their aid.[33]

An eyewitness account describes the clowning of a religious society of the Zuni in 1881.[34] Two of the twelve men of the group were
naked except for breech-clouts of archaic style, which they later removed. Others were dressed in old, cast-off American Army clothing,
with white cotton nightcaps. One wore a long rubber garment and
a pair of goggles painted white, as a take-off on a Mexican priest.
Another was dressed like a young woman. Preliminary activities
included a song ridiculing the three white guests, which evoked uncontrolled merriment among the spectators of both sexes and all
ages crammed into the ceremonial room. The principal feature was
a parody of a Roman Catholic rite, and the performance ended with
the consumption by the clowns of large quantities of human urine.

The dancers suddenly wheeled into line, threw themselves on their knees
before my table, and with extravagant beatings of breast began an out-
landish and fanciful mockery of a Mexican Catholic congregation at
vespers. One bawled out a parody upon the pater-noster, another mumbled
along in the manner of an old man reciting the rosary, while the fellow
with the India-rubber coat jumped up and began a passionate exhortation
or sermon, which for mimetic fidelity was incomparable. This kept the
audience laughing with sore sides for some moments. . . .

The dancers swallowed great draughts [of urine], smacked their lips,
and amid the roaring merriment of the spectators, remarked that it was
very, very good. The clowns were now upon their mettle, each trying
to surpass his neighbors in feats of nastiness. One swallowed a fragment
of corn-husk, saying he thought it very good and better than bread; his
vis-à-vis attempted to chew and gulp down a piece of filthy rag. Another
expressed regret that the dance had not been held out of doors, in one of
the plazas; there they could show what they could do. There they always
made it a point of honor to eat the excrement of men and dogs.[35]

[33] *Ibid.*, p. 197.
[34] J. G. Bourke, *Scatalogic Rites of All Nations.*
[35] *Ibid.*, pp. 5-6.

Ritual reversals of the American Indians have other characteristics that distinguish them from the African rites we have thus far described, and they shade off into behavior for which the term "rites of rebellion" seem poorly applicable. Although the burlesque and mimicry of ritual leaders seems generally to have been approved as an occasion for laughter, it is interesting that in a few societies the audience was prohibited from laughing at these performances.[36] Sometimes the acts were in a wholly secular context, although they seem little different from the behavior in a religious context of other tribes. In the Great Plains area, contrary behavior was a characteristic of various societies of warriors, who pledged themselves to foolhardy bravery in war. Members of these societies said the reverse of what they meant, and indulged in much other unusual behavior. Their acts have been called "antinatural" because they were nonnatural in the sense of being extraordinary, of departing from the normal. Some acts, as we have noted, were direct reversals of the customary; some were ludicrous, and others on certain occasions violated moral norms. But the antinatural also prominently included behavior that was not humorous or immoral. The contraries madly ignored danger in war and performed remarkable feats such as plunging the arm into a boiling stew to remove a piece of meat.[37]

North American Indian clowns were also practical jokers who did such things as throw water on the spectators, tear off their loin cloths, drop live coals down their backs, and deliberately awaken others at night or prevent sleep by their noisiness.

The roles of the American Indian buffoons were sometimes multiple and included serious acts of a kind different from those we have discussed. Pueblo clowns served as police during ceremonies to ensure that people attended performances and that they obeyed the taboos during ritual periods. Clowns might be given considerable power over others at these times, and their role as agents of social control has often been pointed out. Among the pueblo Indians clowns are also disciplinarians for children, and are used as bogey-

---

[36] V. F. Ray, *op. cit.;* and J. H. Stewart, *op. cit.*
[37] *Ibid.*

men. Wearing masks and impersonating supernatural beings, they threatened to whip children and frighten them in other ways.

Interpretations by American scholars of the various Indian rites of reversal and burlesque have emphasized their value as entertainment, "comic relief," and, by projection, as a means of easing tensions. Referring to the Zuni, Bunzel states, "Undoubtedly the great delight in the antics of the clowns springs from the sense of release in vicarious participations in the forbidden."[38] The rites have never received thoroughgoing interpretation along the lines given to similar customs among African peoples; that is, they have not often been related to the social order and to conflicts in interests. Some of the rites appear to lend themselves to this kind of interpretation; that is, it seems plausible that they serve a positively functional role in supporting the social order and, in some measure, resolving conflicts. For other reversals and burlesques, this interpretation is ill-suited. In between, the borderline in the American Indian cases is indistinct because the necessary ethnographic data are not available. Men sometimes burlesqued the behavior of women and occasionally women acted as men, for example, but it is difficult to see in these acts—at least from the descriptions available to us—any expression of group or even individual dissatisfaction with the roles accorded to the sexes. It is very probable that circumstances leading to sex antagonism could be found in social customs of these tribes, but there is probably little doubt that conditions fostering antagonism between the sexes exist in all societies, whether or not they have rites of rebellion.

It is not clear from Gluckman's account to what extent the African ritual reversals in question are regarded by the people themselves as comic. Ethnographic reports on African societies make it fully clear, however, that ritual ribaldry resembling that of the American Indians is well established among various African peoples. Clowns appear to be fairly common, as is ritual obscenity, although scatology seems less prevalent than among the Indian tribes. Gluckman appears to have excluded from his interpretation many African ceremonial acts that "flout convention" and to have concentrated

[38] Ruth L. Bunzel, *Introduction to Zuni Ceremonialism*, p. 521.

on symbolic expressions of social conflict, especially rebellion against authority and sex antagonism. These are the rites most amenable to the interpretation he has presented. If "rituals of rebellion" is broadly defined to embrace the gamut of ritual breaches of convention described here, their significance appears to cover a broad range. It is not limited to the support of social values and the uniting of society through the controlled expression of conflict and the dramatization of propriety by reverse action.

As we have seen, the buffoonery and antinatural behavior of the American Indians embrace acts of many kinds. All cannot be viewed as rebellions against the specific conventions they express in reverse. Reversals and burlesques do indeed dramatize proper behavior, and they may be said thereby to support social values. Ritual lewdness and the ridicule of personal failings may be given this interpretation, and many other acts might be viewed as diffuse or generalized protests against social restrictions of propriety. Few would contend, however, that it is useful in any society to point out the impropriety of eating excrement or drinking urine by having clowns do so in an atmosphere of burlesque. The view that ritual reversals and burlesques are means of resolving social conflict, an interpretation always in doubt for lack of means of verification, cannot be applied very satisfactorily to one category of American Indian rites. Indian customs of burlesquing members of other societies seem qualitatively like customs that burlesque members of one's own society. The role of these acts as a means of expressing and relieving feelings of hostility seems obvious. In this sense, they may "resolve conflict." But they can hardly be held to resolve such actual conflicts of interest as exist between the societies in question. Reversals of normal procedures and other sharp contrasts with customary behavior constitute a comic theme that is certainly very common and perhaps universal; and the principal significance of many of the American Indian rites may indeed lie in the psychological and social implications of comic relief.

We have already expressed in our Introduction additional reservations and doubts concerning interpretations of the kinds discussed in this chapter, and shall add here only a few additional remarks.

Most of these concern the problem of verification. We are by no means always given evidence indicating that the people feel in fact the stresses which the rites are held to relieve, although this question could probably be settled by psychological tests and quantitative data on such things as incidence of quarrels, suicide, nervous ailments, divorce, and litigation. Even when evidence of these kinds indicating emotional strains is cited, we cannot be certain that rites of rebellion and the practice or accusation of witchcraft reduce or ameliorate the strains. It seems reasonable that they might do so— so far only this can be said with assurance. A recent study of practices of child training in the United States seems pertinent here. We are told that there is no decrease in the expression of aggression in phantasy among children raised by "permissive" parents.[39]

Richards complains that psychological interpretations of religious ceremonies are heads-I-win and tails-you-lose: "If a woman behaves submissively in ritual, the explanation offered is that she is expressing the sex role that is proper to a woman in a society in which meekness in woman is admired; if she swaggers the explanation is that she is reacting from this submissive role."[40] In both cases, of course, the rites are seen as giving support to the social order. It is possible that both interpretations are valid, but the feeling that the outcome is predetermined is not a reassuring one. Richards also notes that we lack means of accurately measuring the degree of social unity and disunity in societies, such as those here described in Africa, which are always united, societies with "unchallenged social orders."

It is evident that institutionalized rebellion may exist in some societies without leading to social disintegration. It is plausible that rebellion may serve as a social binder, but its value to this end is hard to appraise. Much remains to be done toward verifying these interesting hypotheses.

[39] R. R. Sears and others, "The Socialization of Aggression."
[40] A. I. Richards, *Chisungu*, p. 119.

Chapter 12. Religious

Therapy

One of the greatest domains of religion in human affairs until recent times has been the curing of illness and injury, and it has often included therapeutic techniques which we view today as naturalistic if sometimes outmoded. Ideas of the causes of illness and death are closely intertwined with supernaturalism everywhere in primitive society. How much of the primitive world attributes every kind of injury and pathology and every death to supernatural cause is unknown. Ethnological accounts sometimes report a complete absence of naturalistic explanation; other accounts report its presence in some measure, particularly for common minor ailments and injuries which the afflicted individual may see occur. For many societies, no information on this subject is available.

Although published data fully supporting his view are lacking, Sigerist is probably correct in stating, "Primitives almost universally distinguish between minor, common, and therefore obvious ailments that they can handle themselves, and serious sickness that is mysterious and cannot be cured unless it has been explained, a process that requires the special knowledge and skill of the medicine man."[1] This statement is well documented for certain African societies, where coughs and cold, fever, rheumatism, toothache, snake and scorpion bites, and even measles and yaws are treated as unexceptional occurrences calling for home remedies.[2]

Invariably, however, supernaturalistic interpretation and treatment of pathology are important and, it is probably safe to say,

[1] H. E. Sigerist, *A History of Medicine*, vol. 1, p. 126.
[2] G. W. Harley, *Native African Medicine, with Special Reference to Its Practice in the Mano Tribe of Liberia*, p. 21.

213

dominant. It seems certain also that disease is more frequently given a supernaturalistic explanation than is injury. In a review of reports on aboriginal medical practices of the many dozens of Indian tribes of South America, Ackerknecht finds only three in which diseases were sometimes regarded as the result of natural agencies.[3] He refers elsewhere to "countless tribes which do not know natural causes for disease."[4]

Naturalistic interpretation of illness does not, of course, prohibit recourse to supernaturalism in therapy, as witness circumstances in our own society, and whether illness and injury are deemed as supernatural or natural in the primitive world, curative measures lie principally within the realm of the supernatural. It is difficult, in fact, to separate medicine and supernaturalism in the beliefs and practices of primitive societies, and it seems that primitive peoples themselves seldom do so in any clear-cut way.

These words in no way imply that primitive medicine is irrational. It is eminently rational if not scientific when one looks at primitive concepts of supernatural power and ideas of the genesis of sickness and death. The bulk of supernaturalistic concepts of pathogenesis found among all societies of the world fall within narrow confines, and these several ideas are repeated again and again throughout the world, separately and in various combinations. Three ideas of the cause of illness and death stand out prominently: bodily loss of that which is necessary, and bodily gain of that which is foreign to it and harmful; violation of certain rules of behavior; and witchcraft.[5] Expressed in other terms, the first of these theories embraces the ideas of intrusive harmful spirits, intrusive objects, and loss of soul; and the second refers to breach of taboo, failure to meet ritual requirements, and sin. Other less prominent interpretations include attacks and other harmful acts by chronically malevolent spirits, and disarrangement of internal organs, brought about in various ways or occurring spontaneously. Sometimes, too, supernatural cause is assumed but its nature is undetermined or unspecified.

[3] E. H. Ackerknecht, "Medical Practices" in J. H. Steward, ed., *Handbook of South American Indians*, vol. 5, pp. 621-622.

[4] E. H. Ackerknecht, "Problems of Primitive Medicine," p. 506.

[5] See F. E. Clements, *Primitive Concepts of Disease*.

The belief in intrusive evil spirits is nearly world-wide. In the history of the Old World possession by spirits was a common explanation of abnormal behavior of various kinds. As we may recall, the theory that insanity is caused by demons entering the body was abandoned only recently in Europe. Traces of its former prevalence remain firmly implanted in modern English usages of the words "devil" ("full of the devil"; "I don't know what devil got into me") and "possessed." Pathological possession is also well known elsewhere, but the borderline between pathology and normalcy is very difficult to draw, and it seems wiser here to use instead the expression "intrusive spirits." A more cogent reason for using this term with reference to primitive societies is that many forms of pathology, whether of the body or the "mind," may in these societies be attributed indiscriminately to spirit intrusion and receive the same therapy. Data on mental disease in primitive society is both scanty and difficult to interpret. There is no doubt that insanity exists, but we can say little with assurance about its incidence or its forms. In our discussion of primitive religious practitioners we noted that behavior regarded as psychotic in our society occurs frequently in contexts which make it valued and normal for the primitive societies in question.[6] In any event, the incidence of mental disease is probably everywhere less than that of the total of all illnesses of other kinds, and it is risking little to think that spirit intrusion as the cause of disease in primitive society refers most frequently to illnesses which are not psychopathological.

We may note in passing that the theory of intrusive spirits giving rise to disease has been well known in some very complex non-European societies, including China, Japan, and India. The belief retains life among rural folk of Japan, where illness is still sometimes attributed to possession by spirits of the dead which have not been accorded proper obsequies. When persons die at sea or in other manner so that their bodies are not recovered, they do not receive the funerals necessary to send their souls to the other world. The spirits therefore wander about in the world of human beings searching for a host, and are capable of entering bodies and causing sick-

[6] See, in this connection, Ruth Benedict, "Anthropology and the Abnormal."

ness until appropriate ceremonial is held to send them off to the other world.[7]

In the Western world diabolic possession has been used to explain immoral behavior, especially gross violations of mores.[8] In primitive societies, where religion and morality are not often intimately connected, we might reasonably expect this interpretation to be uncommon. Pertinent information on this subject is both scarce and unclear, yet it is evident that rationalization of flagrant and heinous violations of codes of prescribed behavior sometimes follows similar lines for primitive peoples. We have noted that any antisocial behavior may be blamed upon witchcraft power in the bodies of people called witches, and that among the Ifaluk of Micronesia, bad spirits are the cause of all antisocial behavior. Among the Ojibwa and Cree of Canada, the loathsome supernatural being called Windigo or Wiitiko may once have served to rationalize cannibalism, although modern forms of the "Windigo complex" seem better described as psychotic obsession since they appear to occur in the absence of any real threat of starvation which might override the loathing of cannibalism. Among these Indian tribes cannibalism was violently detested and was never the behavior of the normal person. It was the act of the individual who had been transformed by witchcraft into a Windigo or had become possessed by the loathsome Windigo spirit and was thus compelled to do its bidding. Once transformed or possessed, the individual has a compulsive desire to eat human flesh. Cooper, in discussing the Cree, interprets the cannibalistic craving as originally arising from periodic threats of death by starvation imposed by the harsh environment which sometimes drove the people to cannibalism despite their abhorrence for it.[9]

The harboring in the body of a harmful spirit has its impersonal counterpart in the belief in intrusive objects as the cause of illness. Absent or thin only in Asia, the idea of intrusion by objects is extremely widespread and, except for the Eskimo, is probably uni-

---

[7] E. Norbeck, *Takashima, A Japanese Fishing Community*, pp. 120, 136-37.

[8] See, for example, Aldous Huxley, *The Devils of Loudun.*

[9] J. M. Cooper, "The Cree Witiko Psychosis," pp. 20-24. See also Ruth Landes, "The Abnormal Among the Ojibwa," pp. 14-33.

versal among Indian tribes of the Americas. Because of its great distribution, some scholars have regarded this concept as the oldest theory of disease. Foreign substances, not in themselves ordinarily pathogenic, are thought to be projected into the body by witchcraft, by harmful spirits, or in unspecified manner. Substances which enter the body are extremely varied, and they are occasionally invisible, as among the Carib and Arawak of South America where illness might be attributed to invisible arrows. For the most part, however, intrusive objects are not only tangible but, by means of sleight-of-hand on the part of the religious practitioner who "extracts" them, are displayed to the invalid. Their range is limited principally by size—they must be small—and, of course, by the range of such things, material objects or small living organisms, within the environment of the people concerned. Dixon's account of the Northern Maidu of California gives an idea of the variety of intrusive objects:

The shaman, in choosing the object or objects to be extracted apparently from the man's body, as a rule, bears in mind the habits of the patient. If, for example, he is addicted to chewing tobacco, he may extract a piece of tobacco; if the man is known to be over-fond of fish, the object may be a bundle of sharp fish-bones; etc. Such things as broken glass, broken crockery, arrow-points, bugs or worms of various kinds, young mice, deer-bones, fragments of rock, buttons, bits of wood, bear's teeth, squirrel bones or teeth, grasshoppers, or bits of iron or nails,—these and many other things are among those apparently removed from the sufferer's body. The worms, insects, etc., are always alive when extracted. The patient is allowed to look at the object, whatever it is; and it is buried by the shaman.[10]

Loss of the soul as the cause of illness, a theory with a wide but spotty distribution has perhaps its most elaborate development among the Eskimo. Loss may come about in various ways. (Universally, the soul or the multiple souls of an individual leave the body sometime after death, however caused, although they must sometimes be dispatched to the supernatural world by ritual.) Souls are captured by supernatural beings and by witchcraft, and they also simply become lost in mechanical ways. Supernatural beings might

[10] R. B. Dixon, *The Northern Maidu*, p. 270.

seize souls out of sheer malevolence, as a punishment for transgressions of any kind, or under the compulsion of human sorcerers who control them. Sometimes, as we noted among the Manus, soul substance is viewed in a quantitative way; loss of a little results in sickness and prolonged withholding or loss of much causes death.

Loss of the soul which involves no act by witch or supernatural being may come about in many ways. The soul might escape through orifices of the body while an individual is asleep—and therefore we find injunctions to keep the mouth closed while sleeping. Souls are not only separable from the body but, as we earlier noted, they are sometimes viewed as being only insecurely seated so that sudden, violent movements such as sneezing or starting from a fright might expel them and lead to sickness or death. In primitive societies where the soul is conceived as normally wandering while one sleeps, death might come from failure to find its way back to the body before the individual is fully awake. It may then be hazardous to awaken any sleeping person suddenly before his soul has received warning and time to return.

Witchcraft may cut across other types of supernatural pathogenesis by causing intrusion of spirits, loss of soul, and so on. As we have noted, it makes extensive use of contagious and imitative magic to bring about its effects. Illness and death which come as the result of violations of rules of behavior have already been discussed, and we need add here only that the nature of the illnesses so derived probably covers the complete range of human pathology, with much variation according to society and according to specific breach of norm.

Illness held to be of supernatural cause generally has some supernaturalistic cure. The major but far from invariable exception is the violation of taboos, which may be thought to result inevitably in illness or death. Occasionally, too, primitive peoples flee from a sick person or, rarely, even kill him.

Where more than one interpretation of cause of illness and death is held, the first step of therapy is diagnosis; and where individuals other than the afflicted or the deceased may be blameful, this procedure may include determination of both cause and human

agent responsible. Resting heavily on divination, diagnosis is usually left in the hands of specialists, who may by convention make
this step of curing one of the most elaborate of tribal ceremonials.
Once diagnosis has been made, remedies follow in logical fashion,
and, since they depend upon a limited number of theories of cause,
the principles they describe are also few.

Therapeutic measures for illness caused by intrusive spirits or
objects are simple in theme: remove the cause. Removal from the
body of unwanted spirits may involve any of the personalized techniques of propitiation and coercion; it may also involve any of the
forms of magic and any combination of magical and nonmagical
religious acts. Most commonly, therapy is by means of mechanical
acts of exorcism, sometimes symbolic but often very real in the sense
that they include or consist of physical acts to draw or force out
the spirit as if it had sensory capacities like those of man. Many
formulas center upon making the body as inhospitable as possible:
have the patient swallow or smear him with urine, excrement,
menstrual blood, or other things that are evil tasting, evil smelling,
or regarded for any reason as abhorrent. Fumigate the invalid with
smoke from tobacco or other substances; make his body hot by fire,
water, or steam bath; make it cold; make it alternately hot and
cold; and cauterize it with hot metal or coals. Starve the patient;
massage, press, and step on his body; or beat it with fists, sticks,
and nettles. Force the spirit out by wearing horrifying masks, by
shrieking and otherwise creating as much noise as possible; and
draw it out by emetics, cathartics, enemas, and venesection. The idea
of transference embodied in these latter measures finds additional
use in practices of bringing objects or forms of life into contact with
the afflicted and then killing, destroying, or otherwise disposing of
these new repositories of the spirit and illness. Ritual objects which
are anathema to the spirit may also be manipulated, and it is even
possible to scandalize the intruding spirit into departure by performing revolting or immoral acts. In the Marquesas, a wife sat
naked upon her sick husband's body or naked females leaped over
men to drive out spirits.[11] Local convention might also enlist the

[11] E. S. C. Handy, *Polynesian Religion*, p. 245.

aid of supernatural beings to bring about expulsion. We may recall that the Christian rite of exorcism centered upon a stern command, uttered in the voice of the Lord, for the possessing devil to depart.

Hospitable means such as enticing the spirit out by food or other desirable things or promising to grant its wishes as disclosed by divination are also employed but appear to be far less common than the inhospitable.

The standard treatment for sickness due to intrusive objects is removal of the objects by suction. Most frequently accomplished by direct application of the lips to the body of the invalid, sucking may also be done through the medium of a reed, bone, horn, or other tube, or by symbolic means. Techniques include true cupping, the creation of a vacuum by placing tinder on the body, lighting it, and quickly clapping a horn or other cup-like object over the flame. Sucking might also be done by placing one end of a piece of string at the seat or assumed seat of pain and the other end in the mouth of the primitive curer, a procedure which probably seems no more remarkable in primitive society than actual physical sucking. Cicatrization may precede sucking, but even among the many societies where the skin of the patient is left unbroken, blood presumably drawn from his body may be spat out by the primitive doctor together with the small objects or forms of life which he produces as evidence of success. Like other primitive healing, removal of intrusive objects may be elaborated into ceremonial with many aspects including ritual song and dance. Evidence of strenuous effort on the part of the medical practitioner is often given:

Slowly approaching the patient, he applies his lips to the seat of pain, and sucks violently. After some minutes, he crawls away, acting as if suffering greatly. Returning to the patient, the sucking is repeated, and again the shaman crawls away. The process is repeated several times, till at last the shaman remains by the side of the patient, making great efforts apparently to extract something from his throat. At last, after prolonged retching and effort, the supposed cause of the pain is successfully gotten out, generally with some force, and either through the nose or the mouth.[12]

[12] R. B. Dixon, *op. cit.*, p. 270.

The removal of intrusive objects is sometimes quite symbolic, a circumstance which reveals much about the philosophy of primitive medicine of the societies concerned. Objects may be "removed" by the medicine man with the full knowledge of the patient and other members of the society that they were never actually lodged in the body. Here we have a kind of symbolism which is similar to that which underlies imitative magic—these acts might in fact be interpreted as either imitative magic or as objectification of fears. "An invisible force is dealt with visibly by means that are meant and understood to be symbolic."[13]

Lost souls must, of course, be recovered, and recovery often depends on manner of loss. If the soul has been seized by a supernatural being in punishment for sin or other transgressions then confession, expiation, and purification may be in order. Witches who steal souls must be forced to make restitution, and for this purpose they must generally be identified. Souls, especially those which wander and lose their ways, may be enticed back into the body by offers of food or other desirable things, or it may be necessary for the medicine man to send his own soul to search for them or to have helpful supernatural beings do so. In the Marquesas, lost souls were lured back to the sick person by setting out food by him. The curer then caught the soul and placed it back in the body through the ear. The Hawaiian curer massaged the soul back into place, introducing it under the nail of the big toe and massaging it into the chest.[14] The wide variety of procedures of recovery might also seek to arouse the sympathy of the lost soul itself so that it returns. Among the natives of the central Celebes, in aboriginal times the patient was whipped with the hope that the soul might be moved by this emotion and return.[15] With the major exceptions of washing, steam bathing, and other unconsciously hygienic measures involved in purification, the curative value of procedures for retrieving souls appears to depend chiefly upon the power of suggestion.

[13] R. R. Marett, *Psychology and Folklore*, p. 208.
[14] E. S. C. Handy, *op. cit.*, pp. 185, 246.
[15] M. Bartels, *Die Medizin der Naturvölker*, p. 201.

Ailments resulting from violations of rules of behavior are as varied as human ailments are varied. Like sicknesses due to soul-loss, they may require confession, expiation, and purification. Where harmful power is transmitted to the body by violations of taboos, rites of contagious magic including lustration and other forms of transference are common remedies. Again like measures for re-capturing souls, the value of therapy directed against illness laid to these causes appears to be principally psychological.

Since witchcraft may cause any kind of disease or injury, treatment is expectably various. Counter-witchcraft is standard procedure, and it covers much of the range of supernaturalistic behavior we have discussed. Counter-witchcraft is also sometimes supplemented by measures doubtless regarded by the people concerned as being wholly naturalistic—the banishment, physical beating, or killing of the suspected witch.

Our discussion of primitive medicine began with a statement that it has often included practices which modern science regards as empirically effective. What we see as naturalism in these practices appears seldom to be viewed in this light in primitive society. One can argue that modern man of the civilized world does not understand how his medicines work, that he uses them on faith, and that they are therefore in some degree magical, but his attitude toward them is naturalistic. In primitive society potency is thought to be due to the supernatural power inherent in the objects used and the acts performed. From the standpoint of modern medical theory, the *scientifically* illogical nature of primitive medicine is clearly evident in such customs as treatment of persons other than those afflicted and the extension of dietary and other restrictions to relatives and associates of the invalids. To state the case more directly, primitive medicine is largely supernaturalism but it has often had genuine therapeutic value, and it has served as the foundation of scientific medicine.

Our brief review has omitted much, but it has also mentioned many practices which are ancestral to therapeutic techniques of civilized society, still in use or only recently abandoned. Massage, cauterization, hydrotherapy, heat therapy, venesection, cupping, emetics, cathartics, and enemas—in civilized society all of these forms of therapy have lost their supernaturalism. The analogies of modern homeopathic medicine find many counterparts in the primitive world, and the principle upon which it is founded is, of course, the same as that of imitative magic.

Of the major fields of medicine, surgery is the most poorly developed in primitive society, and the degree to which it is placed in a supernaturalistic context is not always clear from the reports available to us. Fairly effective practices of lancing, bone-setting, and rarely, of using prosthetic devices are, however, recorded.[16] Trephining, the surgical removal of pieces of bone from the skull, presumably to allow harmful spirits to escape, is known from archeological evidence to have existed in Europe in the New Stone Age, and it has also been found here and there among historically known primitive societies. Circumcision and other genital operations are common, but they are done for wholly social and religious rather than therapeutic reasons, and cannot be viewed as true surgery. As might reasonably be expected, surgery tends to be more highly developed among the more elaborate primitive cultures which provide the economic base to allow the development of specialization in labor. Inca medicine represented one of the primitive heights of development of therapy of all kinds and was very impressive to the Spanish conquerors, a circumstance which is less surprising if one reflects upon the state of medicine in Europe during the sixteenth century.

Medicinal plants are particularly plentiful in the pharmacopoeia of primitive societies, and a considerable number of scientific medicines, now sometimes outmoded, have been derived from this source. Mooney states that approximately one-third of the twenty herbs used in sacred curing by the Cherokee were used correctly, in the light of scientific medicine of the late nineteenth century.[17] McKenzie lists 137 modern botanical remedies as undoubtedly emanating from folk medicine (which if not representing primitive societies probably finds its roots there), and lists 42 additional remedies

[16] See E. H. Ackerknecht, ''Primitive Surgery.''
[17] James Mooney, ''The Sacred Formulas of the Cherokees.''

as probably or dubiously so derived.[18] The pharmacopoeia of South American Indian tribes alone has provided scientific medicine with a large number of drugs including ipecac, curare, coca, cascara sagrada, and Peruvian balsam as well as other medicines once used in Europe but now long obsolete.

These statements do not intend to imply that most medicinal plants of primitive society have been scientifically judged to be useful. Ackerknecht's statement that, "From twenty-five to fifty per cent of their pharmacopoeia is often found to be objectively active," seems optimistic.[19] The number whose usefulness has been demonstrated is nevertheless impressive, and it undoubtedly represents the findings of research on only a small fraction of the total. With some notable exceptions such as certain African societies, the Inca of Peru, and various other American Indian tribes, the herbal lore of primitive societies is not well recorded. We can speculate on the basis of aboriginal practices of the Paiute and Shoshonean Indians of Nevada, peoples as culturally impoverished and crude as could be found anywhere in the world but who nevertheless used approximately three hundred species of plants for medicinal purposes.[20] If these circumstances are at all indicative of the primitive world as a whole, an inventory of its botanical remedies must be extremely bulky, and, given only a small percentage as empirically useful, the total would indeed be impressive. Leaving speculation aside, we may note that the results of scientific tests made long ago on primitive medicinal herbs were adequate to stimulate some research in this field on the part of national governments and that an American pharmaceutical concern has recently offered subsidization to anthropologists for the collection of primitive medicinal plants.

How the substantial percentage of objectively useful plants in the primitive pharmacopoeia might have been derived is an open question. It is true that we have no evidence of a process of selection

[18] Dan McKenzie, *The Infancy of Medicine*, pp. 182-184.

[19] E. H. Ackerknecht, "Problems of Primitive Medicine."

[20] Percy Train and others, *Medicinal Uses of Plants by Indian Tribes of Nevada*. No indication is given as to whether these plants were used with attitudes of naturalism or supernaturalism; it is assumed here that most were used because of the supernatural power thought to inhere in them.

by trial and error. Those who have argued against trial and error hold that if, as we are repeatedly told, the plants are employed because of the supernatural power imputed to them, a process of empirical selection is not conceivable. But this argument seems an inconclusive reason for rejecting the theory of a process of trial and error. Supernaturalism has very often bent to naturalism, and remained supernaturalism. A very slow process of trial and error over centuries and millennia might well escape observation at the moment but, like biological evolution, eventually show visible results. And if trial and error are rejected, little is left to explain successful selection except supernatural insight, a theory even less satisfactory. Sigerist has attempted to deal with this question by an interpretation based on instincts: man instinctively chose the suitable plants in the same manner as ailing lower animals eat herbs and lick their wounds.[21]

Few who have concerned themselves with the history of medicine object to seeing the roots of modern medicine in primitive practices such as we have discussed, even though the philosophies of the two are vastly different. It has also been common to regard the primitive medical practitioner as the ancestor of the modern physician. This view has met with objections from Ackerknecht on the grounds that the two share in common only the treatment of disease (to most of us probably quite an adequate reason for regarding them as lineally related). Following the view earlier expressed by Marett, he states that their philosophies are so vastly different that they are antagonists rather than colleagues, and the medicine man is instead the ancestor of the priest, who was for centuries the antagonist of the physician.[22] This argument derives from the view that much of the effectiveness of primitive medicine lies in its psychological aspects.

Primitive medicine certainly does not end with the direct procedures we have discussed; all of primitive medicine may be viewed as unintentional psychotherapy. Primitive psychotherapy has been little studied but it is clear that the fundamentals of modern prac-

[21] H. E. Sigerist, *op. cit.*
[22] E. H. Ackerknecht, *op. cit.*, *p.* 508; R. R. Marett, *The Sacraments of Simple Folk.*

tices are found in these ancient curing ceremonies. The power of suggestion, working sometimes to cause illness and death, operates unconsciously in curative fashion against illness due to suggestion and also doubtless against illness of any other origin. How much primitive psychotherapy might actually contribute toward the recovery and well-being of the patients is impossible to estimate, but it seems hardly less difficult to make confirmable appraisal of the efficiency of modern psychotherapy. The weight of opinion is surely, however, that the positive contributions of modern practice are considerable, and the same may be said of primitive equivalents. In primitive society at least, the therapeutic value of ritual is not always limited to the patient. As we noted in our discussion of religious practitioners, it may also serve the physician in good stead as psychotherapy.

Many similarities between the practices of the primitive curer and the modern psychologist or psychiatrist have been pointed out.[23] The patient is made the center of attention, made to feel cherished, given the support of other human beings, of powerful supernatural beings, and of procedures believed to be effective—and is thus psychologically bolstered. Success of the treatment in both worlds depends upon the patient's trust and faith in the practitioner and his techniques, and the power of suggestion is strongly brought into play. Of the elaborate curing ceremonies of the Navaho, we are told: "There can be no doubt that treatments carried out for nine days and nights on such a high emotional pitch must give results in many cases, and not only hysteria. The very unity of primitive medicine, the fact that it never addresses itself to either body or mind but always to both, explains many of its results also in the somatic field. That a ceremonial in the course of which the patient comes into complete harmony with nature and the universe must have a strong psychotherapeutic value goes without saying."[24]

The psychological value of confession is unquestioned, even if, as

[23] See, for example, J. J. Honigmann, *Culture and Personality*, pp. 420-423; and John Gillin, *The Culture of Security in San Carlos.*

[24] A. H. Leighton and D. C. Leighton, "Elements of Psychotherapy in Navaho Religion."

happens when illness or tension arise from breaches of supernaturally sanctioned rules, both cause and cure are sometimes religious. Speaking of primitive medicine as a whole, we may say that however misguided it might be from the standpoint of scientific theory of disease, it holds the positive if unconscious theory that some action is better than none and infuses confidence and hope into the afflicted.

Like the account given here, most ethnological reports dealing with primitive medicine have emphasized concepts of disease and techniques of diagnosis and cure. Prophylactic measures often escape attention. Dietary and other taboos are very abundant in primitive society; by definition, they involve negative supernatural sanctions and these often enough take the form of disease and death. In addition to the observance of taboos, an enormous variety of other acts and of objects are believed to prevent disease and death. Bodily decoration—painting, tattooing, scarification, the use of ornaments in the nose, ears, and lips—may involve prophylactic as well as aesthetic motives. No systematic research has been done on the subject of the practical prophylaxis of these primitive practices. It is probably impossible to find value in most of them, and some are doubtless harmful or potentially harmful. Yet it is not difficult to see the unconscious prophylactic value of such common primitive customs as abandonment of the dwelling in which someone has died, destruction of the possessions and avoidance of the bodies of the dead, burial or hiding of bodily excretions for fear of exuvial magic worked through them, and isolation of the sick.

And now a final question suggests itself. Our discussion has had little to say about the negative or harmful aspects of primitive medicine. This course of action has been partly one of choice, but it has also been one of necessity because scholars of primitive medicine have also emphasized strongly its positive aspects and the contributions it has made to modern medicine. Perhaps this circumstance reflects human optimism. It undoubtedly reflects in part the interests and objectives of many of the scholars concerned; those who engage in research in the history of medicine are concerned chiefly with lines of development of therapeutic techniques rather than assessments of the collective value of those techniques at any point in time. It is very clear that scholars of primitive medicine assume that its positive aspects considerably outweigh the negative, and this assumption is probably justified. But it is also clear that the question has not been faced and that presently available data do not in any conclusive way support either one view or the other.

Chapter 13. Religious Movements

Organized religious movements under the leadership of divinely inspired prophets promising temporal aid or spiritual salvation to the faithful are abundant in the history of the Western World. Prophets and revelations are familiar elements in the backgrounds of Christianity, Judaism, and Islam, and many of the later forms of Christianity have also stressed them. The emergence of these religions has been correlated with disturbed social conditions, very frequently in the forms of threats to economic security. This is an interpretation which has met with general scholarly acceptance. Carrying the interpretation further, it seems warranted to describe all rapidly emerging new religions—new in the sense that they represent sharp departures from the past—as arising from conditions critical to the welfare of the human beings concerned. The criteria of crisis need not, of course, be objective; to regard oneself as being in danger is in a very real sense to be endangered.

In the brief history of the United States, messianic sects have risen with great frequency. Their continued emergence today, at a time of great national prosperity when economic conditions and standards of health and education have reached their greatest heights, might seem to argue against the interpretation that the religious movements are markers of crisis. Yet potential sources of distress are undoubtedly manifold in a nation as large, socially differentiated, culturally diverse, and rapidly changing as ours, and attempts to seek relief are correspondingly various, following at the same time lines of social class. Christianity has traditionally offered psychological comfort and aid, and those whose attitudes have been least affected by the growth of naturalistic philosophy make greatest

229

use of their religion in forms regarded by others as obsolete. The salvation sects of the modern United States have arisen among the economically and socially least favored sectors of the population. They have been called "refuges of the poor," and their development has been convincingly shown to be associated with economic distress. It has also been noted that these sects quickly lose their messianic tone when the critical conditions faced by the founders cease to be encountered by subsequent generations of their offspring.[1]

In the primitive world, where such social stratification as exists rarely implies subsocieties and subcultures, religious movements of similar sort embracing the whole society have been extremely common in the past several centuries. But let us note that the prophets, messiahs, millennia, and salvation so characteristic of new Western religions represent but one of the many forms which the religious movements of primitive society have taken. All have shared the aims of gaining benefits, whether couched as salvation of the soul, as more earthly boons of economic security and social equality, or as a combination of all, but they have sought these ends in various ways. We have no standardized generic term for these religious upsurges nor do we have fully conventionalized names for the several bents which they take. Wallace has suggested the useful term "revitalization movements" to cover all types, and also any organized, conscious secular movements which "seek to create a more satisfying culture."[2]

In the rapidly emerging movements to which we refer—our concern here is not with the slow, gradual change which applies to all religions and cultures—religion is usually employed in a highly specific manner as a means to explicitly formulated goals, and it is often variously combined with entirely naturalistic actions aimed at the same objectives. Thus military efforts, political maneuvers, economic embargoes, and rules of ethics may be combined with wholly supernaturalistic acts and may be interpreted as religious acts. The relative proportion of supernaturalism in these efforts at

[1] See, for example, E. T. Clark, *The Small Sects in America;* and Michael Argyle, *Religious Behavior.*

[2] A. F. C. Wallace, "Revitalization Movements."

self-aid varies greatly and the borderlines between religious movements, nationalism, and even war is sometimes vague. In many instances, however, the path toward the various goals has been limited to religious acts.

Following European discovery and control over the Americas, Africa, the islands of the Pacific Ocean, and Asian countries, religious movements have arisen again and again among native peoples, and in some areas of the world they continue to rise and wane. The circumstances under which they have emerged appear everywhere to be much alike, unrest and demoralization as the result of contact with Europeans and Americans, the loss of much of the traditional culture without satisfactory adjustment to newly introduced ways, and often also great loss of life from warfare with the newcomers and the diseases introduced by them. Economic distress caused by loss of lands or depletion of natural resources, as so often applied to American Indian tribes, has also frequently been involved. A contributing factor often discernible in movements arising during recent years has been an awareness of inequality with Europeans and Americans in social and economic status and privilege.

A theme frequently associated with these religious movements is an attempt to seek self-aid by reviving conditions of the past or by attempting to perpetuate traditional customs which appear to be threatened by extinction. We are familiar with this idea in our own society in revivalistic religions and even in songs such as "Give Me that Old Time Religion." A similar attitude—we sometimes call it conservatism—is familiar also in many secular contexts, especially in the expressed sentiments of elderly individuals. Disturbed conditions of any kind—war, economic difficulties, tension in international affairs, or a rising incidence of crime and juvenile delinquency —may be attributed to a departure from the "true" American way or, as is popular with professionals in religion, to religious defection. The young who disregard or hold in low esteem long-established traditions of their elders are familiar with the admonition "I don't know what this younger generation is coming to!" Former times are the good old days, and the traditional ways are the good, the tried, and the true ways.

This attitude of clinging to old habits, secular and nonsecular, may be found among mankind everywhere. In the form of organized religious movements, it has come forcibly to the attention of colonial administrators of Western nations controlling primitive tribes. These developments have been given the name "nativistic movements," a label which is presumably also applicable to secular movements seeking to uphold the indigenous culture. Developments described as organized nativism seem always, however, to include religious elements even when the important goals are economic, political, or military, and the movements have often centered upon religious means to these secular goals. Stripped of their supernaturalism, certain movements might be called nationalism, although the connotations of this term make it seem appropriate only for developments among the largest of primitive societies, such as certain African peoples.

To avoid confusion with nationalism or simple conservatism, we may define nativistic movements as organized, witting movements among primitive peoples arising at times of crisis and seeking to provide self-aid through the revival or perpetuation of selected traditional elements of culture.[3] Our definition allows movements to be either religious or secular, but, we repeat, as far as the record of developments given this name goes, religion has always been included, and often in such strong proportion as to warrant the name religious nativism.

In no nativistic movement on which we have information adequate to allow statements of this kind has there been complete rejection of newly introduced elements of culture. Even when the expressed aims demand rejection of all that is new, such things as metal tools, guns, and new varieties of domesticated plants and animals are exempted. In the field of nonmaterial culture, circumstances are less clear but at least unconscious retention of the foreign must frequently occur. In place of truly wholesale rejection, emphasis is generally placed upon following certain traditional ways to ensure the welfare of the people or the return of conditions of the past which have, in comparison and retrospect, become highly desirable.

[3] Adapted from a definition by Ralph Linton, in "Nativistic Movements."

Adherence to traditional religious practices has often enough been the major focus of activity, but revival or retention of other aspects of the indigenous culture may also receive emphasis in conjunction with the religious.

Nativistic movements involving prophets and revelations have thickly dotted the post-European history of the Indian tribes of North America, and it is this region of the earth on which we have the most detailed records on this subject. The messianic nature of Christianity as it came to the Indians has doubtless served to influence the form which most of these movements have taken, but revelations and many other traits of Christianity find similarities and parallels in aboriginal beliefs and it is not always possible to distinguish the indigenous from the foreign in the developmental backgrounds of these new religions.

The earliest nativistic movement of which we have record in North America occurred among the Tewa Indians of New Mexico in the late seventeenth century. Its features follow a pattern which in general outlines serves to describe many of the subsequent developments in primitive society: Under the leadership of Popé, a prophet of established fame as a medicine man, the Tewa sought independence from the heavy-handed rule of the Spanish and return to the ways of old, including the native religion. Unlike most of their brethren of primitive society, they succeeded in driving out the foreigners. This event occurred in 1680 and was accomplished by the use of force. To what extent supernaturalism entered as an element deemed essential to achieve the expulsion is unclear, but the course of events after the expulsion has been recorded: "Those who had been baptized as Christians were washed with yucca suds, the Spanish language and all baptismal names were prohibited; where not already consumed by the burning of the churches, all Christian objects were destroyed and everything done to restore the Old Order of Things."[4]

The rise of religious movements, nativistic in varying degree, among other North American groups roughly coincides with the progress of white settlement of the land. Among the central and

[4] James Mooney, *The Ghost Dance Religion*, p. 659.

easterly tribes, the seventeenth and early eighteenth centuries saw
the birth of many religions, of which the best documented are those
led by "the Delaware Prophet," associated with Pontiac; the Iroquois prophet Handsome Lake, and "the Shawnee Prophet," brother
of Tecumseh. These three religions stressed revealed ethical prescriptions and ritual purification; nativism was included but it was
not one of their most outstanding elements.

The total number of distinguishably different religions arising
among the central and easterly tribes is unknown but it is unquestionably great. Referring to the Delaware alone, Wallace states:

Over a period of three hundred years, some Delaware Indians in the
Oklahoma line participated, as converts or innovators, in varying numbers and with varying enthusiasm, in no less than fifteen separate *new*
religious movements. This is a minimum number; there were almost certainly other movements which I have failed to include. Even with the
minimum number, however, the *average* rate of new-religion-acceptance
by a noticeable part of the population was once every twenty years.[5]

It is noteworthy that religious activities of this kind among the
Delaware began after approximately 1730, when the Delaware first
suffered strongly the effect of white contact. It is noteworthy also
that the first new religion of the Delaware was Christianity, by
conversion, and it may be considered as simply one of the many religious forms which the Delaware employed, shifting from one to
another as the attitude of crisis continued to exist or resurge.

In California, where many of the tribes were early exposed to
contact with the Spanish, an incompletely documented record describes a nativistic movement arising in 1801 in the southern part
of the state.[6] Beginning among the Chumash Indians of the coast
and spreading to tribes of the interior valley and the Sierra Nevada,
the movement centered on the revival of aboriginal religious beliefs.
Circumstances surrounding the emergence appear to have been
oppression by the white overlords coupled with more acute and im-

[5] A. F. C. Wallace, "New Religions among the Delaware Indians, 1600-1900,"
p. 13.

[6] R. F. Heizer, "A California Messianic Movement of 1801 among the Chumash."

mediate anxiety from the heavy loss of life caused by an epidemic of Spanish-introduced disease. California was to have its greatest religious fever at a later time, however, after the native tribes had borne the brunt of the Gold Rush.

During the nineteenth century new religions arose and spread widely among tribes of the Midwest and West, which until this time had escaped contact with white invaders sufficiently strong to endanger their livelihood or seriously to threaten their aboriginal cultures. In the West as well as in the East, the growth of these religions did not immediately follow the arrival of critical times. A period of some years of crisis and demoralization before the emergence of a religious movement appears to be the general pattern everywhere. Once started, however, some of these movements spread like grass fires. Beginning as local conflagrations, they raced to other areas, skipping uninflammable ground here and there, burning fiercely for a time, and dying out. This description best fits the two upsurges (circa 1870 and 1890) of the Ghost Dance religion, which eventually reached dozens of tribes but made no impression on others in its path. Other outstanding western movements have been the Shaker religion of tribes of the northwest coast, beginning about 1882 and deriving its name from the fact that its ritual involved trembling movements of the body,[7] and the Peyote religion, to be discussed shortly.

As the last sentence implies, not all of these religions of the North American Indians are dead. The Peyote religion is not only alive but still spreading. Although their earlier qualities of urgency have been lost, the "Good Message" of Handsome Lake survives in altered form and the Shaker religion appears far from moribund.

In South America, where the Indians were early exposed to sustained and telling contact with Europeans, messianic movements arose quickly. Early records are scanty on details, but they tell us that about 1540 a salvation movement led by a native prophet sent a group of Tupinamba Indians from Brazil to Peru in search of an earthly paradise where they could evade the cataclysm prophesied for the world. Whether Christianity was influential in determining

[7] See H. G. Barnett, *Indian Shakers*.

the form which this movement took is unclear, since the idea of
paradise exists in Tupinamba mythology as well as in Christianity.
During the second half of the sixteenth century and the early
seventeenth century, a number of similar messianic outbursts involving long migrations and incorporating elements of Christianity
with native beliefs are reported among the numerous Tupinamba
and Guarani tribes of Brazil, who were then being enslaved or
driven from their lands by the Portuguese. The last of these mi-
gratory movements is described by Métraux:

> In 1912, a Brazilian scientist, C. Nimuendajú, met on the seashore, not
> far from São Paulo, a pathetic group of Guarani Indians who had been
> halted by the ocean in their quest for the Terrestrial Paradise. They had
> danced tirelessly for several days in the belief that, their bodies made light
> by the constant motion, they could fly across the sky until they arrived at
> the mansion of "Our great mother" who waits for her children in the East.
> Disappointed, but with faith unbroken, they turned back, convinced that,
> having used European clothes and eaten European food, they had become
> too heavy for the celestial adventure.[8]

A messiah arose among the Indians of the old Inca empire in
Peru in 1750 and attracted a following who sought to escape Spanish
rule. The aim of the movement was to perpetuate not the aboriginal
culture but the mixed Spanish-Indian culture of the time, with the
Indians rather than the Spanish dominant. Expressed goals were
military, political, and economic as well as religious, and, as with
many other movements promising salvation, the religious aspects
seem best viewed as techniques for reaching other goals.[9]

As among North American tribes, the total number of new religious movements among South American Indians which appear
to have been responses to European contact is uncounted but great.
Frequently recurrent features of these movements were leadership
by prophetic messiahs, native or *mestizo*, who claimed divinity and
supernatural power of many kinds including the gift of divine healing. Military opposition to the Spanish or Portuguese was some-

---

[8] A. Métraux, "Messiahs of South America," p. 54.
[9] A. Métraux, "A Quechua Messiah in Eastern Peru."

times involved, but it seems frequently to have had less emphasis than salvation by ritual observance. Perpetuation and revival of old traits of culture appear from the often fragmentary records to have had no great prominence as stated aims. With the possible exception of the very earliest of these South American movements, the influence of messianism and other Christian ideas seems strong.

History records an abundance of similar events in other areas of the world among primitive societies whose traditional ways and values have become inadequate or impossible to maintain in the face of contact with Europeans. The native populations of Asia, Africa, and most of Oceania have all produced prophetic saviours, and many of the religious movements they have led may be viewed as incipient nationalism with religious expression. In recent years Melanesia has held a stellar role in the primitive world in the number and vigor of reactionary religious movements.

Religious cults arising in Africa are recorded among the Moslem Arabs from the eighth century.[10] Many cults have subsequently arisen in the Moslem world of Africa, but their total number is dwarfed by that of new religions emerging in Negro Africa during the past century. The grand total—again uncounted—of all new African religions of which record is available surely reaches into the thousands, although many of this number may be regarded as somewhat different local manifestations of common religions.

For information on most of the cults of Negro Africa one must go to mission publications rather than to the accounts of anthropologists because these new religions are nominally Christian offshoots. Anthropologists have seldom regarded conversion to Christianity in the same light as the rise of new native and non-Christian (or essentially non-Christian) religions, a course which seems reasonable enough when conversion has come about as part of a general pattern of assimilation of European culture. It is possible, however, that adoption of Christianity is a phenomenon of the same sort as the rise of native religions. Conversion to Christianity as a possible revitalization movement appears to have escaped the attention of anthropologists for still another reason. So much attention had been

[10] Katesa Schlosser, *Propheten in Afrika.*

given to nativistic elements in new primitive religions that a tendency to view nativism as diagnostic of religious movements in primitive society has been fairly prevalent until very recent times. Ex-
pecting to find no nativism in putatively Christian religions, one
might well pass these African sects by as merely ordinary events of
acculturation.

Sundkler lists the astounding total of 847 native separatist
churches in Africa as of August 1, 1945, and reports the addition of
123 in the ensuing period of less than two years to May 30, 1947.[11]
All of these sects are nativistic in at least the sense that they interpret Christianity after native beliefs or combine the two. Sundkler
describes many of them as being ''deliberately nativistic,'' but the
extent to which nativism represents conscious efforts is not wholly
clear. Whether consciously nativistic or nonnativistic, they are very
likely part and parcel of the phenomenon of religious responses to
stress. The great number of separatist churches, however, can hardly
be used as an index of the severity of crisis. It is also likely that they
are in part reflections of the common tendency to social fission of
these large African societies. As the groups split into smaller divi-
sions, their churches have also become independent and have thereby
caused the total of separatist churches to swell.

Outstanding features of these African sects are prophetic leaders,
revelations, prophesies, and talking in tongues. In these and other
respects the religions conform so closely to the native molds that
Sundkler speaks of them as reversions to native religions.

Other prominent elements are a strong emphasis on ritual observances, conceptions of a Black God, and the belief that admission to
heaven is reserved for Negroes. As may be inferred from the foregoing, these religions have a strong flavor of nationalism. Sundkler
states in this connection: ''The desire of the Zulus or the Fingos or
the Sothos for a tribal church was at the outset not necessarily
caused by . . . nativistic tendencies. The phenomenon of the tribal
church is rather a symptom of awakening Bantu race-consciousness
and nationalism, the African's reply to the colour-bar of the
Whites.''[12]

[11] B. G. M. Sundkler, *Bantu Prophets in South Africa.*
[12] *Ibid.*, p. 298.

Christianity is, of course, not alone in Africa as a missionizing religion. Rapid conversion to Islam has also occurred and is still occurring among African negro tribes, and may be viewed in the same manner as conversion to Christianity. When, for example, a whole community or people suddenly embraces Islam and disavows its own religion to the extent of destroying or otherwise disposing of all idols and paraphernalia of the native faith, grounds are ample for thinking that these events are not simply the orderly, normal result of culture contact.[13]

Factors behind the many new religions of Africa appear to be like those behind similar movements in other areas of the primitive world. Perhaps, as in Melanesia, feelings of inequality with the white man have been of greater importance in Africa than among American Indians and other non-Negroid societies of the world.

For lack of data is is possible to say little of circumstances among primitive peoples under the control of either czarist or communist Russia, and the Communist government has presumably discouraged religious activity of any kind. Ethnographic data on Russian-controlled native peoples is generally very sparse, but a casual search nevertheless yields evidence of at least three nationalistic religious developments. One of these, called Burkhanism, arose in 1904 among the Turkic-speaking Oirot, a herding and hunting people of the Altai region of Siberia.[14] Combining with religion the political goal of independence, this messianic, nativistic movement was soon suppressed by the Russians. A messianic movement with similar objectives arising in the same year among natives of Tanna Tuva, Outer Mongolia, stressed the opposite of nativism—the old faith was to be rejected.[15]

The *Kugu Sorta,* "Big Candle," a name derived from the cult practice of using giant candles made of beeswax, of the Cheremis emerged earlier than the foregoing religions and, losing its nationalism, had a longer life.[16] Until their subjugation by the Russians in the sixteenth century the Cheremis, who speak a Finno-

---

[13] See J. S. Trimingham, *Islam in West Africa.*
[14] Lawrence Krader, ''A Nativistic Movement in Western Siberia.''
[15] R. H. Lowie, *Primitive Religion,* p. 362.
[16] T. A. Sebeok and F. J. Ingeman, *Studies in Cheremis: The Supernatural.*

Ugric tongue and occupy the region between the Volga and Vyatka rivers, had lived as nomadic hunters and gatherers of wild foods. The Big Candle arose in the late nineteenth century at a time of heavy economic oppression from the Russians. After long exposure to Islam while they were under Tatar control before the sixteenth century, the Cheremis were first strongly exposed to Christianity through the Russians in the eighteenth century. The Big Candle movement, in expectable fashion, thus includes features of three religions, Islam, Christianity, and the native pagan belief. Once nationalistic with ideals of an independent Cheremis state, the religion changed to pacifism, emphasizing industry, cooperation, and brotherly love. Here the available record makes no mention of a prophetic saviour, and supernaturalism plays only a small role as a way of controlling the course of events of temporal life. Whether the Big Candle continues to exist today is uncertain; latest available information reports it still vigorous during the 1930's.

With the curious exception of Australia, no major area of the primitive world has failed to produce religious movements after contact with European culture. An inventory of the total is not the objective here, but before we turn to concluding remarks on the nature and functions of these religions, it is useful to examine a few of them in greater detail. For this purpose we have chosen four complex movements, two from North America, one from Melanesia, and one from Africa. At the time of this writing, probably only one of the four, the Ghost Dance religion of North America, may be described as wholly dead as a religious movement.

THE GHOST DANCE RELIGION

The Ghost Dance religion arose from the same tribal source twice, and spread widely in different directions on each occasion. Detailed descriptions of the prophets, their doctrines, and the growth and spread of the religion have been published, and we shall attempt only a brief summary.[17] The movements take their name from the doctrinal belief that the spirits or ghosts of dead relatives would be

---

[17] The earliest major publication is James Mooney, *op. cit.* See also later works by Cora DuBois and A. H. Gayton.

revived as living human beings. The point of origin in both instances is among prophets of the Northern Paiute (also called Paviotso) living at Walker Lake, Nevada. An impoverished people who hold an inconsequential position in the recorded history of Indian-white relations, the chief claim to historic note of the Northern Paiute probably lies in giving birth to the Ghost Dance religion.

In about 1869 a Northern Paiute called Wodziwob began to preach of events supernaturally revealed to him. He was soon joined by another prophet, Weneyuga, who preached the same doctrine. Both were men claiming special power enabling them to communicate with spirits of the dead, and the common prophecy they made had come to them during periods of trance when they had visited the spirit land of the dead. This prophecy was couched in highly specific terms: those who followed the revealed doctrine would find their parents and other close relatives revived. The formula the two prophets espoused to achieve this end was simple, sustained performance of a traditional Northern Paiute dance accompanied by singing divinely revealed songs.

By the time the prophet Weneyuga had converted the neighboring Washo around Reno in 1871 or 1872 he predicted the disappearance of the white people at the time the Indian dead returned, and also a great increase in wealth. The movement spread widely and quickly into California and southern Oregon, receiving locally different interpretation as it advanced, and developing in California into three submovements. Local prophets with their own predictions appeared, and hope and excitement were high for a time. Disillusionment followed when the prophecies failed to come true, and, although some of the local ritual survives today, the religion died as a cult of revitalization after several years of feverish activity.

A resurgence of the Ghost Dance religion occurred about 1889. Predictions came this time from a Northern Paiute called Wovoka, also known by the European name Jack Wilson, who was the son of a follower of the original prophet Wodziwob. The promise was again disappearance of the whites, return of dead relatives, and the return of better conditions of life if revealed rites were followed.

The spread of the doctrine this time was chiefly to the east, especially among the tribes of the Great Plains, where it moved with greater speed and force than the earlier manifestations, and again underwent local modifications. In this area the promise of return to conditions of the past came to include the idea that the now nearly extinct buffalo were to pour back onto the surface of the earth. Although the movement is generally described as pacifistic, magically bullet-proof "ghost shirts" of coarse, white cotton trade cloth became a prominent part of ceremonial regalia. Dancing was prolonged, continuing until many individuals collapsed in a state of trance. As an active nativistic movement, this second Ghost Dance religion died quickly and violently. Disappointment in the failure of predictions to materialize was doubtless a strong factor contributing to its abandonment, but more important was the death in 1890 from the bullets of white soldiers of nearly all of a group of approximately three hundred Dakota Indians, men, women, and children, gathered at Wounded Knee Creek, South Dakota for the performance of Ghost Dance ritual. As with the earlier movement in California, elements of the second wave lingered here and there in ritual performances essentially lacking the active idea of salvation, and certain of these ritual elements probably continue to survive.

The ideas of revelation and salvation of the Ghost Dance religions doubtless reflect in some measure the influence of Christianity, but they also fall within the scope of the aboriginal religion of the Northern Paiute and probably of most other tribes affected. Spier has presented a body of data to support his view that the roots of the Ghost Dance may be traced to the earlier Prophet Dance, which originated among Indians of the Columbia plateau region and spread widely as a religious movement in the nineteenth century before the birth of the Ghost Dance.[18]

Most groups exposed to the doctrines of the Ghost Dance accepted them eagerly or even feverishly but others found no appeal in them. A common explanation of the failure to embrace the cult has been that the exposed but rejecting tribe had not reached the point of cultural disintegration necessary. This reasoning appears to be sound enough for some tribes, but it is clear that even when condi-

[18] Leslie Spier, *The Prophet Dance of the Northwest and its Derivatives.*

tions of cultural decay appeared to offer the greatest encouragement to accept the Ghost Dance other factors prohibited it. The California and Oregon tribes which were exposed to the first Ghost Dance had been hard hit by contact with white Americans. Some, however, had reached a point of sophistication as the result of contact with white culture whereby magical nativism was no longer acceptable. DuBois states that the Hupa and other tribes which rejected the Ghost Dance did so in part because of ''insufficient deterioration'' and in part because it was antagonistic to traditional attitudes. Among the Hupa, the mixed bathing of purification which followed dancing was shocking to the sensibilities; a real fear of ghosts inhibited the idea of resurrection, and a strong sentiment prevailed against speaking of the dead. In some areas of California the predicted death of the whites was interpreted to include individuals of mixed white-Indian ancestry, an idea which was not well received.[19]

The second movement into the Great Plains reached tribes which had in a short period gone from relative economic plenty to abject poverty and demoralization. The buffalo had gone by 1880; the Indians were confined to reservations, and they were supported by scanty government rations. The old and highly valued social order which bestowed social prestige on the basis of feats of valor in war was impossible to maintain and no new order had replaced it. Life as farmers, the future which the United States government had plotted for them, appealed to few, and the Dakotas, as new farmers, had suffered a disastrous drouth. Under these conditions, the Ghost Dance religion generally found the way paved for acceptance.

Again, however, various tribal groups encountered in the spread of the second movement failed to be drawn into it. The Navaho, who were comparatively prosperous at the time and also had a great fear of the dead, found in it no appeal. The harder pressed Apache had produced a religious movement of their own beginning in 1881. Among the pueblos to the southwest, only Taos was touched. States of trance, revelation, and frenzied dancing to the point where the participants lost consciousness found precedents in the religions of most tribes of the West, but these characteristics were far outside

[19] Cora Du Bois, ''The Ghost Dance of 1870 in South-Central California.''

the pattern of life and religious behavior of the more staid puebloans.

The status of the two Ghost Dance religions held among the Nevada Indians which gave birth to them is curious. In their home environments skepticism seemed always to surround Wodziwob and the other Paiute prophets, and the movements never reached among the Northern Paiute the state of excitement and group-wide participation which it had elsewhere. The Nevada Shoshoni, easterly neighbors of the Northern Paiute and culturally very similar to them, appear to have been unaffected by either movement although knowledge of the content of these religions must surely have reached them. A field study of the White Knife Shoshoni of north central Nevada conducted in 1937 when many individuals survived who were young adults in 1889 turned up no evidence that the Ghost Dance had caused even a ripple of excitement.[20]

The lack of interest in the Ghost Dance religions on the part of the Nevada Indians is interesting because there is no shred of doubt that the conditions of life of these tribes were deporable, probably as bad from the standpoint of material well-being as might be found among any tribes in the history of Indian-white contact in the United States. Unable to provide for themselves in traditional ways because of loss of their lands, and largely ignored by the national government, which established few reservations in Nevada until the 1930's, most of the Indians subsisted as best they could by attaching themselves to white-owned mines and ranches, and by begging, stealing, and scavenging. A report on the White Knife Shoshoni by a white farmer-agent of the Indian Bureau of the time describes the sifting of horse manure to retrieve such grain and other seeds as might have been undigested.[21]

Even in prewhite times, however, life had been pitifully meager for these tribes and consisted chiefly of a sustained battle to fill empty stomachs.[22] Virtually everything edible which their harsh,

[20] J. S. Harris, "The White Knife Shoshoni of Nevada," in Ralph Linton, ed., *Acculturation in Seven American Indian Tribes.*

[21] J. S. Harris, *op. cit.*

[22] J. S. Steward, *Basin-Plateau Aboriginal Sociopolitical Groups.*

semidesert environment offered was consumed. Large game animals were few, and the scarcity of sizeable streams seldom allowed fish to be an important item of diet. Roots, bulbs, and seeds of wild plants, gophers, rabbits, and grasshoppers and other insects formed their principal items of diet. The supply of these foods was inadequate to support anything but small face-to-face living groups or to allow more than a very crude development of culture. The habit of digging in the ground for food is the inspiration for the name "Digger Indians" given to these and neighboring tribes by early white travelers and settlers, who commonly regarded the Diggers as the lowest and most despicable form of American Indian life.

Ruth Underhill has referred to the Nevada Indians and neighboring tribes living in similar physical environments as "Those Who Had Little to Lose,"[23] and much of their indifference to the Ghost Dance religions appears to lie in just that circumstance. Conditions among the Indians of Nevada in 1869 and 1889 were deplorable by the standards of whites and of many other Indian tribes, but, by contrast with preexisting conditions of life, the cultural change for the worse brought about by the invasion of Nevada was one of the less drastic suffered by American Indians. It is interesting to note that the stark poverty of their aboriginal life and the qualities of malleability and endurance which it forced upon them appear to have served them well from the standpoint of survival under white domination. Estimated to have totaled between 7000 and 8500 individuals at the time of first contact with white men,[24] their number in 1960 was approximately 6000, a figure which represents a high rate of survival as compared with most tribes of the United States.

Aboriginal conditions may also have entered in another way to influence the reaction of the Nevada Indians to the Ghost Dances. In prewhite times the poverty of the environment in natural resources seldom allowed more than a small number of people to live together habitually, and no over-all tribal political unity existed. The largest social units were the loose, small bands of the Northern Paiute, groups which never exceeded a few hundred persons and

[23] Ruth Underhill, *Red Man's America.*
[24] J. S. Steward, *op. cit.*

which were ordinarily dispersed into smaller units most of the year. Among the Shoshoni, clearly recognizable bands hardly existed, and living groups were generally still smaller in size. Lacking social cohesion, the Indians never presented a truly united front on a tribal level to face their common enemy, the white man. Governmental policies of leaving the Nevada Indians largely to shift for themselves also discouraged the formation of large social units. In 1870 they were dispersed about the state, and some still relied partly for subsistence on old practices of nomadic hunting and gathering. Shortly after this time the national government established a few reservations, inadequate for more than a modest proportion of the Indian population, and in 1889 most Indians remained distributed about the state as before. Thus, at no time did the doctrines of the Ghost Dances encounter large and strongly united groups which might engender a spirit of fervor through the contagion of common belief and joint participation in rites by many people.

These hypotheses do no more than suggest a partial explanation of the apathy of Nevada Indians to the Ghost Dance. A thorough examination of the indigenous religions and other aspects of the cultures of these tribes would doubtless tell us more. One wonders, for example, about the influence of Indian attitudes toward their own religious beliefs. The fact that most individuals were credited with visions and special supernatural power of some sort might work to discourage heavy reliance on the claims of prophets who were not by virtue of either their supernatural gifts or their social statuses especially distinguished.[25] Among these peoples, most contacts with the supernatural were on an individual basis, and the receipt of supernatural power by dream or vision was usually kept secret, at least until the recipient presented proof of its possession by conspicuous success. The Nevada prophets of the Ghost Dance appear never to have been outstandingly successful in any line of endeavor.

THE PEYOTE RELIGION

On the heels of the Ghost Dance came another cult of supernaturalism whose appeal for Indians of the Great Plains and adjoin-

[25] See R. H. Lowie, *Primitive Religion*, who argues that the prophet Wodziwob was not a man of high position or forceful personality.

ing areas lay in supernaturalism of a different order. The peyote plant, the central element of this religion, first reached the Great Plains about 1870, but was of little importance until approximately 1885, when it spread among tribes of the southern plains.[26] A full-fledged cult with elaborate ritual quickly developed and spread to the north. Firmly established today among many tribes of the Plains, the Peyote religion has gone well beyond the borders of this region and continues to spread.

Peyote (*Lophophora williamsii*) is a small, spineless cactus resembling in form a small, squat, and somewhat melted ice cream cone. A mature specimen, when fresh, approaches three inches in length from top to root tip. Only the lowly mounded pale green crown, a small portion of the total plant, protrudes above the ground. Known also as mescal, a name which, as we have noted, is confusingly shared with other plants and with liquors distilled from them, peyote contains a number of narcotic alkaloids. Its natural range is parts of Mexico and the southwestern United States, and most cult centers must import it. The plant is also found outside its natural range among the succulents in western plant nurseries and in home gardens, where its purveyors and cultivators are generally ignorant of its narcotic properties and religious significance.

All parts of the plant may be ingested, but it is most common to excise the rounded crown (button), drying it or using it fresh. When fresh, the button or whole plant may be eaten as is; once dried to a shriveled, leathery consistency it may be preferable or necessary to prepare infusions from it. Physiological effects include "visual, olfactory, and auditory hallucinations, as well as kinaesthetic and synaesthetic derangements."[27] An outstanding feature is hallucinatory color visions, often described as being of dazzling brilliance. Slotkin has given a subjective description of its physiological effects:

After midnight I began to notice the effects of the Peyote. . . . There were slight, visual effects: the fire was the most beautifully colored I've ever seen, and the shadows cast by the fire flickered in time to the drumming. . . . I could hear whispers at the other side of the tipi . . . and at

[26] Weston LaBarre, *The Peyote Cult.*

[27] Weston LaBarre, "Primitive Psychotherapy in Native American Cultures: Peyotism and Confession."

first these whispers seemed to come from right behind me. In all, there was much distortion in auditory acuity and direction. Suddenly I realized as I sat with my eyes closed, that the drumming seemed to be coming from inside of me. I paid some attention to this, and discovered that the distinction between my self and non-self disappeared when I closed my eyes. Puzzled, I explored a little further, and found that my sense of touch was fairly well-gone. For instance, I couldn't feel my [eye]glasses on my face; I had to touch them with my hand in order to make sure they were on. . . . When I concentrated on anything, all my immediate experience fused with it harmoniously, with no distinction between internal and external aspects of experience. I found it very easy to become absorbed in any idea which I contemplated. . . . The Peyote permits one to have a sustained series of mystical experiences lasting for hours.[28]

Many reports have described the euphoric effects of peyote and, as Lewin puts it, the "superior spheres of perception" which it induces.[29] The most glowingly enthusiastic account comes from Aldous Huxley, who subjectively describes the effects of mescalin, one of the alkaloids found in peyote, and recommends as salutary its occasional use by humanity at large as a means of leaving the world of ordinary sensory experience and passing through "The Doors of Perception" to self-transcendence.[30]

Scientific investigators of the effects of peyote are unanimous in stating that its use does not lead to addiction and that they have found no evidence of harmful physiological after-effects such as are produced by cocaine, morphine, and other narcotics. No federal law prohibits its use, but various states have enacted such legislation, presumably on the mistaken grounds that it leads to sexual immorality and violent behavior as well as to harmful addiction. Fearing legal action, Indians of some states are secretive about its use, and fully detailed information on its present distribution in all states is not easily available. Most of the history of the use of peyote by Indians of the United States and Canada is, however, well known to scholars of the subject, who have recorded it in painstaking detail.

Peyote (from the Aztec *peyotl*) was known and used in divina-

[28] J. S. Slotkin, *Menomini Peyotism*, p. 569.
[29] Louis Lewin, *Phantastica, Narcotic and Stimulating Drugs*, p. 107.
[30] Aldouh Huxley, *The Doors of Perception*.

tory ritual by the Aztecs of Mexico before the arrival of the Spanish in the sixteenth century, but was a comparatively unimportant feature of their elaborate ceremonial procedures. Also used by Indians of more northerly areas of Mexico in various rites, it appears to have reached the Great Plains through the Apache. In the late nineteenth century conditions in the Plains were highly favorable to its acceptance. The difficult conditions of life which had made the Ghost Dance seem so attractive still prevailed, and much of the pre-existing supernaturalism was in sympathy with the beliefs and practices of the Peyote religion. Great Plains' conceptions of mana-like supernatural power fitted themselves well to ideas of the properties of peyote. From a mixture of Christianity and Indian beliefs, peyote came to be regarded as the repository of supernatural power placed in it by the Great Spirit (God) for the benefit of the Indians. Power inherent in the plant enables the Indian to communicate directly with the supernatural world by means of the visions which follow its consumption. This pattern of direct contact with supernatural beings is an ancient and well established feature of the religions of the Great Plains, and it is among American Indians whose religions emphasized divine visions that peyote was most acceptable. Some of the beliefs and ritual which grew up about peyote also appears to find precedence in supernaturalistic practices surrounding the use of the coral bean, *Sophora secundiflora,* which has narcotic properties, although ritual involving the coral bean appears never to have approached the importance of the peyote religion.[31]

Still another feature of peyote—the curative properties attributed to it—strongly stimulated its spread. It is regarded as a specific cure for any and every kind of ailment from drunkenness and insanity to injury, disease, and malnutrition, and in addition is credited with prophylactic qualities. Introduction of the peyote religion has often been through the agency of famed Indian peyote doctors whose services have been requested by members of outside tribes.[32]

[31] J. A. Howard, ''The Mescal Bean Cult of the Central and Southern Plains.''

[32] Weston LaBarre, ''Primitive Psychotherapy in Native American Cultures: Peyotism and Confession.''

As we have intimated, ingredients of the Peyote religion are numerous. Outstanding features of indigenous provenience to which we have alluded are native conceptions of supernatural power, herbal curing, and the employment of unusual physiological states interpreted as visionary experiences of religious significance. Added to these and other native beliefs and practices are various elements of Christianity, commonly including the Trinity, the cross and other Christian symbolism, baptism, and Christian prayers. Some scholars have referred to the Christian elements as a veneer, but although the native component seems generally dominant, the two religions are intermingled or blended rather than layered. Sanction of moral codes is also included and probably finds its history in a combination of native custom and Christianity.

Ritual meetings of peyotist groups are night-long observances held weekly or at longer intervals. It is customary to conduct them on Saturday night, and the following day, in accord with white American practice, is a day of rest from the fatigue of the lengthy meeting. Ceremonies begin after darkness falls and are characteristically held in a tepee rather than in a structure of European style. A crescent-shaped, earthen altar on which a large "Father Peyote" is placed serves as the focus of ritual procedures. Participants are seated on the ground. Ritual lays stress on the number four, which, as in aboriginal times among many of the tribes concerned, is invested with special supernatural properties. Within the crescent a fire burns. Rites are typically conducted by four officials and include, in order of precedence, the smoking of cornshucks and tobacco, blessing by rubbing oneself with the smoke of incense cedar placed on the fire, purification by rubbing sagebrush over one's body, and, finally, consumption of peyote. The number of plants ingested varies greatly. When fresh and whole, only two or three might produce the desired effects, but the consumption of as much as forty buttons is reported.

After these preliminaries, most of the night is given to the singing of special peyote songs in ritually prescribed order and manner, each individual in turn singing four songs to the accompaniment of the beating of a drum and the rattling of a gourd. At midnight and at four o'clock in the morning, water-bringing ceremonies are conducted. Prayers to the Christian God and to Indian deities are also made. At dawn, public confession of sins follows, and the assembled individuals are baptized, a rite which involves passing from hand to hand the ceremonial drum, an iron trade kettle containing a little water and various other objects of symbolic value over the top of which a drumhead is stretched. Baptism consists of rubbing oneself with a little of the water or drinking it. Curing may be done at this time, and a ritual breakfast follows as the last religious act. Much of the rest of the morning may be spent resting and talking with friends, recounting and discussing individual visions experienced during the night.[33]

Attitudes of peyotists toward the cultural affiliation of their religion are curious. Although Indian religious elements seem clearly dominant, many peyotists nevertheless regard themselves as Christians. On the other hand, some individuals refer with pride to their religion as being Indian. Despite the existence of this latter attitude and the strong leaning toward aboriginal elements, the Peyote religion seems hardly classifiable as consciously and strongly nativistic, certainly not as being nativistic in the same sense as the Ghost Dance of the Great Plains. It does not seek to reject the white man's culture or to reinstate the Indian. Nor is it messianic; it prophesies neither a millennium nor the coming of a saviour, and, except to the extent that certain peyote doctors are famous, it has no outstanding, forceful figures as leaders and saviours.

In other respects—its goals, the means of achieving these goals, and the circumstances surrounding its emergence—the Peyote religion is an example of the larger phenomenon of religious revitalization. We have noted that its welcome was most enthusiastic among the troubled tribes of the Great Plains whose indigenous beliefs were sympathetic to its acceptance. (Much of the present form of the religion, of course, represents incorporation or adaptation of Plains beliefs and rites which did not originally accompany the introduction of the peyote plant.) In its northward spread from Mexico, peyote reached and found acceptance among some Navaho, then

[33] Drawn principally from Westen LaBarre, *ibid.*

facing troubled times which had not existed when they rejected the Ghost Dance. The pueblo cultures, whose own religions accorded no better with peyotism than with the Ghost Dance, for the most part again passed it by. During the past several decades, the Peyote religion has reached tribes of Nevada and adjoining areas of the Great Basin and its peripheries; again, as with the Ghost Dance, interest and participation among these tribes have not been intense.

The quality of urgency of the modern Peyote religion seems less than that associated with the Ghost Dance or with religious movements among many other societies of the primitive world. It appears, nevertheless, to be much greater than that of prewhite supernaturalism, and its growth and spread have been amply swift to place it in the category of rapidly rising, revitalizing religions. We may also note that circumstances beyond the control of the Indians have served to inhibit its development and sometimes to threaten its existence—i.e., the difficulties in getting the plant itself because of legislation in various states prohibiting its use and the factors behind this prohibition. Particularly forceful opposition to the Peyote religion as being inimical to aims of converting the Indians to Christianity came from American missionary societies, whose representatives had long held positions of influence in the Bureau of Indian Affairs and, until 1930, had control of education on reservations. The common attitude of lay whites that the use of peyote, a narcotic, is immoral has doubtless also had its effects on the Indians. This idea appears to have become communicated to many Indians so that they share rather than endure or suffer from it. Some Indians violently condemn the use of peyote, and probably no tribe has to the last individual joined the Peyote religion.

Yet the movement is both vigorous and expanding. The Peyote religion in organized form exists today among over fifty Indian tribes of the United States and Canada and had a membership in 1956 estimated to exceed 40,000 persons.[34] Most peyotists are members of the Native American Church, an organization first chartered in Oklahoma in 1918. As of 1955, twelve additional states and the Canadian province of Saskatchewan had issued charters to the

[34] O. C. Stewart, ''Peyote and Colorado's Inquisition Law,'' p. 89.

several denominations of the Peyote religion. Indian peyotists themselves are waging a vigorous campaign to have state laws changed to allow the use of the plant. By 1957 these activities had met success in seven of eleven western states.

THE CARGO CULTS

The numerous movements of Melanesia called the Cargo Cults have reached into far more lives than either the Ghost Dance or the Peyote Religion. Beginning in the second half of the nineteenth century with the Water Baby and Tuka or Immortality cults of Fiji,[35] new religions involving native prophets have appeared frequently in Melanesia, and they have waxed and waned with mercurial speed during the past two decades. Most of the twentieth-century movements have been lumped under the title Cargo Cults because they share the common theme of acquiring through supernaturalistic means supplies of European goods ("cargo"—rendered as "kako" or "kago" in Melanesian Pidgin English) to come to them by ships or airplanes. Included under this heading are the Vailala Madness, and the more recent Masinga Rule (or Marching Rule), the Manseren Cult, the John Frum movement, and many other local developments. With the exception of the Vailala Madness, which swept Papua in 1919, cults with a unified set of beliefs and practices have seldom embraced large areas or large numbers of people. The general trend has been toward proliferation in locally somewhat different form, and even local versions applying to a single small area have also changed rapidly. An idea of their abundance may be gained from the fact that a bibliography of writings on these cults published in 1952 totals nearly sixteen pages.[36]

All may be described as xenophobic, anti-British, anti-Dutch, and, during World War II, anti-Japanese. All thus have what might also be called political aims. They seek independence from white domination; but it is utterly impossible as yet to think of a

[35] Laura Thompson, *Fijian Frontier*, pp. 114-121; A. B. Brewster, *Hill Tribes of Fiji.*

[36] Ida Leeson, *Bibliography of Cargo Cults and Other Nativistic Movements in the South Pacific.*

Melanesia politically united in whole or even in any substantial part. Under aboriginal conditions, political unity in Melanesia did not extend beyond the single community or a small number of neighboring communities. Hostility toward all except one's most immediate neighbors was the rule, and this state of affairs was encouraged by the multiplicity of mutually unintelligible dialects of the Papuan and Malayo-Polynesian languages spoken by the peoples of Melanesia. The development of Pidgin English after the coming of Europeans has encouraged tribal intercommunication, and it is often through this *lingua franca* that the ideas of the Cargo Cults have spread from one people to another. A common source of stress, a common if not altogether adequate language, and a religion held more or less in common have served to reduce traditional intergroup enmities, and these factors may also be said to have at least cultivated the ground for the development of Melanesian nationalism.

Like the indigenous religions of the Melanesians, the Cargo Cults are highly specific and concrete in objectives and ritual acts. Goals are not spiritual salvation, transcendental experience, or moral well-being for its own sake (although the Vailala Madness sought to establish European conceptions of morality as a means toward other goals). Instead these movements aim at equality with the white man and free access to cargo, the objects of Western material culture with which he is so abundantly supplied. Arising among societies whose native religions lay great stress on magical means of gaining material ends, these new religions have also emphasized magical manipulation.

Against the background of these general statements, description of the cult as it existed among one of the Melanesian groups, the Garia of New Guinea, will serve us better than further generalities to convey a picture of the nature of the Melanesian religious attempts at self-aid.[37] It is to be remembered that other movements vary greatly in detail and ritual emphasis.

Numbering about three thousand individuals, the Garia live in village communities about forty miles southwest of Madang, and

[37] From Peter Lawrence, "Cargo Cult and Religious Beliefs Among the Garia."

subsist chiefly by simple horticulture. Their first sustained contact with Western culture occurred after World War II by way of Lutheran missionaries and white officials administering native affairs. Many conversions to Christianity were made during the 1930's, but, as seems ever the circumstance when a new religion is first imposed over an old, the result of missionizing was the creation of a third religion, an interpretation of Christianity strongly reflecting the nominally displaced native religion.

In native belief all things of Garia culture are of divine origin, created by a pantheon of gods which human beings may control by propitiation and magic. Spirits of ancestors, which serve as the messengers of the gods, are also important; if properly approached they bring items of material culture from the gods to man. Native interpretation of Christianity conceives Western material culture— the canned goods, cloth, ships and all other cargo—as being God-given and as having existed from the beginning in its present form. God created Paradise, all flora and fauna, and all cargo. He placed Adam and Eve in Paradise with cargo, but cast them out without it because they cohabited. No cargo existed in the world until the time of Noah, who escaped the flood in a vessel identical with modern steel ships. Noah obeyed God's word and was rewarded with cargo, as were his three sons. Shem and Japheth continued to follow God's word and became the ancestors of white men, who still have cargo. Ham was arrogant, lost the privilege of receiving cargo, and went to New Guinea, where his progeny are the New Guinea natives, without cargo because of Ham's defection.

On the basis of interpretations of this kind, Cargo Cult observances of the Garia have consisted of ritual, supernaturally revealed to prophetic leaders, to induce God to send cargo from Paradise.

In an interval of less than ten years from 1944, the Garia became interested in ten different cult prophecies, all but one of which came to them from outside peoples. Formulas have included banning native deities in favor of the Christian God and, at another time, turning against all Christian belief and practice in favor of the native. Conceptions involved in the various prophecies and ritual formulations have, like those of the native religion, been highly concrete. Paradise was conceived as being in the heavens above Sydney, Australia. There God, as the deity of cargo, presided over warehouses full of goods. If the proper rites of control were learned, spirits of dead ancestors would transport the cargo from Paradise down a ladder to Sydney and on to the Garia. Ideas of many kinds circulated: the whites kept the formula of control secret, especially by failing to tell the true name of their god; cargo for the Garia had in fact come down in boxes bearing their names but the whites had changed the names and appropriated it; the God in the teaching of the whites was false and only the New Guinea gods were true. Prophecies also included the idea that Europeans would be wiped out or driven out by the natives with the aid of weapons to come to them in cargo. One prophet—soon placed in jail—predicted the arrival of cargo and the return of the Japanese to help expel the Europeans.

No set of beliefs and practices took firm form or hold. When predictions failed, disillusionment took the form of substituting other but in principle fundamentally similar prophecies, which served to give hope until disappointment came again.

THE MAU MAU RELIGION

In 1952 the British government of Kenya declared a state of emergency as a result of the activities of the Mau Mau organization of the Kikuyu tribesmen of that colony. Even the most casual reader of newspapers is familiar with the terrorism and warfare which followed. The international press devoted much space to these activities, describing them as rebellion by force of arms and giving virtually no indication that religion played a large if auxiliary role. This seems hardly surprising when it is learned that the foremost authority on Kikuyu culture, L. S. B. Leakey, only belatedly saw the importance of the religious aspects of Mau Mau. Leakey, born and bred among the Kikuyu, intimately acquainted with their customs, and speaking their language "as well as, if not better, than English,"[38] in 1952 identified the Mau Mau movement with two earlier Kikuyu political associations which had been banned.[39] In 1954 he

[38] L. S. B. Leakey, *Mau Mau and the Kikuyu*, p. vii.
[39] *Ibid.*

wrote, "What I did not realise then, and in fact have only come to appreciate fully in the past few months, was that Mau Mau, while to some extent synonymous with these political organisations, *was in fact a religion and that it owed its successes to this fact more than to anything else at all.*"[40]

Leakey has provided us with the lone substantial body of data on the Mau Mau religion, and from it emerges a picture of a religion which differs conspicuously from others we have described in being deliberately and shrewdly planned as a means of furthering other and more important aims. Since the Kikuyu represent the culturally most elaborate, the largest, and the socially most complex primitive society of those we have considered, this sophistication is perhaps not surprising. The Kikuyu leaders had, moreover, a background of considerable contact with British culture and experience in political maneuvers.

In Leakey's two accounts of the Mau Mau we find a rich accumulation of the kinds of circumstances which have in other societies fostered the emergence of religions, and we find the birth of not one but several religions. At the end of the nineteenth century the Kikuyu, who subsist by farming and raising cattle, sheep, and goats, experienced a number of catastrophes—an epidemic of smallpox, an outbreak of rinderpest among their cattle, an intense drouth and consequent famine, and a devastating invasion of locusts. As a result of these misfortunes, the population was greatly reduced. Early in the nineteenth century the Kikuyu were dispossessed of a portion of their lands by British settlers, a matter which then, at a time when the population was low, was not a very serious concern. Contact with British culture became close at this time, and under the impact of this association native customs changed very greatly in the interval of approximately fifty years to the time of emergence of the Mau Mau movement in 1948 or 1949. During this period European-introduced medicine and practices of hygiene had brought such an increase in population that farming lands were inadequate. Other sources of discontent and social disturbance lay in the effects of European economy on native social organization, the failure of the new British-imposed educational system to serve all the func-

[40] L. S. B. Leakey, *Defeating Mau Mau*, p. 41.

tions of its traditional counterpart, and in incompatibilities between mission-taught Christianity and native customs.

Traditional marriage customs included "marriage insurance," livestock given by the groom's family to the family of the bride. Since divorce meant that the valuable livestock must be returned, this custom had done much to assure stable unions. After contact with the British it became impossible to follow the old marriage customs for a variety of reasons, the chief of which was poverty. Reduction of lands through alienation and distribution among a greater number of people made the raising of the required livestock difficult or impossible. Under the new order of things in the now heavily populated land, parents and marriageable sons were sometimes so widely separated geographically as to make the normal marriage arrangements unfeasible for that reason alone. Yet the weight of tradition called for the "insurance," which now took principally the form of money, a sum so large that young men forced to rely upon their own earnings had difficulty in finding wives.

A vital feature of traditional Kikuyu customs was a program of extensive training in tribal standards of morality, given to the young in fairly organized form before they underwent the initiation rites at puberty which advanced them to the status of adults. With education left largely in the hands of mission-dominated schools, the importance of initiation rites diminished; little of the former training in morality came to be given; and—an important development— the force of old social sanctions to conformity became greatly weakened. Aboriginal Kikuyu society was organized into several kinds of social units, of which one of the most important in ensuring conformity to norms of behavior by its members was age-graded societies to which all individuals belonged. The diminished strength of this and other social units with punitive functions served to encourage theft, drunkenness, and sexual immorality in the form of premarital intercourse resulting in illegitimate children, breaches of proper conduct which were formerly uncommon.

Mission-taught Christianity was the source of discontent because of its prohibition of native customs of polygyny, circumcision at puberty, and the sacrificial offering of animals in religious rites. The Kikuyu appear long to have had a surplus of females, and the indictment of polygyny left surplus women with no honorable means of earning a livelihood, so that many became prostitutes in towns and cities. Circumcision (of young men; clitoridectomies were performed on adolescent females) at puberty was a custom of great social import as the symbol of advancement to adult status. An important reason for objection to mission prohibitions of these customs came through British-taught literacy: Kikuyu who read the Old Testament (usually in the *lingua franca* Swahili) could find no words proscribing these acts; rather, they found the Old Testament religion was much like their native beliefs and that at least circumcision and sacrifice were also practiced by the ancient Jews.

Added unrest among the Kikuyu sprang from an awareness of social and economic inequality with Europeans. The acquired desire for foods, clothing, and other goods introduced by the British and also for additional secular education of the young had become strong—but Kikuyu economy provided little beyond subsistence. Racial discrimination in both economic and social matters added to their feelings of inequality.

Against this background, we shall sketch the history of Kikuyu religions from the turn of the century. The native faith included a conception of a powerful creating god and goddess, often equated with Adam and Eve, who received homage and who exercised supernatural sanctions over the people. Spirits of ancestors were also important. As we have suggested, much of their religion is described as similar to that of the Old Testament Jews. Added to the personified conceptions of gods and ancestral spirits to which prayer and other forms of propitiation were directed were well developed ideas of ritual pollution from forbidden acts and a complex of beliefs of witchcraft and other magic.

The first course of change in Kikuyu religion was a widespread conversion to Christianity. As time passed and the lack of European ministers brought natives to the pulpit, Kikuyu Christianity came to have an increasingly strong flavor of the indigenous religion. The next step, held in common with many other areas of Negro Africa,

was the establishment of native separatist churches, although a part
of the population remained members of the mission churches. Then
came the Mau Mau religion, a development which was not simul-
taneous with the Mau Mau organization but a later development—
as Leakey sees it, deliberately planned by leaders of that organization to give it the strength which it had lacked as an insurgent
political movement. It is significant that during the time of the revolt a revival of Christianity springing up among the Kikuyu
population was suppressed by the Mau Mau organization.

Chief aims of the Mau Mau (a name reported by Kikuyu tribesmen to be without meaning in their language) were independence,
the abolition or subjugation of all foreigners, the recovery of alien-
ated lands, and the destruction of Christianity. To these were added
the stated aims of abolishing soil conservation, increasing secular
education, and restoring ancient customs whenever possible. The
first two of these latter goals are described as measures designed to
win certain sectors of the population to the cause. Kikuyu women,
who performed most of the agricultural tasks, viewed British-
enforced policies of soil conservation as merely irksome and unnecessary tasks which took them away from the important work of raising
crops. Increased secular education had special appeal for young
men. The restoration of ancient customs was never seriously considered except in such matters as polygyny, initiation ceremonies
and sacrifices to ancestral spirits, and it was used chiefly as a
shibboleth to rouse spirits to the cause. Such attempts at prohibition
of British customs as were made—smoking cigarettes, wearing hats,
drinking English beer—generally met with little enthusiasm.

As an important part of identifying the Mau Mau organization
with religion, leaders attempted to bring the separatist churches
into the fold, reinterpreting their teachings to suit organizational
ends.

The leaders . . . realized that if they could set up a religion . . . they
could achieve much they had never achieved before. . . . Since the vast
majority of those who were to be won over to Mau Mau were people who
already knew the outward forms of the Christian religion . . . Mau Mau
had to be largely based (in its presentation) upon Christianity. A creed

was drawn up, based upon the Apostles' Creed . . . on the cover of the printed form was an exhortation to all who considered themselves to be "true children of Mumbi and Gikuyu" (the Eve and Adam of the tribe) to learn this creed by heart, to say it every morning and evening and to have faith in it. It was a creed affirming faith in Almighty God, but also in His supposedly chosen leaders of the tribe, the leaders of Mau Mau, with Jomo Kenyatta taking the place of Jesus Christ. . . . The religion of Mau Mau was the true religion, and God would bless those who believed in it. Those who opposed it were the opponents of truth and justice and must be fought and resisted by every possible means.[41]

The singing of hymns from Christianity had been popular and this was also taken over. Making use especially of the more emotional hymns, new words were written and books of hymns extolling the native gods were printed and widely circulated.

Probably the most important single element of religion in supporting the Mau Mau cause was the deliberate use of a binding oath at the time of initiation into the organization. Induction into Mau Mau became a religious initiation, replete with impressive symbolism. Full advantage was taken of the psychological impact of traditional ritual acts and inductions were made to resemble the youths' rites of initiation to adult status, the most solemn moments of the individual's life. Ceremonial of induction also required an oath of support and secrecy, imposing upon the initiate extreme supernatural sanctions for violation of his promise. "The fear of supernatural punishments that will follow the breaking of the oath are so much greater (for the majority at least) than the fear of physical consequences, such as imprisonment or a death sentence, that the first easily overcomes the second, until it almost ceases to exist in the awareness of the person concerned."[42]

Leakey's account leaves little doubt that religion was unscrupulously used as a tool. Unwilling tribesmen were made by force to take the oath (behavior quite contrary to Kikuyu custom, whereby the oath was an important but entirely voluntary act in cases of law), and a series of seven or eight graded oaths was developed.

[41] *Ibid.*, pp. 47-48.
[42] *Ibid.*, p. 84.

With each succeeding step the individual was further bound to forget all ties and considerations except the goals of the Mau Mau. Ordinary members took only the first or second oaths. The small number of individuals who took the advanced oaths were fettered to organizational objectives by religious conceptions of another kind. As a part of the oaths they were obliged to perform debasing acts violently contrary to native custom, acts so horrible and degrading that the individual becomes a pariah, polluted and uncleansable. Leakey regards these requirements of the oaths as being so vile that he refrains from describing them. He gives an idea of the enormity of their offensiveness in the eyes of the Kikuyu by stating that they are inconceivable to the average tribesman, so beyond the pale that they were not taken into account in drawing up Kikuyu law (which does impose penalties for incest with one's mother and for some forms of bestiality—offenses which render the guilty person irredeemably polluted). The individual who takes the advanced oaths and commits these acts, Leakey states, is deliberately made into an outcast who can no longer be a member of normal society. People who have taken these oaths are rendered "so abnormal and unnatural that . . . no act of arson or massacre, or disembowelling of victims, can seem to be anything but mild."[43]

At its height, the Mau Mau movement attracted approximately 70 per cent of the population, whereas the earlier political organizations out of which the movement arose had only small followings. This great and intense participation Leakey unequivocally attributes to the role which religion was made to play.

Taking stock of the preceding accounts of rapidly rising religions, we see that messiahs, revelations, prophecies, prayer, magic, adherence to moral codes, and so on—in short, the whole range of distinguishable kinds of religious behavior—may be found in various combinations and with various emphases. Many of the religions have stressed revival or perpetuation of elements of the native culture, and it is for this reason the tendency emerged among ethnologists to call nativistic any religious movement among primitive peoples except conversion to Christianity. It has long been clear, however,

[43] *Ibid.*, p. 84.

that nativism is not the fundamental point at issue and that conscious nativism may be absent, or present in any degree from small to great. In the Peyote religion, for example, a clear-cut focus on nativism is difficult to see, and the Cargo Cults have often favored the new and foreign or have sometimes alternated between the new and the old. From the standpoint of their significance as religious phenomena, it matters not at all whether movements are nativistic or nonnativistic. As we have already suggested, rapid tribal conversions to nominal Christianity or Islam, probably represent events of the same order as movements oriented along indigenous lines. It is also probable that Christianity has exerted its influence upon the form of most of the recorded religious movements of the primitive world and has helped to inspire the rise of some, but the fundamental factors involved in their emergence have always existed as long as religion itself has existed.

All movements are responses to stress and all are, in fact, reinterpretive. It is difficult to imagine any religious upsurge of the magnitude of a movement which might be other than reinterpretive, whether manifest aims focus upon the new or the old. Even those movements which have consciously sought to eradicate the new and exotic in favor of the old and native have reinterpreted the old. Many of the observed religious developments among primitive peoples have been nativistic in the sense that they look primarily to the interest of the in-group and oppose the interests of out-groups; but this attitude is better called nationalism or incipient nationalism.

We have seen that the new religions have frequently been accompanied by militarism or other nonreligious activity. The secular aspects have frequently been supported by the religious, but sometimes the religious have tried to meet objectives unaided by other means. Man has always adjusted himself to his universe by secular and religious techniques, singly and in combination, and the religious have prevailed in areas where he has had no known naturalistic means of control. It is not at all surprising that many peoples placed in tight corners have given religion special significance in the face of the apparent failure of other techniques or in bolstering combination with them.

And now a question arises: have similar movements emerged in native societies untouched by European contact but under stress from indigenous conditions such as epidemics of disease, drouths, and other natural catastrophes, losses in warfare with neighboring tribes, or internal social disturbances? Following the reasoning advanced here that crisis has often been met by organized religion, we could reasonably surmise that religious reorientations have been events of countless frequency in man's history. Unfortunately, of course, the ethnologist has not been present to observe any of these hypothesized events; or, to state the case in another way, where the ethnologist has been present, his culture has generally preceded him. The answer to the question is nevertheless yes—probably, and some small pieces of data may be mustered in its support.

The first religion-inspired migrations of the Tupinamba Indians of South America to which we earlier referred appear to have arisen before any telling contact with Europeans occurred but, unfortunately, available data tell us nothing about the nature of social disturbances presumably stimulating these movements. In North America, the spread of the Prophet Dance may also in some instances have been a response to internal stress. In its early forms this religious complex consisted of native beliefs and practices (Christian elements were added in the nineteenth century), and Spier has suggested that phenomena of this sort were endemic in northwestern America rather than merely a response to the presence of Europeans.[44] Suttles has suggested that the adoption, beginning about 1840, of the Prophet Dance by various tribes of the Coast Salish is partly attributable to causes within the native society itself, specifically to inadequacy of leadership stemming from the "poverty of political institutions" of these societies.[45] Salisbury provides a report of a New Guinea cult which he regards as indigenous in form and inspiration, and argues reasonably that outside pressures are not necessary to the formation of movements of this kind.[46]

Archeologists have occasionally suggested that certain of the re-

[44] Leslie Spier, *op. cit.*
[45] Wayne Suttles, "The Plateau Prophet Dance Among the Coast Salish."
[46] R. F. Salisbury, "An Indigenous New Guinea Cult."

mains of extinct cultures suggest the rise of cults. The "Southern Death Cult" of the Mississippi Valley and the southeastern United States, dating from approximately A.D. 1450 to A.D. 1650, is inferred from the distribution and distinctive form of various implements, ornaments, and art styles that appear rather abruptly in a number of sites. Conspicuous among these items are lavish headdresses in which copper is used. It has been suggested that these paraphernalia indicate a religious revival, caused by "a premonition of impending doom" from rumors of the Spanish conquest of Mexico; the barbarous treatment of the southwestern Indians by the Spaniards; the cruelty and killing by DeSoto's expedition; and perhaps by such misfortunes as epidemics of new and strange diseases and crop failures. These contacts with the white man did not occur, however, until the sixteenth century. Presumably for this reason, the curious hypothesis has been presented that the cult activity which the obpects suggest began approximately a century after the date the objects first appear in archeological sites.[47] The existence of a similar indigenous cult among Indians on the Columbia River in prehistoric and early historic times has been suggested on the basis of carvings in wood, bone, and stone.[48] Changes or innovations in art, architecture, and ritual objects in pre-Spanish Mexico in the "cult of Quetzalcoatl" have also been interpreted as suggesting the introduction of a new religion.[49] A thorough comparative examination of archeological finds in these and other areas such as Peru, Mesopotamia, and the Indus Valley should be rewarding.

Another question one might wish to ask concerns the value of religious movements to the peoples concerned. It is true that most of the historically known movements of primitive society have not reached their stated objectives, but they have probably never been unqualified failures. Perhaps all have succeeded in giving hope for weeks, months, or years until the final disappointment, or until needs and desires were met in other ways.

[47] P. S. Martin, G. I. Quimby, and D. Collier, *Indians Before Columbus*, pp. 361-366.

[48] W. D. Strong, "Occurrence and Wider Implications of a 'Ghost Cult' on the Columbia River Suggested by Carvings in Wood, Bone and Stone."

[49] See G. C. Vaillant, *Aztecs of Mexico*.

In the past, religious movements of primitive societies have been matters of interest in the Western World chiefly to scholars, and to colonial administrators and officials of bureaus of native affairs as irritants or as obstacles standing in the way of aims of the controlling nations. Except when the religions have included or centered upon military and political objectives, they have generally failed to come to the attention of other members of the dominating societies or have been regarded as events of little import. In a world where conceptions of the proper role of human being to human being is changing to give less weight to differences of race and culture, the religious strivings of primitive societies, as indices of stress, carry significance beyond that of serving merely as subjects of academic interest.

Chapter 14. Religion,

Primitive and Civilized

This discussion has omitted much and given short shrift to much else. This is in part a reflection of personal interest, and needs no apology. In other instances, sketchy treatment and omission represent scarcity of information or difficulty in presentation. It is not possible in a few or even quite a few pages to present with any fidelity the content of studies of individual primitive religions that point out the intricate enmeshing of religious beliefs and acts with the economy, social and political structure, and other aspects of the culture of the people concerned. Interesting recent studies of this kind are in print, but they are suitable for reading only in their original forms.[1] A cogent reason for slighting these books is that this survey attempts to make some general observations about primitive religions. The studies in question are concerned with single religions, societies, and cultures, which they treat as self-contained, closed systems. They are poorly suited to comparative study because they do not seek to generalize and they do not always present their data in a form suitable for comparison.

It is unfortunately true that very few comparative studies of primitive religion of any sizeable compass have been attempted in America during the past two decades; and none has been attempted in England, where a common view seems to be that we must understand every detail of the social and cultural context of each religion from the native viewpoint before any kind of comparison is attempted. We seriously doubt that a full comprehension of the native view—something which seems hardly attainable—is necessary for

[1] See, for example, E. E. Evans-Pritchard, *Nuer Religion*.

the comparative study of many aspects of religion or that it constitutes the most desirable basic data for a study of anything except
comparative theology or eschatology.

There is no doubt of religion's alliance with the rest of culture,
and an interplay is evident in many ways. To cite the most obvious
kinds of examples, farmers do not worship gods of the sea, hunters
have no rites for the Corn Mother, and educated citizens of the modern nations have no gods that cause disease or thunderstorms. Religion has often given support to the social scheme, the political
hierarchy, the economic organization, and to customs that are important in maintaining social order. The most exhaustive study of
religions, both primitive and civilized, will doubtless tell us little
more than this about the societally integrative role of religion. It
seems most doubtful that study will reveal blanket support of the
social *status quo* or of the whole of culture as a universal trait of
religion, although it will doubtless point out manifold linkages of
various kinds. One of the few recent comparative studies of primitive religions tells us, with respect to economics, only what anyone
moderately familiar with primitive society has doubtless concluded
without painstaking "inductive" study, that religion may both
encourage and inhibit man's economic affairs: ". . . the religious
system helps to motivate, guide, distribute, and validate the produc-
tive energies of the individuals in it, not always in the most efficient
way."[2] Similar statements are made concerning the relationship
between religion and the family, and religion and "political action."

We repeat, religion may often be seen to give societal support,
although this support is not uniform in all societies and we have no
assurance that the supportive effects always outweigh the disruptive.
The ingenious dedication with which scholars have worked to see
these probable effects, their redefinition of religion to suit these
theoretical ends, and the willing acceptance of their ideas by much
of the educated public are themselves subjects for investigation.
They suggest the defense of a cause.

Among scholars as well as other citizens there appears to be a
dedication to the idea that religion is "good," a dedication, con-

---

[2] W. J. Goode, *Religion Among the Primitives*, p. 137.

scious or unconscious, to the idea that religion is and must be imperishably with us. Religion is something to be defended, and it appears to be defended even by those who are unable to see themselves doing so. Three decades ago V. F. Calverton published an essay on a subject he called "cultural compulsives," customs of our culture which have assumed such value to us, have become so thoroughly established that they seem the only right and true ways, and are so surrounded by emotion that we defend them wittingly and unwittingly.[3] Calverton discussed in particular monogamy and the attempts at the end of the nineteenth century by the anthropologist Edward Westermarck to defend this institution of his own society by arguing on the basis of selected evidence, dubious even at the time, that apes are monogamous. Calverton and others have noted that monotheism and the institution of private property have been defended in similar fashion.[4]

Perhaps religion—not merely monotheism but, however interpreted, something called religion—is receiving the same treatment in our society today. It is inconceivable to many citizens that any of his fellows could lack religion, and any philosophy of life or set of ethical mandates is given this name. Scholars of religion in the social sciences often express similar views by defining religion secularly in such a way as to credit every member of society with it. The sociologist Talcott Parsons, for example, states: "Religious beliefs then are those which are concerned with moral problems of human action, and the features of the human situation, and the place of man and society in the cosmos, which are most relevant to his moral attitudes, and value-orientation patterns."[5] Another characteristic is added by Parsons to distinguish the religious. Ideas that are merely intellectual or cognitive, concerned with intellectual problems, are not religious. They become religious when they involve "commitment" in emotion and action, when they are "taken seriously."[6] Essentially the same view of religion is current outside

---

[3] V. F. Calverton, "Modern Anthropology and the Theory of Cultural Compulsives," in V. F. Calverton, ed., *The Making of Man.*

[4] See L. A. White, *The Evolution of Culture*, pp. 255-258.

[5] Talcott Parsons, *The Social System*, p. 368.

[6] *Ibid.*

the world of professional scholars in the United States. For many Americans, religion has come to mean ideas, ideals, or goals about which one feels strongly or desires intensely. Attachment to Communism, money, moral codes, and compulsive behavior of various kinds have been called religion.

This definition is unquestionably Western, and it reflects a changing culture with concomitant change in conceptions of religion. It seems also to reflect the history of Christianity. Christianity has traditionally involved strong emotional attitudes, laid great stress on worldly morality, and it has been dogmatic. The term dogma has, of course, more than one meaning. We refer here to the authoritative laying down of doctrine without regard to empirical evidence, thereby implying defense and persistent retention of the doctrine. Dogma so defined revolves about the coexistence of belief and skepticism that has marked the history of Christianity. We judge an individual as religious or nonreligious on the basis of whether or not he holds religious beliefs, and those who pass judgment often demand that he hold the same religious beliefs as they. Not one but many views obtain, and mutual accusations of dogmatism have been common. The very authoritativeness of Christian religious doctrines is, in fact, contingent upon the existence of differing views and of skepticism directed toward them. Christianity emerged and spent its infancy in an atmosphere of opposition and skepticism, and as a militantly exclusive and missionizing religion it has continued to meet opposition. In its later history, after the rapid expansion of science, it met strong skepticism directed toward traditional interpretations of the Bible.

Dogmatism in the sense of emotional defense of a belief or custom is, of course, not limited to religion. We have already referred to monogamy and private property, which, although supported by Christian doctrine, were probably never viewed as religious issues by the scholars who rose to their defense. With the growth of science, skepticism has been extended toward all kinds of philosophy and rationalization including the scientific itself, and unreasoning defense of scientific views has not been remarkably unusual. In our history, however, this sort of defense has been most violent when the scientific view has seemed to challenge or threaten to displace the religious view.

We have noted that under conditions of stress primitive religions have often changed, but dogged retention of the old is by no means always the pattern. In this respect, most primitive religions differ sharply from those of the West. A frequent response of primitive people to the new and foreign in supernaturalism is one of interest and welcome, and it is often accompanied by secrecy about one's own religious beliefs and acts. Like the civilized housewife who collects recipes, primitive peoples often eagerly accept foreign practices of supernaturalism, viewing them as additional techniques for mastery of the universe rather than as replacements of the traditional. This is not to say that conflict and resistance to the new do not exist; foreign religious elements antithetical to indigenous beliefs certainly may not find ready acceptance. Primitive and civilized religions are, however, similar enough not to be complete and utterly incompatible strangers. The growth of skepticism and the rejection of the traditional religion have occurred frequently enough among primitive societies exposed to Western civilization, even though under these circumstances the new religion has always been a hybrid of the old and the new.

Under aboriginal conditions, primitive peoples appear seldom to examine their religious beliefs critically. No fundamentally different and opposing interpretation ordinarily exists, and the traditional beliefs are simply accepted as another part of tradition. It is probably true that the existence of skeptics, individuals who doubt the religious interpretation of their society, is not limited to modern times. Paul Radin has held that skeptics are a normal part of all societies including the primitive. Radin does not, however, support this seemingly reasonable idea with much factual evidence, and, in any case, his statements concerning primitive skeptics convey the idea that they are passive individuals carried along with the crowd rather than aggressive dissidents.[7] Whatever the incidence of skeptics in primitive society might be, it seems clear that their skepticism has not reflected or brought about any fundamental change in reli-

[7] Paul Radin, *Primitive Religion.*

gious beliefs. The issue in primitive society has not been one of
naturalism versus supernaturalism.

In short, available information suggests that during most of the
period of man's existence religion has not been an issue whose basic
validity has been subjected to active debate or dispute. Supernaturalistic beliefs and practices have been matters for routine acceptance as a part of a greater body of traditional learning which
provided few or no alternate conceptions. The superstructure of
ritual and myth and the roster of supernatural beings and objects
have doubtless changed repeatedly. We can reasonably surmise that
religious conflict arose from time to time, especially when man's
culture underwent great economic change or at times of stress, and
we have already presented some evidence suggesting that events of
this kind have occurred. As judged from archeological evidence,
most of the period of man's existence in the world has seen little
revolutionary change in his culture. During this long span of a
half-million or more years until approximately eight thousand years
ago man remained a hunter and gatherer of foods whose culture
was very simple. Crises doubtless arose frequently during this time,
but we have no evidence to lead us to think that they inspired any
change in religion beyond substitution of fundamentally similar
ideas and acts for those which might have appeared to be false or
to have failed. If, indeed, it is true that religion is closely linked
with other aspects of culture, we could hardly expect to find change
in religion during most of man's history that would indicate any
fundamental change in world view.

The great change in conceptions of the nature of the universe
and in religion in the West arose with the growth and acceptance of
science. Before that time there were no truly basic differences between Western religions and those of primitive society. At least, the
similarities are far more striking than the differences. With the
growth of science, much that traditionally fell within the scope of
religion moved into the realm of science, often only after a long and
bitter struggle. The pattern itself of the growth and acceptance of
scientific interpretation is significant. Emerging first in astronomy
and other physical sciences and representing the sectors of man's

universe least intimately concerned with and influencing his ideas, ideals, and behavior, scientific interpretation gradually drew closer to man until it finally took to examination of man himself and his culture.[8] Objectivity emerged first where it was easiest to gain, and we are yet far from reaching a detached, scientific viewpoint in our observation of ourselves and our culture. It is much easier for us to reject the explosion theory of the creation of the universe in favor of the steady state theory than it is to accept the idea that polygamy does not inherently involve a moral issue or to deny the idea of free will.

With rare exception until recent times religion has been defined one way or another on the basis of supernaturalism. It is possible to argue that religion has always served the roles imputed to it by nineteenth- and twentieth-century scholars and, therefore, the definition of religion should be based upon those roles. But this stand ignores trends of change that are outstanding and significant. Radcliffe-Brown has argued that Confucius regarded the supernaturalistic aspects of religion as unimportant and viewed it as a device for unifying society and supporting social values.[9] There have doubtless been other early philosophers who have looked upon religion in this way, but until modern times they represent a tiny minority.

In this connection it is useful to look at some of the recent trends of religious development among the general population of our own nation. Increasing latitude is allowed to those regarded as religious in their interpretations of man and the universe. The fundamentalist is by and large the person least exposed to scientific philosophy, and the name given to him implies changing ideas of religion. For the nonfundamentalist religious majority, conceptions of God tend away from the concrete and anthropomorphic toward the remote, abstract, and vague; and religious doctrine tends increasingly away from rigid dogma toward broad philosophy, often relating to morality. Most of the above statements may be summarized in the observation

---

[8] See L. A. White, ''The Expansion of the Scope of Science,'' in *The Science of Culture*.

[9] A. R. Radcliffe-Brown, ''Religion and Society.''

that religious change has been toward increasing secularization. By
the standards of yesterday, many, perhaps most, Americans and
Europeans are heretics. Religion in its older form has survived
where man has the least control by naturalistic means or the least
acquaintance with scientific interpretation.

Our discussion suggests a number of questions. Is the growing
trend toward redefinition of religion in secular terms a reflection of
scholarly observation that has seemed to reveal its prime significance
as social or moral? Is this tendency only a religious retrenchment
following the growth of scientific thought that gives increasingly
small room to supernaturalism? Does the new definition of religion
bear any relation to the vested theoretical interests of social scientists in deducing social value from our beliefs and customs, or represent the influence upon their theorizing of Western religions that
have emphasized emotionalism and morality? Returning to the ideas
of Calverton, does it represent unconscious defense of a cultural
trait that has been doggedly defended for many centuries and has
repeatedly retrenched through modification?

The answers to these questions are not forthcoming, but it is evident that they and the circumstances they imply all indicate pro-
found cultural and religious change. As culture-bearing animals
and members of society, our scholars have been carried along by
the cultural currents about them. Like other words of language, the
term religion has no inherent meaning, and redefinition in keeping
with a changed significance seems altogether in order.

There is no reason to think that religion will not continue to
evolve. The evolution of religion, religion in a generic sense rather
than the historic developments of individual religious complexes, is
a subject that has received little scholarly attention since the nineteenth century. After the beginning of the twentieth century any
kind of theorizing, and particularly ideas of cultural evolution, were
looked upon with strong disfavor in anthropology. With a few
notable exceptions, for two decades or more ethnological writings
on primitive religions were generally descriptive and historical.
After analytic interpretation and generalization again became re-
spectable, interests turned chiefly to the customs and institutions

that make the social order possible, as these chapters amply testify. With the exception of histories of individual religions and native religious movements such as we have discussed, little attention was directed toward religious change.

Yet there is no question that great change has taken place in the religions of the great industrialized nations. A question at issue is whether it is apt to use the term evolution or whether we must simply call it change, a word that arouses less antagonism. Treating all of the known cultures of mankind, it seems both possible and useful to attempt to make correlations between types of religion and types of culture or society, and some small attempts have been made to do so.[10] Theology and the acts of religion depend upon the social or cultural environment to which a people are exposed, and this cultural environment in turn reflects their technology, the natural environment, and the influence of past conditions. If evolutionary theory is fruitfully applicable to culture as a whole, it must be equally applicable to religion.

But first, much remains to be done in formulating religious, cultural, and social types. It is clear enough that supernatural beliefs and practices of primitive peoples such as we have described are incompatible with the culture of modern industrialized society, but this observation is hardly a generalization or law. At present we have no scientifically validated laws allowing us to predict religious patterns that will be associated with particular institutions or levels of technological development. No doubt illuminating generalizations on religious evolution can be formulated, although attempts to link types of religions or theology directly with types or stages of technological development may well be difficult. Probably, also, generalization may be more easily couched in terms of the naturalistic or scientific philosophy upon which technological development has depended. What will probably prove most feasible is a correlation of types of philosophy including religion with cultural or societal types, and formulation of the latter will surely depend in large measure upon economic considerations.

[10] See, for example, E. K. Nottingham, *Religion and Society;* and L. A. White, *The Evolution of Culture.*

Anthropologists have lengthily pointed out to all who would listen that culture follows patterns. And, of course, everyone who has ever considered the matter knows that all classes of phenomena of our universe including biota, heavenly bodies, atomic structures, the currents of mountain streams, the structure of snowflakes, and forms of human mental derangement are patterned. If culture and religion represent valid scientific categories, it would be most remarkable to find them lacking in patterns, either patterns at fixed points in time or patterns of change.

We have noted in the foregoing chapters great diversity in the religions of mankind but also very much that is held in common. Although we do not clearly know its boundaries, the range of men's cultural behavior surely falls within a restricted scope; and the patterns and potentials of religion, as a part of culture, are also limited. Much further comparative study is necessary before we may safely venture to offer many generalizations on the nature of religion and religious change. Reviewing the data presented here we may, however, make a number of statements concerning the nature and functions of religion among both primitive and civilized societies.

Religion does not stand by itself discretely but, as a part of culture, is intimately linked with other parts of the whole. Like the rest of culture, religion undergoes constant, if often slight and inconsequential, change. As other important parts of culture change significantly, religion also changes to correspond, and it, in turn, exerts its own influence toward change. There seems to be no evidence to indicate that religions independently spring full blown as motivating or fundamental factors in the integration of society and the growth of civilizations. Rather, religions emerge and change as the result of more fundamental factors, the manner of gaining a livelihood and the related ordering of society. Once instituted, however, religious beliefs and customs, like other customs and attitudes, seem to have a kind of autonomy, a value beyond their intrinsic value, and, especially because religious values involve the emotions, they may exert great influence on the rest of culture. We have only to think here of such examples as the numerous religious prohibitions against eating certain foods, against intercaste social relations of various kinds in India, religiously dressed rules favoring or prohibiting polygamy, and the religious support in some societies of industry and thrift. Social and economic organization have without doubt been the influential factors in the original establishment of these customs, but, once established as religious ideas, they have considerable tenacity in the face of change in the conditions that gave them birth. Despite this autonomy and tenacity, religion has changed greatly among the industrialized nations, and it seems doubtful that it can anyplace be so surrounded with affect that it is able to remain unaltered by substantially changed conditions of life.

Many persons have called attention to a heightening of religious activity in the United States that began about 1940.[11] Although statistics supplied by churches disagree, it seems clear that membership in the major churches and sects and church attendance have grown considerably faster than the rise in population. Some have called these events a religious revival, a term which seems particularly inept because it suggests a resurgence of traditional religion. Whatever these developments indicate, it is clear that they are not revival movements.

Popular thought has linked these events with crisis, and it is current fashion to say that modern life is beset with anxiety. This is an idea with a substantial history, reaching back into earlier days of the industrial revolution and, coincidentally, to the time of the first real acquaintance of Europeans with primitive peoples. Rousseau's conception of primitive life as an idyll of simplicity is surely not unique to him but represents thought current in educated circles of the time. Since the days of Rousseau this theme has received ever-wider currency. The stresses and strains of modern civilization, we are told on every hand, are growing intolerable, and civilized man needs some form of aid to withstand them.

On the side of caution, it must be stated that we lack evidence to indicate that anxiety and the factors which give rise to it are inevitable features of elaborate, industrialized civilizations. Only the

[11] See, for example, Michael Argyle, *Religious Behaviour;* and J. M. Yinger, *Religion, Society and the Individual.*

slightest acquaintance with the conditions of life in many primitive societies leads to extreme skepticism of the idea that cultural simplicity and freedom from anxiety are necessary or even common companions. The sources of insecurity of modern Americans, for example, seem trifling as compared with those we can infer for ancient Paleolithic men, and they seem equally small as compared with observed conditions among a good many modern primitive tribes. There is probably much, however, in another idea, that a competitive and rapidly changing culture rather than merely a complex one imposes problems of adjustment and readjustment for many individuals.

The prevalence of the idea that modern civilization imposes psychological strains of critical proportion is probably also in part a function of man's increasing awareness of and interest in his own psychological state. Thus it may be viewed as one facet of a general philosophical trend of the past several centuries, as a part of the growth of science during this period. Turning objective eyes to the phenomena of the universe, man has not neglected attention to himself. He has become aware of the tensions which the events of human life produce, and he has consciously sought both secular and religious means to alleviate them.

The complexity of modern life seems for more than one reason questionable as an explanation of the heightened religious activity in the United States. Our culture is surely complex, but few of us participate in more than a small fraction of the total culture. If compensation, solace, or relief from tension are increasingly necessary to prevent psychological disintegration, we have no clear evidence in the form of increased and intense religiosity of traditional sort by the population at large to indicate these needs are met by recourse to religion. Religion may indeed be an aid for most of the American population, but, if we exclude members of the fundamentalist and salvation sects, it does not take traditional form, and it is variously displaced or augmented by reliance on such secular devices as professional and amateur psychotherapy, drugs, alcohol, and secular philosophy.

Popular theories concerning the apparent increase in religious activity in the United States have also included the ideas that heightened interest in religion is part of an increased intellectual curiosity associated with rising standards of education, and that church affiliation and attendance represent a search for reassuring stability in a society undergoing rapid change.

A comparison of religious behavior in the United States and Great Britain casts doubt on some of these ideas, and offers another explanation, one that takes us back to the subject of religious change. Church membership and attendance in the United States are reported to be proportionately two to three times greater than in the British Isles. A plausible explanation, offered to account for the difference is that official religion in America has changed the more so that it accords with the values of the American middle class. Religion in the United States, as we have noted, has become liberal and secular, whereas the official religion of Britain's churches has clung more closely to a traditional form so that it has little pertinence or interest for most of the population.[12]

The foregoing leads to the question of the future of religion. If religion means only fallacious supernaturalism, then it appears to be doomed as soon as scientific interpretations are advanced and have demonstrated their validity and usefulness by the results they achieve. For more than one reason this seems to be an unrealistic view. There may indeed be naturalistic explanations for all phenomena, but we do not know that we will ever be able to formulate them or that they will give satisfaction. Man does not live by cool reason alone. We do not choose our spouses or conduct much of our lives in a wholly rational, matter-of-fact way. Our habitual diets are not made of the foods that we know to be the most nutritious, digestible, or otherwise suitable to health and pocketbook. Well-being can be measured in many ways. The importance of religion to many men seems to lie in its nonrational character, in the emotional satisfaction it provides. For these, religion in the form of supernaturalism will doubtless long continue to be preferred.

We have been both victims and beneficiaries of religion as supernaturalism. For a society to survive, it must share goals and values;

12 Michael Argyle, *op. cit.*

and religion in supernaturalistic form has often served man well by justifying and supporting social ideals. We have no doubt that the contributions of religion to the welfare of man have outweighed the harm it has done, that it has had survival value for the human species, and that it will continue to have this significance for many. Perhaps we too are swayed by the tradition that religion is good, for we can offer no wholly satisfactory support for these opinions. This endorsement—that religion is good—does not mean to say that religion in any form is necessary or that it is the most efficient or even the most satisfying invention of man for the uses to which it has been put. A substantial part of the population of the great societies of the modern world refuses to be credited with religion, and for these people the roles which religion continues to fill for others are presumably handled in secular ways. But the question of the value of religion, however religion is conceived, is one that can be answered satisfactorily only in retrospect, from a vantage point sometime in the distant future.

The future trend of religious change appears to be toward increasing secularization, but whether this trend will carry on to the disappearance of supernaturalism is uncertain. Religion as supernaturalism is far from moribund, and long survival in this form seems assured. It also seems certain, whether or not supernaturalism dies, that something called religion will long be with us and that its nature will continue to change.

BIBLIOGRAPHY

Abbreviations

AA	American Anthropologist
AAA	American Anthropological Association
AES	American Ethnological Society
BAE	Bureau of American Ethnology
BHM	Bulletin of the History of Medicine
JRAI	Journal of the Royal Anthropological Institute
SWJA	Southwestern Journal of Anthropology
UCAR	University of California Anthropological Records
UCPAAE	University of California Publications in American Archaeology and Ethnology

Aberle, D. F., and Stewart, O. C. *Navaho and Ute Peyotism.* University of Colorado Studies, Series in Anthropology No. 6. Boulder: University of Colorado Press, 1957.

Ackerknecht, E. H. "Problems of Primitive Medicine," *BHM,* 11 (1942), 503-521.

Ackerknecht, E. H. "Psychopathology, Primitive Medicine and Culture," *BHM,* 12 (1942), 545-574.

Ackerknecht, E. H. "Natural Diseases and Rational Treatment in Primitive Medicine," *BHM,* 19 (1946), 467-97.

Ackerknecht, E. H. "Primitive Surgery," *AA,* 49 (1947), 25-45.

Ackerknecht, E. H. "Medical Practices." In Steward, J. H. (ed.). *Handbook of South American Indians. BAE,* Bulletin 143, 5 (1949), 621-643.

Aescoly, A. Z. *Jewish Messianic Movements: Sources and Documents on Messianism in Jewish History.* Vol. 1. Ed. Yehuda Even-Shmuel. Jerusalem, Israel: Mosad Mialik, 1956.

Alvarez, W. C. "The Emergence of Modern Medicine from Ancient Folkways," *BAE, Annual Report, 1937* (1938), 409-430.

Argyle, Michael. *Religious Behavior.* Glencoe: The Free Press, 1959.

Barber, Bernard. "Acculturation and Messianic Movements," *American Sociological Review,* 6 (1941), 663-669.

Barnett, H. G. *Indian Shakers.* Carbondale: Southern Illinois University Press, 1957.

Barnouw, Victor. *Acculturation and Personality among the Wisconsin Chippewa. AAA,* Memoirs (1950), 72.

Bartels, M. *Die Medizin der Naturvölker.* Leipzig: T. Grüben, 1893.

Barton, R. F. *The Religion of the Ifugaos. AAA,* Memoirs (1946), 65.

Bascom, W. R. *The Sociological Role of the Yoruba Cult Group. AAA,* Memoirs (1944), 63.

Bascom, W. R. "Four Functions of Folklore," *Journal of American Folklore,* 67 (1954), 333-349.

Bateson, Gregory. *Naven.* Cambridge: Cambridge University Press, 1936.

Belo, Jane. *Bali: Rangda and Barong. AES,* Monographs (1949), 16.

Belo, Jane. *Bali: Temple Festival. AES,* Monographs (1953), 22.

Belo, Jane. *Trance in Bali.* New York: Columbia University Press, 1960.

Belshaw, C. S. "The Significance of Modern Cults in Melanesian Development," *The Australian Outlook,* 4 (1950), 116-125.

Benedict, Ruth. *The Concept of the Guardian Spirit in North America. AAA,* Memoirs (1923), 29.

Benedict, Ruth. "Anthropology and the Abnormal," *Journal of General Psychology,* 10 (1934), 59-82.

Benedict, Ruth. "Religion." In Boas, Franz (ed.). *General Anthropology.* New York: D. C. Heath and Company, 1938.

Bennett, Wendell, and Zingg, R. M. *The Tarahumara: an Indian Tribe of Northern Mexico.* Chicago: University of Chicago Press, 1935.

Bernatowicz, A. J. "Teleology in Science Teaching," *Science* (December 5, 1958), 128, 1402-1405.

Berndt, R. M. "A Cargo Movement in the Eastern Central Highlands of New Guinea," *Oceania,* 23 (1952), 40-65, 136-158, 202-234.

Bettelheim, Bruno. *Symbolic Wounds.* Glencoe: The Free Press, 1954.

Biswas, Praphallachandra. "Concepts of Disease among the Primitive People of India," *Journal of the Department of Letters, Calcutta,* 25 (1937), 1-28.

Boas, Franz. "The Central Eskimo," *BAE, Sixth Annual Report, 1884-85* (1888), 409-669.

Boas, Franz. *The Mind of Primitive Man.* New York: The Macmillan Company, 1911.

Boas, Franz. "Tsimshian Mythology," *BAE, Thirty-first Annual Report, 1909-1910* (1916), 29-1037.

Bogoras, Waldemar. *The Chuckchee—Religion.* Memoirs of the American Museum of Natural History. No. 11, Part 2. New York: American Museum of Natural History, 1907.

Bourke, J. G. *Scatalogic Rites of All Nations.* Washington: W. H. Lowdermilk & Co., 1891.

Bourke, J. G. "The Medicine Men of the Apache," *BAE, Ninth Annual Report, 1887-1888* (1892), 443-603.

Bowers, A. W. *Mandan Social and Ceremonial Organization.* Chicago: University of Chicago Press, 1950.

Brant, C. S. "Peyotism among the Kiowa-Apache and Neighboring Tribes," *SWJA,* 6 (1950), 212-222.

Brewster, A. B. *Hill Tribes of Fiji.* London: Seeley Service, 1922.

Briffault, R. "Birth Customs," *Encyclopaedia of the Social Sciences.* 1930, Vol. II.

Buck, P. H. *Regional Diversity in the Elaboration of Sorcery in Polynesia.* Yale University Publication in Anthropology, 2. New Haven; London: H. Milford; Oxford University Press, 1936.

Bunce, W. K. *Religions in Japan.* Rutland, Vermont: Charles E. Tuttle Co., 1955.

Bunzel, Ruth L. *Introduction to Zuni Ceremonialism, BAE,* Bulletin 47 (1932).

Burkitt, M. C. *The Old Stone Age.* New York: The Macmillan Company, 1933.

Callaway, Henry. *The Religious System of the Amazulu.* London: Trubner & Co., 1870.

Calverton, V. F. "Modern Anthropology and the Theory of Cultural Compulsives." In Calverton, V. F. (ed.). *The Making of Man.* New York: The Modern Library, 1931.

Cannon, W. B. "The 'Voodoo' Death," *AA,* 44 (1942), 169-181.

Carpenter, Edward. *Intermediate Types among Primitive Folk.* London: George Allen & Co., 1914.

Chamberlain, A. F. "New Religions among the North American Indians," *Journal of Religious Psychology,* 6 (1913), 1-49.

Chamberlain, B. H. (trans.). *Kojiki.* Supplement to vol. 10. Transactions, Asiatic Society of Japan, 1882.

Chapple, E. D., and Coon, C. S. *Principles of Anthropology.* New York: Henry Holt and Company, 1942.

Childs, G. M. *Umbundu Kinship and Character.* London: Oxford University Press, 1949.

Chinnery, E. W. P., and Haddon, A. C. "Five New Religious Cults in British New Guinea," *The Hibbert Journal,* 15 (1917), 448-463.

Clark, E. T. *The Small Sects in America,* rev. ed. Nashville, Tenn.: Abingdon-Cokesbury Press, 1949.

Clements, F. E. *Primitive Concepts of Disease. UCPAAE,* 32, no. 2, (1932).

Codrington, R. H. *The Melanesians.* Oxford: The Clarendon Press, 1891.

Collins, J. M. "The Indian Shaker Church: A Study of Continuity and Change in Religion," *SWJA,* 6 (1950), 399-411.

Cooper, J. M. "The Cree Witiko Psychosis," *Primitive Man,* 6 (1933), 20-24.

Cooper, J. M. "Stimulants and Narcotics." In Steward, J. H. (ed.). *Handbook of South American Indians. BAE,* Bulletin 143, 5 (1949), 525-558.

Corlett, W. T. *The Medicine-Man of the American Indian and His Cultural Background.* Springfield and Baltimore: Charles C. Thomas, 1935.

Cornford, F. M. *From Religion to Philosophy.* New York: Henry Holt and Company, 1913.

Cumston, C. G. *History of Medicine.* New York: Alfred A. Knopf, 1926.

Cutten, G. B. *Speaking with Tongues.* New Haven: Yale University Press, 1927.

Czaplicka, M. A. *Aboriginal Siberia, a Study in Social Anthropology.* Oxford: The Clarendon Press, 1914.

Dabbs, J. A. "A Messiah among the Chiriguanos," *SWJA,* 9 (1953), 45-58.

Deardorff, M. H. "The Religion of Handsome Lake: Its Origin and Development." In Fenton, W. N. (ed.). *Symposium on Local Diversity in Iroquois Culture. BAE,* Bulletin 149 (1951), 79-107.

De Bruyn, J. V. "The Mansren Cult of Baik," *South Pacific,* 5 (1949), 1-10.

Devereux, George. "Primitive Psychiatry," *BHM,* 11 (1942), 522-542.

d'Harcourt, Raoul. *La médicine dans l'ancien Pérou.* Paris: Librairie maloine, 1939.

Dixon, R. B. *The Northern Maidu.* Bulletin of the American Museum of Natural History, 17. New York: American Museum of Natural History, 1905.

Dixon, R. B. *The Shasta.* Bulletin of the American Museum of Natural History, 17. New York: American Museum of Natural History, 1907.

Dorsey, J. O. "A Study of Siouan Cults," *BAE, Eleventh Annual Report, 1889-1890* (1894).

Du Bois, Cora. *The Religion of the Luiseño Indians of Southern California. UCPAAE,* 8 (1908), 69-186.

Du Bois, Cora. *The 1870 Ghost Dance. UCAR,* 3, No. 1, Berkeley (1939).

Du Bois, Cora. *The People of Alor.* Minneapolis: University of Minnesota Press, 1944.

Durkheim, Emile. *The Elementary Forms of the Religious Life.* Glencoe: The Free Press, 1954.

Eduardo, Octavio Da Costa. *The Negro in Northern Brazil. AES,* Monographs (1948), 15.

Elkin, A. P. "Studies in Australian Totemism," *The Oceania Monographs,* 2, Sydney (1937).

Ellis, W. *Polynesian Researches,* 2nd ed. London: Fisher Son & Jackson, 1831.

Evans, I. H. N. *The Religion of the Tempasuk Dusuns of North Borneo.* New York: Cambridge University Press, 1953.

Evans-Pritchard, E. E. "The Morphology and Function of Magic: a Comparative Study of Trobriand and Zande Ritual and Spells," *AA*, 31 (1929), 619-641.

Evans-Pritchard, E. E. "The Zande Corporation of Witchdoctors," *JRAI*, 62 (1932), 291-336; 63 (1933), 63-100.

Evans-Pritchard, E. E. "Witchcraft," *Africa*, 8 (1935), 419-422.

Evans-Pritchard, E. E. *Witchcraft, Oracles and Magic among the Azande.* London: Oxford University Press, 1937.

Evans-Pritchard, E. E. *Nuer Religion.* Oxford: The Clarendon Press, 1956.

Evans-Pritchard, E. E., and others. *The Institutions of Primitive Society.* Glencoe: The Free Press, 1954.

Field, M. J. *Religion and Medicine of the Gã People.* London: Oxford University Press, 1937.

Firth, Raymond. *The Work of the Gods in Tikopia,* 2 vols. London: The London School of Economics and Political Science, 1940.

Firth, Raymond. "Religious Belief and Personal Adjustment," *JRAI*, 78 (1948), 25-43.

Firth, Raymond. "Function." In Thomas, W. I. (ed.). *Yearbook of Anthropology.* New York: Wenner-Gren Foundation, 1955.

Flannery, Regina. "Two Concepts of Power." In Tax, Sol (ed.). *Selected Papers of the Fifth International Congress of Americanists.* Chicago: University of Chicago Press, 1952.

Forde, Daryll. "Integrative Aspects of the Yakö First Fruits Ritual," *JRAI*, 79 (1949), 1-10.

Fortes, M. "Ritual Festivals and Social Cohesion in the Hinterland of the Gold Coast," *AA*, 38 (1936), 590-604.

Fortes, M., and Evans-Pritchard, E. E. *African Political Systems.* London: Oxford University Press, 1940.

Fortune, R. F. *Sorcerers of Dobu.* London: G. Routledge & Sons, 1932.

Fortune, R. F. *Manus Religion.* Memoirs of the American Philosophical Society. Vol. 3. Philadelphia, 1935.

Frazer, J. G. *The Golden Bough: a Study in Magic and Religion,* abridged, one-vol. ed. New York: Macmillan and Company, 1922 (12 vol. ed. London: Macmillan, 1911-1915).

Freeland, L. S. *Pomo Doctors and Poisoners. UCPAAE,* 20 (1923), 57-73.

Freud, Sigmund. *Moses and Monotheism* (trans. by Katherine Jones). London: Hogarth Press & Institute of Psycho-Analysis, 1939.

Freud, Sigmund. *The Future of an Illusion* (trans. by W. D. Robson-Scott). London: Hogarth Press, 1949.

Freud, Sigmund. *Totem and Taboo* (trans. by James Strachey). New York: W. W. Norton & Company, 1950.

Gayton, A. H. *The Narcotic Plant Datura in Aboriginal American Culture.* Unpublished Ph.D. dissertation. University of California, Berkeley, 1928.

Gayton, A. H. *Yokuts-Mono Chiefs and Shamans. UCPAAE,* 24 (1930), 361-420.

Gayton, A. H. *The Ghost Dance of 1870 in South-Central California. UCPAAE,* 28 (1930), 57-82.

Geertz, Clifford. "Ritual and Social Change: a Javanese Example," *AA,* 59 (1957), 32-54.

Gelfand, Michael. *Medicine and Magic of the Mashona.* Capetown: Juta and Co., 1956.

Gerth, H. H., and Mills, C. W. *From Max Weber: Essays in Sociology.* New York: Oxford University Press, 1958.

Gillin, John. *The Culture of Security in San Carlos.* Middle American Research Institute. Publication 16. New Orleans: Tulane University, 1951.

Gluckman, Max. "Zulu Women in Hoe Culture Ritual," *Bantu Studies.* Vol. 9, 1935.

Gluckman, Max. "The Role of the Sexes in Wiko Circumcision Ceremonies." In Fortes, M. (ed.). *Social Structure: Studies presented to A. R. Radcliffe-Brown.* Oxford: The Clarendon Press, 1949.

Gluckman, Max. *Rituals of Rebellion in South-East Africa.* The Fraser Lecture, 1952. Manchester: Manchester University Press, 1954.

Goldenweiser, A. A. "Religion and Society," *The Journal of Philosophy, Psychology and Scientific Methods,* 14 (1917), 113-124.

Goldenweiser, A. A. "Totemism, an Analytical Study." In *History, Psychology and Culture.* New York: Alfred A. Knopf, 1933.

Goldi, W. H. "Maori Medical Lore." *New Zealand Institute, Transactions,* 37 (1904).

Goode, W. J. *Religion Among the Primitives.* Glencoe: The Free Press, 1951.

Goodwin, Grenville, and Kaut, Charles. "A Native Religious Movement among the White Mountain and Cibecue Apache," *SWJA,* 10 (1954), 385-404.

Grinnell, G. B. "Some Cheyenne Plant Medicines," *AA,* 7 (1905), 37-43.

Grinnell, G. B. *The Cheyenne Indians,* 2 vols. New Haven: Yale University Press, 1923.

Guiart, Jean. " 'Cargo Cults' and Political Evolution in Melanesia," *South Pacific,* 5 (1951), 128-129.

Guiart, Jean. "The Cooperative Called 'Malekula Native Company,' A Borderline Type of Cargo Cult," *South Pacific*, 6 (1952), 429-433.

Guiart, Jean. "John Frum Movement in Tanna," *Oceania*, 22 (1952), 165-177.

Guiart, Jean. "Culture Contact and the 'John Frum' Movements on Tanna, New Hebrides," *SWJA*, 12 (1956), 105-116.

Gunther, E. "The Shaker Religion of the Northwest." In Smith, M. W. (ed.). *Indians of the Urban Northwest.* New York: Columbia University Press, 1949.

Haggard, H. W. *Devils, Drugs, and Doctors.* New York and London: Harper & Brothers, 1929.

Hallowell, A. I. "Primitive Concepts of Disease," *AA*, 37 (1935), 365-368.

Hallowell, A. I. "Some Psychological Characteristics of the Northeastern Indians." In Johnson, Frederick (ed.). *Man in Northeastern North America.* Papers of the Robert S. Peabody Foundation for Archaeology, 3 (1946), 195-225.

Handy, E. S. C. *Polynesian Religion.* Bernice P. Bishop Museum, Bulletin No. 34, Honolulu, 1927.

Handy, E. S. C., Pukui, M. K., and Livermore, K. *Outline of Hawaiian Physical Therapeutics.* Bernice P. Bishop Museum, Bulletin 126, Honolulu, 1934.

Harley, G. W. *Native African Medicine, with Special Reference to Its Practice in the Mano Tribe of Liberia.* Cambridge: Harvard University Press, 1941.

Harris, Grace. "Possession 'Hysteria' in a Kenya Tribe," *AA*, 59 (1957), 1046-1066.

Harris, J. S. "The White Knife Shoshoni of Nevada." In Linton, Ralph (ed.). *Acculturation in Seven American Indian Tribes.* New York: D. Appleton-Century Co., 1940.

Hayley, T. T. S. *The Anatomy of Lango Religion and Groups.* Cambridge: Cambridge University Press, 1947.

Heizer, R. F. "A Californian Messianic Movement of 1801 among the Chumash," *AA*, 43 (1941), 128-129.

Henry, Alexander, and Thompson, David. *Manuscript Journals of Alexander Henry and David Thompson, 1799-1814.* Ed. Coues, E. New York: Francis P. Harper, 1897.

Henry, T. A. *The Plant Alkaloids.* London: J. and A. Churchill, 1913.

Herskovits, M. J. *Dahomey,* 2 vols. New York: J. J. Augustin, 1938.

Hewitt, J. N. B. "Orenda and a Definition of Religion," *AA*, 4 (1902), 33-46.

Hill, W. W. "The Navaho Indians and the Ghost Dance of 1890," *AA*, 46 (1944), 523-527.

Hodge, F. W. (ed.). *Handbook of American Indians North of Mexico*. *BAE*, Bulletin 30 (1907-1910), Parts 1-2.

Hoebel, E. A. *The Law of Primitive Man*. Cambridge: Harvard University Press, 1954.

Hoffman, W. J. "The Midewiwin or 'Grand Medicine Society' of the Ojibway," *BAE, Seventh Annual Report, 1885-1886*, (1891), 143-300.

Holmberg, A. R. *Nomads of the Long Bow*. Institute of Social Anthropology. Publication 10. Washington: The Smithsonian Institution, 1950.

Homans, G. C. "Anxiety and Ritual: The Theories of Malinowski and Radcliffe-Brown," *AA*, 43 (1941), 164-172.

Honigmann, J. J. "Witch-Fear in Post-Contact Kaska Society," *AA*, 49 (1947), 222-243.

Honigmann, J. J. *Culture and Personality*. New York: Harper & Brothers, 1954.

Hörnle, A. W. "Magic and Medicine." In Schapera, I. (ed.). *The Bantu-speaking Tribes of South Africa*. London: George Routledge & Sons, 1937.

Howard, J. A. "The Mescal Bean Cult of the Central and Southern Plains: an Ancestor of the Peyote Cult?" *AA*, 59 (1957), 75-87.

Howells, W. *The Heathens*. Garden City, New York: Doubleday and Company, 1948.

Howitt, A. W. "On Australian Medicine Men," *The Journal of the Anthropological Institute of Great Britain and Ireland*, 16 (1887), 23-59.

Howitt, A. W. *The Native Tribes of South-East Australia*. London: Macmillan & Co., 1904.

Hsu, F. L. K. *Religion, Science and Human Crises*. London: Routledge and Kegan Paul, 1952.

Hutton, J. H. *The Angami Nagas*. London: Macmillan & Co., 1921.

Huxley, Aldous. *The Devils of Loudun*. New York: Harper & Brothers, 1952.

Huxley, Aldous. *The Doors of Perception*. New York: Harper & Brothers, 1954.

James, B. J. "Some Critical Observations Concerning Analyses of Chippewa 'Atomism' and Chippewa Personality," *AA*, 56 (1954), 283-286.

James, William. *The Varieties of Religious Experience*. New York: Longmans, Green, and Co., 1902.

Jenness, Diamond. *The Life of the Copper Eskimo.* Report of the Canadian Arctic Expedition. Vol. 12. Ottawa: F. A. Acland, 1922.

Jenness, Diamond. *The Ojibwa Indians of Parry Island: Their Social and Religious Life.* National Museum of Canada, Department of Mines, Bulletin 78, Anthropology Series 17, 1935.

Jochelson, Waldemar. *Religion and Myths of the Koryak.* Memoirs of the American Museum of Natural History. Vol. 10. Leiden: E. J. Brill; New York: G. E. Stechert, 1905.

Jochelson, Waldemar. *The Yukaghir and the Yukaghirized Tungus.* Publications of the Jesup North Pacific Expedition, 9. Leiden: E. J. Brill; New York: G. E. Stechert, 1926.

Junod, H. A. *The Life of a South African Tribe,* 2 vols. London: Macmillan & Co., 1913.

Kaberry, Phyllis. *Aboriginal Woman, Sacred and Profane.* Philadelphia: New Impression, 1939; New York: Humanities Press, 1950.

Kaempfer, Engelbert. *History of Japan* (trans. by J. G. Scheuchzer). London: the translator, 1727.

Karsten, Rafael. *The Civilization of the South American Indians.* New York: Alfred A. Knopf, 1926.

Kittredge, G. L. *Witchcraft in Old and New England.* Cambridge: Harvard University Press, 1929.

Kluckhohn, Clyde. "Myths and Rituals: A General Theory," *The Harvard Theological Review,* 35 (1942), 45-79.

Kluckhohn, Clyde. *Navaho Witchcraft.* Papers of the Peabody Museum of American Archaeology and Ethnology. Vol. 22, No. 2, 1944.

Koty, J. *Die Behandlung der Alten und Kranken bei den Naturvölkern.* Stuttgart: C. L. Hirschfeld, 1934.

Krader, Lawrence. "A Nativistic Movement in Western Siberia," *AA,* 58 (1956), 282-292.

Krige, J. D. "The Social Function of Witchcraft," *Theoria,* 13 (1947), 8-21.

Kroeber, A. L. *Handbook of the Indians of California. BAE,* Bulletin 78 (1925).

Kuper, Hilda. *An African Aristocracy: Rank Among the Swazi.* London: Oxford University Press, 1947.

LaBarre, Weston. *The Peyote Cult.* Yale University Publications in Anthropology. No. 19. New Haven: Yale University Press, 1938.

LaBarre, Weston. "Primitive Psychotherapy in Native American Cultures:

Peyotism and Confession," *The Journal of Abnormal and Social Psychology*, 42, (July, 1947), 294-309.

LaFarge, Oliver. *Santa Eulalia.* Chicago: University of Chicago Press, 1947.

Landes, Ruth. "The Abnormal Among the Ojibwa," *Journal of Abnormal and Social Psychology*, 33 (1938), 14-33.

Lang, Andrew. *The Making of Religion.* London: Longmans Green, 1898.

Lantis, Margaret. *Alaskan Eskimo Ceremonialism. AES*, 11 (1947).

Lawrence, Peter. "Cargo Cult and Religious Beliefs Among the Garia." *International Archives of Ethnography*, 47 (1954), 1-20.

Leakey, L. S. B. *Mau Mau and the Kikuyu.* London: Methuen & Co., 1952.

Leakey, L. S. B. *Defeating Mau Mau.* London: Methuen & Co., 1954.

Leeson, Ida. *Bibliography of Cargo Cults and Other Nativistic Movements in the South Pacific.* South Pacific Commission, Technical Paper No. 30, Sydney, 1952.

Leighton, A. H. and Leighton, D. C. "Elements of Psychotherapy in Navaho Religion," *Psychiatry,* 4 (1941), 515-523.

LeRoy, A. *The Religion of the Primitives* (trans. by Newton Thompson). New York: The Macmillan Company, 1922.

Lesser, A. "Cultural Significance of the Ghost Dance," *AA,* 35 (1933), 108-115.

Levy-Bruhl, Lucien. *Primitive Mentality* (trans. by L. A. Clare). New York: The Macmillan Company, 1923.

Lewin, Louis. *Phantastica: Narcotic and Stimulating Drugs, Their Use and Abuse* (trans. from the second German edition by P. H. A. Wirth). London: Kegal Paul, Trench, Trubner and Co., 1931.

Li An-che. "Zuni: Some Observations and Queries," *AA,* 39 (1937), 62-76.

Linton, Ralph. "Nativistic Movements," *AA,* 45 (1943), 230-240.

Lott, Milton. *Dance Back the Buffalo.* Boston: Houghton Mifflin Company, 1959.

Lowie, R. H. *Religion of the Crow Indians.* Anthropological Papers of the American Museum of Natural History. Vol. 32, Pt. 2. New York, 1922.

Lowie, R. H. *Primitive Religion.* New York: Boni & Liveright, 1924.

Lowie, R. H. *The Crow Indians.* New York: Farrar & Rinehart, 1935.

MacIver, R. M., and Page, C. H. *Society, an Introductory Analysis.* New York: Rinehart & Company, 1949.

Maddox, J. L. *The Medicine Man.* New York: The Macmillan Company, 1923.

Major, R. H. *A History of Medicine.* Vol. 1. Springfield: Charles C. Thomas, 1954.

Malinowski, Bronislaw. "Culture," *Encyclopaedia of the Social Sciences.* 1931, Vol. 4.

Malinowski, Bronislaw. *Coral Gardens and their Magic,* 2 vols. London: George Allen & Unwin, 1935.

Malinowski, Bronislaw. *Magic, Science and Religion and Other Essays.* Glencoe: The Free Press, 1948.

Mandelbaum, D. G. "Form, Variation, and Meaning of a Ceremony." In Spencer, R. F. (ed.). *Method and Perspective in Anthropology: Papers in Honor of Wilson D. Wallis.* Minneapolis: University of Minnesota Press, 1954.

Marett, R. R. *The Threshold of Religion,* rev. ed. London: Methuen & Co., 1914.

Marett, R. R. *Psychology and Folklore.* London: Methuen & Co., 1920.

Marett, R. R. *The Sacraments of Simple Folk.* Oxford: The Clarendon Press, 1933.

Maringer, J., and Bandi, Hans-Georg. *Art in the Ice Age* (trans. by Robert Allen). New York: F. A. Praeger, 1953.

Martin, P. S., Quimby, G. I., and Collier, D. *Indians Before Columbus.* Chicago: University of Chicago Press, 1947.

Marwick, B. A. *The Swazi.* Cambridge: Cambridge University Press, 1940.

Marwick, M. G. "Another Modern Anti-Witchcraft Movement in East Central Africa," *Africa,* vol. 20, no. 2 (1950).

Marwick, M. G. "The Social Context of Cewa Witchcraft Beliefs," *Africa,* 22, (1952), 120-135, 215-233.

May, L. C. "A Survey of Glossolalia and Related Phenomena in Non-Christian Religions," *AA,* 58 (1956), 75-96.

McGee, W. J. *The Siouxan Indians. BAE, Fifteenth Annual Report, 1893-1894* (1897), 157-212.

McKenzie, Dan. *The Infancy of Medicine.* London: Macmillan & Co., 1927.

Mead, Margaret. *The Mountain Arapesh.* Vol. 2, *Supernaturalism.* Anthropological Papers of the American Museum of Natural History, 37 (1940), 317-451.

Means, P. A. *Ancient Civilizations of the Andes.* New York: Charles Scribner's Sons, 1931.

Merton, R. K. *Social Theory and Social Structure.* Glencoe: The Free Press, 1949.

Métraux, Alfred. "Les Migration Historiques des Tupi-Guarani," *Journal de la Societé des Americanistes de Paris*, 19 (1927), 1-45.

Métraux, Alfred. "Les hommes-dieux chez les Chiriguano," *Revista del Instituto de Etnologia de la Universidad Nacional de Tucumán*, 2 (1931), 16-91.

Métraux, Alfred. "Messiahs of South America," *The Inter-American Quarterly*, 3 (1941), 53-60.

Métraux, Alfred. "A Quechua Messiah in Eastern Peru," *AA*, 44 (1942), 721-725.

Métraux, Alfred. "The Couvade." In Steward, J. H. (ed.). *Handbook of South American Indians*. *BAE*, Bulletin 143, 5 (1949), 369-374.

Mikhailovskii, V. M. "Shamanism in Siberia and European Russia" (trans. by Oliver Wardrop), *The Journal of the Anthropological Institute of Great Britain and Ireland*, 24 (1895), 62-100.

Miller, W. B. "Two Concepts of Authority," *AA*, 57 (1955), 271-289.

Mitchell, J. C. "The Yao of Southern Nyasaland." In Colson, E., and Gluckman, M. (eds.). *Seven Tribes of British Central Africa*. London: Oxford University Press, 1951.

Mooney, James. "The Sacred Formulas of the Cherokees." *BAE, Seventh Annual Report, 1885-1886* (1891), 301-397.

Mooney, James. "The Ghost Dance Religion and the Sioux Outbreak of 1890." *BAE, Fourteenth Annual Report, 1892-1893* (1896), 653-1110.

Mooney, James. "The Swimmer Manuscript, Cherokee Sacred Formulas and Medical Prescriptions, Revised, Completed, and Edited by Frans M. Olbrechts." *BAE*, Bulletin 99 (1932).

Morgan, William, "Navaho Treatment of Sickness: Diagnosticians," *AA*, 33 (1931), 390-402.

Morley, S. G. *The Ancient Maya*. Stanford: Stanford University Press, 1946.

Morton, C. V. "Notes on *Yagé*, a Drug Plant of Southeastern Colombia," *Journal of the Washington Academy of Sciences*, 21 (1931), 485-488.

Müller, F. Max. "Comparative Mythology," *Oxford Essays*. Vol. 2. London: W. Parker and Son, 1856, 1-87.

Müller, F. Max. *Lectures on the Origin and Growth of Religion*. London: Longmans Green, 1878.

Müller, F. Max. *Anthropological Religion*. London: Longmans Green, 1892.

Nadel, S. F. "A Study of Shamanism in the Nuba Mountains," *JRAI*, 64 (1946), 25-37.

Nadel, S. F. "Witchcraft in Four African Societies: an Essay in Comparison," *AA*, 54 (1952), 18-29.

Nadel, S. F. *Nupe Religion*. Glencoe: The Free Press, 1954.

Nadel, S. F. "Two Nuba Religions: an Essay in Comparison," *AA*, 57 (1955), 661-679.

Newcomb, W. W., Jr. *The Culture and Acculturation of the Delaware Indians*. Anthropological Papers of the Museum of Anthropology, University of Michigan. No. 10. Ann Arbor: University of Michigan Press, 1956.

Norbeck, E. "Pollution and Taboo in Contemporary Japan," *SWJA*, 8 (1952), 269-285.

Norbeck, E. *Takashima, a Japanese Fishing Community*. Salt Lake City: University of Utah Press, 1954.

Nottingham, E. K. *Religion and Society*. New York: Doubleday & Company, 1955.

Oesterreich, T. K. *Possession* (trans. by D. Ibberson). New York: Richard R. Smith, 1930.

Park, W. Z. *Shamanism in Western North America*. Northwestern University Studies in the Social Sciences. No. 2, 1938.

Parker, A. C. "Secret Medicine Societies of the Seneca," *AA*, 11 (1909), 161-185.

Parrinder, Geoffrey. *Witchcraft*. Penguin Books, 1958.

Parsons, E. C. *Pueblo Indian Religion*, 2 vols. Chicago: University of Chicago Press, 1939.

Parsons, E. C., and Beals, R. L. "The Sacred Clowns of the Pueblo and Mayo-Yaqui Indians," *AA*, 36 (1934), 491-516.

Parsons, Talcott. "The Theoretical Development of the Sociology of Religion." In *Essays in Sociological Theory Pure and Applied*. Glencoe: The Free Press, 1949.

Parsons, Talcott. *The Social System*. Glencoe: The Free Press, 1951.

Pearson, A. C. "Possession (Greek and Roman)." In Hastings, James (ed.). *Encyclopedia of Religion and Ethics*. Vol. 10. New York: Charles Scribner's Sons, 1920, 127-130.

Pettitt, G. A. *Primitive Education in North America. UCPAAE*, 43, no. 1 (1946).

Pos, Hugo. "The Revolt of 'Manseren'," *AA*, 52 (1950), 561-564.

Potter, C. F. *The Story of Religion*. New York: Garden City Publishing Company, 1929.

Provinse, J. H. "The Underlying Sanctions of Plains Indian Culture." In
    Eggan, Fred (ed.), *Social Anthropology of North American Tribes.*
    Chicago: University of Chicago Press, 1937, 341-374.

Radcliffe-Brown, A. R. *The Andaman Islanders.* Cambridge: Cambridge
    University Press, 1922.

Radcliffe-Brown, A. R. "On the Concept of Function in Social Science,"
    AA, 37 (1935), 394-402.

Radcliffe-Brown, A. R. *Structure and Function in Primitive Society.* Glen-
    coe: The Free Press, 1952.

Radin, Paul. *Crashing Thunder.* New York: D. Appleton-Century Com-
    pany, 1926.

Radin, Paul. *Primitive Man as a Philosopher.* New York, London: D. Ap-
    pleton & Co., 1927.

Radin, Paul. *Primitive Religion.* New York: Viking Press, 1937.

Radin, Paul. *Monotheism among Primitive Peoples.* Basel, Switzerland
    Ethnographical Museum, 1954.

Radin, Paul. *The Trickster.* London: Routledge and Kegan Paul, 1956.

Rattray, R. S. *Religion and Art in Ashanti.* Oxford: The Clarendon Press,
    1927.

Rattray, R. S. *Akan-Ashanti Folk Tales.* Oxford: The Clarendon Press,
    1930.

Ray, V. F. "The Kolaskin Cult: A Prophet Movement of 1870 in North-
    eastern Washington," *AA*, 38 (1936), 67-75.

Ray, V. F. "The Contrary Behavior Pattern in American Indian Cere-
    monialism," *SWJA*, 1 (1945), 75-113.

Read, K. E. "A Recent 'Cargo' Situation in the Markham Valley, New
    Guinea," *SWJA*, 14 (1958), 273-294.

Reagan, A. B. "Some Chippewa Medicinal Receipts," *AA*, 23 (1921), 246-
    249.

Reichard, G. A. *Navaho Medicine Man.* New York: J. J. Augustin, 1939.

Reichard, G. A. *Navaho Religion,* 2 vols. New York: Pantheon Books, 1950.

Reik, Theodor. *The Psychological Problems of Religion.* Vol. I. New York:
    Farrar, Straus, 1946.

Reko, V. A. *Magische Gifte: Rausch-und Bettaubungsmittel der Neuen
    Welt.* Stuttgart: Ferdinand Enke Verlag, 1938.

Richards, A. I. "A Modern Movement of Witch-Finders," *Africa,* 8 (1935),
    448-461.

Richards, A. I. *Chisungu.* New York: Grove Press, 1956.

Riesman, David. *The Lonely Crowd*. New Haven: Yale University Press, 1950.

Riley, C. L., and Hobgood, J. "A Recent Nativistic Movement among the Southern Tepehuan Indians," *SWJA*, 15 (1959), 355-360.

Ritzenthaler, Robert. "The Ceremonial Destruction of Sickness by the Wisconsin Chippewa," *AA*, 47 (1945), 320-322.

Rivers, W. H. R. *The Todas*. London: Macmillan & Co., 1906.

Rogers, S. L. "Disease Concepts in North America," *AA*, 46 (1948), 559-564.

Roscoe, John. *The Baganda: an Account of their Native Customs and Beliefs*. London: Macmillan & Co., 1911.

Roscoe, John. *The Northern Bantu*. Cambridge: Cambridge University Press, 1915.

Roscoe, John. *The Bakitara*. Cambridge: Cambridge University Press, 1923.

Rose, Ronald. *Living Magic*. New York, Chicago, and San Francisco: Rand McNally & Company, 1956.

Rosenthal, T., and Siegel, B. J. "Magic and Witchcraft: an Interpretation from Dissonance Theory," *SWJA*, 15 (1959), 143-167.

Safford, W. E. "Narcotic Plants and Stimulants of the Ancient Americans." *BAE, Annual Report for the Year Ending June 30, 1916* (1917), 387-424.

Safford, W. E. "Daturas of the Old World and New: an Account of their Narcotic Properties and their Use in Oracular and Initiatory Ceremonies." *BAE, Annual Report of the Smithsonian Institution for 1920* (1922), 537-567.

Sahagun, Bernardino de. *A History of Ancient Mexico* (trans. by F. R. Bandelier), 3 vols. Nashville: Fisk University Press, 1932.

Salisbury, R. F. "An Indigenous New Guinea Cult," *Papers of the Kroeber Anthropological Society*. No. 18 (Spring, 1958), 67-78.

Schapera, I. (ed.). *The Bantu-speaking Tribes of South Africa*. London: George Routledge & Sons, 1937.

Schlosser, Katesa. *Propheten in Afrika*. Braunschweig: Albert Limbach Verlag, 1949.

Schmidt, Wilhelm. *The Origin and Growth of Religion* (trans. by H. J. Rose). London: Methuen & Co., 1931.

Schmidt, Wilhelm. *Der Ursprung der Gottesidee*. Münster: Aschendorf, 1954.

Schultes, R. E. "Teonanacatl: the Narcotic Mushroom of the Aztecs," *AA*, 42 (1940), 429-443.

Schultes, R. E. "A New Narcotic Genus from the Amazon Slope of the

Colombian Andes," *Harvard University Botanical Museum Leaflets*, 17, no. 1, (1955).

Schurhammer, George (S.J.). *Shinto, The Way of the Gods in Japan.* Bonn and Leipzig: Kurt Schroeder, 1923.

Schurtz, Heinrich. *Altersklassen und Männerbünde.* Berlin: G. Reimer, 1903.

Sears, R. R., and others. "The Socialization of Aggression." In Maccoby, E. E., Newcomb, T. M., and Hartley, E. L. (eds.). *Readings in Social Psychology.* New York: Henry Holt and Company, 1958.

Sebeok, T. A., and Ingeman, F. J. *Studies in Cheremis: The Supernatural.* Viking Fund Publications in Anthropology. No. 22. New York: The Viking Fund, 1956.

Seligman, C. G., and Seligman, B. Z. *The Veddas.* Cambridge: Cambridge University Press, 1911.

Seligman, C. G. *Pagan Tribes of the Nilotic Sudan.* London: George Routledge, 1932.

Shirokogoroff, S. M. *Psychomental Complex of the Tungus.* London: Kegan Paul, Trench, Trubner & Co., 1935.

Sigerist, H. E. *A History of Medicine.* Vol. I. New York: Oxford University Press, 1951.

Skeat, W. W. *Malay Magic.* London, New York: Macmillan, 1900.

Slotkin, J. S. "Menomini Peyotism," *Transactions of the American Philosophical Society.* Vol. 42, pt. 4 (1952), 565-700.

Slotkin, J. S. "Peyotism, 1521-1891," *AA,* 57 (1955), 202-230.

Slotkin, J. S. *The Peyote Religion: A Study in Indian-White Relations.* Glencoe: The Free Press, 1956.

Smith, W. Robertson. *Lectures on the Religion of the Semites,* rev. ed. London: Adam and Charles Black, 1901.

Speck, F. G. "Penobscot Shamanism." Memoirs, *AAA,* 6 (1919), 239-288.

Speck, F. G. *Naskapi.* Norman: University of Oklahoma Press, 1935.

Speck, F. G. "Catawba Herbals and Curative Practices," *Journal of American Folklore,* 57 (1944), 37-51.

Spencer, B., and Gillen, F. J. *The Native Tribes of Central Australia.* London, New York: Macmillan, 1899.

Spencer, H. L. *The Principles of Sociology.* New York: D. Appleton & Co., 1896.

Spencer, R. F. (ed.). *Method and Perspective in Anthropology.* Minneapolis: University of Minnesota Press, 1954.

Spier, Leslie. *The Sun Dance of the Plains Indians.* Anthropological Papers of the American Museum of Natural History. Vol. 16. New York: American Museum of Natural History, 1921, 451-527.

Spier, L. *The Prophet Dance of the Northwest and its Derivatives: The Source of the Ghost Dance.* General Series in Anthropology. No. 1. Menasha: G. Banta & Co., 1935.

Spier, L., Hallowell, A. I., and Newman, S. S. (eds.). *Language, Culture and Personality.* Menasha: Sapir Memorial Publication Fund, 1941.

Spiro, M. E. "Ghosts, Ifaluk, and Teleological Functionalism," *AA,* 54 (1952), 497-503.

Srinivas, M. N. *Religion and Society among the Coorgs of South India.* Oxford: The Clarendon Press, 1952.

Stanley, A. P. *Lectures on the History of the Eastern Church.* New York: Charles Scribner and Co., 1871.

Steiner, Franz. *Taboo.* Ed. Bohannon, Laura. New York: Philosophical Library, 1956.

Steward, J. H. "The Ceremonial Buffoon of the American Indian," *Michigan Academy of Science, Arts and Letters,* 14 (1930), 187-207.

Steward, J. H. *Basin-Plateau Aboriginal Sociopolitical Groups. BAE,* Bulletin 120 (1938).

Steward, J. H. (ed.). *Handbook of South American Indians. BAE,* Bulletin 143, 6 vols. (1946-1950).

Stewart, K. M. "Spirit Possession in Native America," *SWJA,* 2 (1946), 323-339.

Stewart, O. C. *Washo-Northern Paiute Peyotism. UCPAAE,* 40 (1944), 63-140.

Stewart, O. C. "Peyote and Colorado's Inquisition Law." *The Colorado Quarterly,* 5 (1956), 79-90.

Stone, Eric. *Medicine among the American Indians.* New York: Paul B. Hoeber, 1932.

Strong, W. D. "Occurrence and Wider Implications of a 'Ghost Cult' on the Columbia River Suggested by Carvings in Wood, Bone and Stone," *AA,* 47 (1945), 244-261.

Summers, Montague. *The Geography of Witchcraft.* Evanston: University Books, 1958.

Sumner, W. G., and Keller, A. G. *The Science of Society.* Vols. II and IV. New Haven: Yale University Press, 1927.

Sundkler, B. G. M. *Bantu Prophets in South Africa.* London: Lutterworth Press, 1948.

Suttles, Wayne. "The Plateau Prophet Dance Among the Coast Salish," *SWJA,* 13 (1957), 352-396.

Swanton, J. R. "Religions, Beliefs and Medical Practices of the Creek Indians." *BAE, Forty-second Annual Report, 1924-1925* (1928), 473-672.

Tanner, John. *A Narrative of the Captivity and Adventures of John Tanner During Thirty Years of Residence Among the Indians.* Ed. James, E. Minneapolis: Ross and Haines, Inc., 1956.

Tawney, R. H. *Religion and the Rise of Capitalism.* New York: Harcourt, Brace and Company, 1926.

Thalbitzer, W. "Shamans of the East Greenland Eskimo." In Kroeber, A. L., and Waterman, T. T. (eds.). *Source Book in Anthropology.* New York: Harcourt, Brace and Company, 1931.

Thomas, W. I. "The Relation of the Medicine Man to the Origins of the Professional Occupation." In *Source Book for Social Origins.* Chicago: University of Chicago Press, 1912.

Thompson, Laura. *Fijian Frontier.* American Council, Institute of Pacific Relations, 1940.

Thompson, Stith. *The Folktale.* New York: The Dryden Press, 1946.

Titiev, Mischa. *Old Oraibi.* Papers of the Peabody Museum of American Archaeology and Ethnology. Vol. 22, no. 1, 1944.

Tooth, Geoffrey. *Studies in Mental Illness in the Gold Coast.* Colonial Research Publications. No. 6. London: His Majesty's Stationery Office, 1950.

Train, Percy, Henrichs, J. R., and Archer, W. A. *Medicinal Uses of Plants by Indians of Nevada.* Contributions Toward a Flora of Nevada. No. 33. Washington: U. S. Department of Agriculture, Division of Plant Exploration and Introduction, 1941.

Tremearne, A. J. N. *Hausa Superstitions and Customs.* London: J. Bales, Sons & Danielson, 1913.

Trimingham, J. S. *Islam in West Africa.* Oxford: The Clarendon Press, 1959.

Trollope, Frances. *Domestic Manners of the Americans.* New York: Alfred A. Knopf, 1949 (first published 1832).

Tschopik, H. J. *The Aymara of Chucuito, Peru. Part 1, Magic.* Anthropological Papers, American Museum of Natural History. Vol. 44. New York: American Museum of Natural History, 137-308.

Tylor, E. B. *Primitive Culture,* 2 vols., 3rd American ed. New York: Henry Holt and Company, 1889 (first published 1871).

Underhill, Ruth. *Papago Indian Religion.* New York: Columbia University Press, 1953.

Underhill, Ruth. *Red Man's America.* Chicago: University of Chicago Press, 1953.

Vaillant, G. C. *Aztecs of Mexico.* Garden City: Doubleday & Co., 1947.

Van Gennep, Arnold. *Les Rites de Passage.* Paris: Librairie Critique, Emil Mourry, 1909.

Voget, F. W. "The American Indian in Transition: Reformatism and Accommodation," *AA,* 58 (1956), 249-263.

Wach, Joachim. *Sociology of Religion.* Chicago: University of Chicago Press, 1944.

Wallace, A. F. C. "New Religions among the Delaware Indians, 1600-1900," *SWJA,* 12 (1956), 1-21.

Wallace, A. F. C. "Revitalization Movements," *AA,* 58 (1956), 264-281.

Wallace, W. J., and Taylor, E. S. "Hupa Sorcery," *SWJA,* 6 (1950), 188-196.

Wallis, R. S., and Wallis, W. D. "The Sins of the Fathers: A Concept of Disease among the Canadian Dakota," *SWJA,* 9 (1953), 431-435.

Wallis, W. D. *Messiahs: Christian and Pagan.* Boston: The Gorham Press, 1918.

Wallis, W. D. *Religion in Primitive Society.* New York: F. S. Crofts & Co., 1939.

Wallis, W. D. *Messiahs: Their Role in Civilization.* Washington: American Council on Public Affairs, 1943.

Warner, W. L. *A Black Civilization.* New York: Harper & Brothers, 1937.

Wasson, V. P., and Wasson, R. G. *Mushrooms, Russia, and History,* 2 vols. New York: Pantheon Books, 1957.

Waterman, T. T. *The Religious Practices of the Diegueño Indians. UCPAAE,* 8 (1908), 271-353.

Watt, J. M., and Breyer-Brandwijk, M. G. *The Medicinal and Poisonous Plants of Southern Africa.* Edinburgh: E. & S. Livingstone, 1932.

Weber, Max. *The Protestant Ethic and the Spirit of Capitalism* (trans. by Talcott Parsons). London: George Allen & Unwin, 1930.

Webster, Hutton. *Magic: A Sociological Study.* Stanford: Stanford University Press, 1942.

Webster, Hutton. *Taboo.* Stanford: Stanford University Press, 1942.

Welmers, W. E. "Secret Medicines, Magic, and Rites of the Kpelle Tribe in Liberia," *SWJA,* 5 (1949), 208-243.

Westermarck, Edward. *The Origin and Development of the Moral Ideas,* 2 vols. London: Macmillan & Co., 1908.

Westermarck, Edward. *The History of Human Marriage,* 5th ed., 3 vols. London: Macmillan & Co., 1921.

Weyer, E. M. *The Eskimos.* New Haven: Yale University Press, 1932.

White, L. A. *The Science of Culture.* New York: Farrar Strauss, 1949.

White, L. A. *The Evolution of Culture.* New York: McGraw-Hill Book Company, 1959.

Whiting, B. B. *Paiute Sorcery.* Viking Fund Publications in Anthropology. No. 15. New York: The Viking Fund, 1950.

Whiting, J. M. *Becoming a Kwoma.* New Haven: Yale University Press, 1941.

Whiting, J. M., and Child, Irvin L. *Child Training and Personality: A Cross-Cultural Study.* New Haven: Yale University Press, 1953.

Whiting, J. M., Kluckhohn, R., and Anthony, A. "The Function of Male Initiation Ceremonies at Puberty." In Maccoby, E. E., Newcomb, T. M., and Hartley, E. L. (eds.). *Readings in Social Psychology,* 3rd ed. New York: Henry Holt and Company, 1958.

Whitman, William. "The San Ildefonso of New Mexico." In Linton, Ralph (ed.). *Acculturation in Seven American Indian Tribes.* New York and London: D. Appleton-Century Co., 1940.

Williams, F. E. *Orokaiva Magic.* London: Oxford University Press, H. Milford, 1928.

Williams, F. E. "The Vailala Madness in Retrospect." In Schapera, I. (ed.). *Essays Presented to C. G. Seligman.* London: Trench, Trubner & Co., 1934, 369-379.

Wilson, Monica. *Good Company: A Study of Nyakyusa Age Villages.* London: Oxford University Press, 1951.

Wilson, Monica. "Witch Beliefs and Social Structures." *American Journal of Sociology,* 56 (1951), 307-313.

Wilson, Monica. "Nyakyusa Ritual and Symbolism," *AA,* 56 (1954), 228-241.

Wilson, Monica. *Rituals of Kinship Among the Nyakyusa.* New York: Oxford University Press, 1957.

Wilson, Monica. *Communal Rituals of the Nyakyusa.* New York: Oxford University Press, 1959.

Wisdom, Charles. "The Supernatural World and Curing." In Tax, Sol, and others (eds.). *Heritage of Conquest: The Ethnology of Middle America.* Glencoe: The Free Press, 1952.

Wissler, Clark. "Smoking Star: Blackfoot Shaman." In Parsons, E. C. (ed.). *American Indian Life*. New York: B. W. Huebsch, 1922.

Wissler, Clark, and Spinden, H. J. "The Pawnee Human Sacrifice to the Morningstar," *American Museum Journal*, 16 (1916), 49-55.

Wolff, K. H. (trans. and ed.). *The Sociology of Georg Simmel*. Glencoe: The Free Press, 1950.

Worsley, P. M. "Totemism in a Changing Society," *AA*, vol. 57, no. 4 (1955).

Worsley, P. M. *The Trumpet Shall Sound*. London: Macgibbon & Kee, 1957.

Yinger, J. M. *Religion, Society, and the Individual*. New York: The Macmillan Company, 1957.

INDEXES

Index of Names

Index of Subjects

Abnormal behavior, *see* Psychosis;
Sexual aberration
Acculturation and religion, 231-266,
271
Africa, 61, 62, 68, 79, 85-86, 91, 92,
94, 96, 102, 104, 105, 106, 118, 147,
148, 151, 154-159, 165, 167, 172-173,
179-182, 189, 190, 194, 196, 197, 198,
200, 205, 206, 207, 209, 210, 212,
213, 224, 237, 238, 239, 240, 256-262
See also specific tribal names
Afterworlds, conceptions of, 175-177
See also Sanctions, supernatural
Agnostics, ethical codes of, 186
Albinos, 105
Alcohol, 95-96, 98, 100, 278
Algonquin Indians, 43-44, 199-200
See also specific tribal names
Amazulu, 86
American Indians, *see* Indians
Ancestor worship, 20, 172-173, 259
Angakok, 112
Anglo-Egyptian Sudan, 179
Animism, 17, 169
Anthropocentrism, 8, 135
See also Projection
Anthropology, views of religion, 4-13
Anthropopsychic gods, 77
Anthroposocial gods, 77
Antisocial rites, *see* Rites of rebellion
Anxiety, *see* Tension
Apache Indians, 105, 243, 249
Arabs, 147
Arawak Indians, 217
Archeological evidence of religion, 25-
31, 60, 61, 272
Art, and prophylaxis, 227; and reli-
gion, 73; Paleolithic, 27-30, 55

Aryans, 178
Astrology, 60, 63
Atea, 77
Atomized societies, 198-201
Aurignacian, art of the, 30
Australian aborigines, 55, 91, 120, 121,
147, 191, 240
Autosuggestion in trance, 93-94
Avebury, ruins at, 31
Azande, 62, 197, 202
Aztecs, 66-67, 97, 102, 104, 106, 175-
176, 248-249, 265

Bali, trance-dancing of, 93
Banisteriopsis, 96, 97
Bantu, 173, 205, 238
See also specific tribal names
Barakka, 45
Bemba, 154-159
Berdache, 106
Big Belly Indians, 94-95
Big Candle, 239-240
Birth rites, *see* Crisis rites
Bismarck Archipelago, 38, 70, 182
Black Mass, 55
Blood, pollution from, *see* Pollution
Bloodletting, *see* Venesection
Bogey-men, 209-210
Borneo, 106
Brazil, 70, 235, 236
Buddhism, 72, 74, 122; Zen sect, 185
Bugis, 106
Buha, 44
Bull-roarer, 121
Burkhanism, 239
Burlesque in ritual, *see* Rites of re-
bellion
Byzantine Rome, 72